A Classical Republican in Eighteenth-Century France

JOHNSON KENT WRIGHT

A Classical Republican in Eighteenth-Century France

THE POLITICAL THOUGHT OF MABLY

STANFORD UNIVERSITY PRESS
STANFORD, CALIFORNIA
1997

Stanford University Press
Stanford, California

Printed in the United States of America

CIP data are at the end of the book

Last date below indicates year of this printing:
05 04 03 02 01 00 99 98 97

Preface

Where would the history of ideas be without that familiar figure, the "unjustly neglected" thinker who enjoyed a vast reputation in his or her lifetime, only to fall into an unaccountable oblivion at some later point? Often enough, of course, closer inspection reveals either that this neglect has been exaggerated for rhetorical purposes, or that it is in fact perfectly justified. Nevertheless, it does sometimes happen that important thinkers escape the attention they deserve from historians of ideas. The subject of this study, Gabriel Bonnot de Mably, is surely one of these. By any reckoning, Mably, whose public career as a writer extended from 1740 to the eve of the French Revolution, was a major figure in the intellectual life of eighteenth-century France. It is impossible to work in the fields of the Enlightenment and the French Revolution without encountering his name at every turn. Indeed, the Revolution may have raised Mably's reputation to a higher level than he enjoyed in his lifetime, winning him notoriety that persisted throughout most of the nineteenth century.

Yet for all his contemporary and posthumous fame and impact, Mably has never been the subject of more than a very modest scholarly literature. This neglect is nowhere more evident than in the world of Anglo-American scholarship—it has been more than sixty years since the appearance of the only survey of his life and thought in English. The chief purpose of this book, whose form is that of an intellectual biography, is simply to fill this gap. At the same time, this study also presents a novel interpretation of Mably's thought. When twentieth-century scholars have looked at Mably, they have tended to portray him in two sharply contrasted ways—either as a fundamentally progressive thinker, one of a handful of utopian communists of the French Enlightenment and thus a "precursor" of nineteenth-century socialism; or as a deeply conservative or even reactionary figure, misanthropic moralist and inveterate enemy of the Enlightenment. There is something to both of these views. But this study will argue for a different reading of the character of Mably's thought, one which restores an emphasis on its fundamentally *political* nature. To reduce it to a formula: Mably was quite clearly a *classical republican*, in just the sense this term has acquired in recent years for students of early modern European political thought. Not only that, I argue that he was in fact the author of perhaps the most extensive and important body of republican thought to be produced in eighteenth-century France. The novelty and force of these claims are discussed at some length in the introduction to the book; I return to them in the last chapter, which draws some conclusions about the specific character of classical republicanism in France and about the French contribution to a wider "Atlantic republican tradition."

Like many first books, this one has taken an inexplicably long time to complete—but not long enough to eliminate all of its errors and shortcomings, the responsibility for which is mine alone. I cannot, however, say the same for whatever merits it may possess. These I am happy to share with Keith Baker, who directed the doctoral dissertation at the University of Chicago from which it has evolved. It was Keith who first suggested that Mably's thought represented a French variant of early modern civic humanism—in fact, he may well have contemplated writing a monograph on Mably himself at one time. It is typical of his generosity and dedication that he so willingly passed this and so many other ideas along to me, and then oversaw the slow emergence of the work itself with so much care, encouragement, and patience. I also want to thank another member of my dissertation committee, Charles Gray, for his expert guidance and advice. And I owe a special debt to my friend Robert Morrissey, not just for his own contributions to the dissertation, but for many happy years of intellectual comradeship.

Much of the original research for this study was made possible by generous grants from the Georges Lurcy Trust and the John M. Olin Foundation. During the evolution from doctoral thesis to book, I acquired a number of debts of a more personal nature as well, to friends and colleagues at Chicago and elsewhere. For all variety of intellectual stimulation, encouragement, and kindness, I wish to thank Dwight Allman, Ray Birn, Hans Bödeker, John Brooks, François Furet, Jan Goldstein, Dan Gordon, Istvan Hont, Carroll Joynes, Tom Kaiser, Ralph Lerner, Colin Lucas, Bernard Manin, Peter Miller, Bill Sewell, and Dale Van Kley. I especially want to express my gratitude to my friend Dale Van Kley, both for active interventions on my behalf at various points, and for the inspiring model of his own scholarship; and to thank Bill Sewell, for helpful suggestions about final revisions to the text. I am grateful as well to Iain Hampsher-Monk and colleagues at *History of Political Thought*, for comments on my article, "Conversations with Phocion: The Political Thought of Mably," published in that journal (Vol. XIII, no. 3 [1992], pp. 391–415), as well as for permission to use portions of it here in Chapter 4. My thanks also to Stanford University Press, for their skill and care in seeing the manuscript into print—as well as for their patience in waiting for it. The final preparation of the text was helped along by the welcome I have received at Arizona State University; I owe particular thanks to Charles Dellheim, Director of the Interdisciplinary Humanities Program at ASU.

My debts do not quite end there. There are three friends to whom I owe more than I could properly say—David Pelizzari, Jay Schleusener, and Max Ziff. I am deeply grateful to my parents for their support and encouragement over the years. And finally, I wish to dedicate the book to Ann Hobart, with thanks and love.

J.K.W.
July 1996

Contents

A Classical Republican in Eighteenth-Century France

CHAPTER I

Introduction: Placing Mably

In 1819, Benjamin Constant delivered a famous lecture in Paris under the title "The Liberty of the Ancients Compared with that of the Moderns." The talk was a distillation of two decades of reflection on the meaning of the French Revolution. Constant's central claim was that the First Republic had represented a vain attempt to transform France into a modern Sparta—an attempt, in other words, to establish a political order based on the "ancient" conception of liberty, which Constant defined as the "active and constant participation in collective power."[1] Such a goal, however, was a dangerous anachronism in a modern commercial nation such as France. The predictable result of the Jacobin experiment was not the restoration of the direct democracy of the ancient city-state, but rather the heedless destruction of a wholly distinct form of liberty, the "peaceful enjoyment of private independence." The latter was the specific product of *modern* civilization, and was entirely unknown to classical antiquity. What then had led to the attempt in the first place—how could the French have to come to believe that a restoration of "ancient liberty" was both possible and desirable in a modern setting?

The chief culprits here, in Constant's view, were two Enlightenment writers who had devoted their careers to fostering just this delusion. One of these, of course, was Jean-Jacques Rousseau—much of the interest of Constant's lecture in fact derives from his exasperated yet sincere admiration for the author of *Du contrat social.* His real venom was reserved for the abbé de Mably, a figure far less likely to be familiar to twentieth-century readers, but whom Constant believed bore an even greater responsibility than Rousseau for having glamorized the idea of "ancient liberty." Both Rousseau and Mably had failed—with dire consequences for the succeeding generation—to see that the pure democracy of the classical city-state had been lost forever with the decline of antiquity. The unforgettable lesson of the French Revolution, Constant concluded, was that freedom in the modern world could best be secured by combining ironclad guarantees of individual liberty with "representative government"—in which, he conceded, political self-direction for the vast majority of the populace would necessarily be reduced to an "abstract supposition."[2] The experience of the Terror would serve henceforth as a standing warning against any further experiments with a more direct democracy.

Constant was not alone in this judgment on the French Revolution. The belief that the Jacobin cult of Graeco-Roman antiquity was somehow central to its meaning was widely shared in the nineteenth century, and not merely among Constant's fellow liberals. Karl Marx, for one, was no less struck by Jacobin and Napoleonic imitation of classical political and cultural forms, as famous pages from *The Holy Family* and *The Eighteenth Brumaire* remind us. Today, however, any reconsideration of "The Liberty of the Ancients Compared with that of the Moderns" must confront an initial paradox. Constant's lecture has long since come to be seen as a founding document of modern political liberalism—indeed, the notion of a contrast between competing forms of liberty, ancient and modern, has been a staple of liberal polemic for decades. Yet for all its current celebrity, the substance of his interpretation of the Revolution itself is virtually without resonance in twentieth-century historiography. The phenomena to which he drew attention—the classical republicanism of writers such as Rousseau and Mably, and the Revolutionary cult of antiquity that is supposed to have been inspired by it—have largely been ignored by contemporary historians of the Enlightenment and the Revolution; it has been decades since either has attracted serious and sustained scholarly attention. The general indifference to these topics appears still more paradoxical, in light of the recent emergence of a substantial body of scholarship on classical republicanism elsewhere in early-modern Europe, synthesized some time ago in J. G. A. Pocock's *The Machiavellian Moment*. Surprisingly enough, there have been no efforts to find a place in Pocock's "Atlantic republican tradition" for the Jacobin Republic of Virtue, and remarkably few attempts even to restore the political thought of Rousseau to its wider European context. As for the abbé de Mably, who for Constant and many others was the central figure of French republicanism in the

Enlightenment, this disregard has been nearly total. Indeed, it is difficult to think of any eighteenth-century thinker of comparable stature and interest who has received so little scholarly attention over the years. Among other indices of neglect, the surprising fact is that there exists no recent authoritative survey of Mably's thought in either French or English—the only study in the latter language was published nearly seventy years ago.

The chief purpose of the book at hand is to remedy this gap, at least in regard to Mably. In form an intellectual biography, its primary goal is to sketch an accurate and complete portrait of its subject by means of a contextual study of his life and works. At the same time, this book also has a wider ambition. It is perfectly clear that a major reassessment of the political usages of classical antiquity in eighteenth-century France—from the "Quarrel of the Ancients and the Moderns" early in the century to the Jacobin Republic of Virtue itself—is long overdue. What better starting point for such an assessment than with Mably? The larger purpose of this book will be to demonstrate not only that the *dominant* political language in Mably's writing, which gave it coherence and direction over a long intellectual career, was indeed a French variant of classical republicanism, recognizably belonging to a larger "Atlantic republican tradition," but that Mably was in fact the author of the most important, extensive, and varied corpus of republican thought produced in eighteenth-century France—perhaps in Europe. Such will be the general claims of this study. In order to grasp their specific novelty and force, however, it is necessary to take a closer look both at the career and reputation of Mably and at the current state of scholarship on French republicanism.

Mably's Reputation: Celebrity and Eclipse

Let us begin with some simple facts about Mably's life and work. He was born into the provincial *noblesse de robe* at Grenoble in 1709. Although he was educated in preparation for an ecclesiastical career—as was his younger brother, Etienne Bonnot de Condillac—he was never ordained. A brief period of employment in the diplomatic bureaucracy of the French monarchy in the 1740s left an indelible mark on his thought. But by mid-century Mably had abandoned what was evidently a promising career in the service of church or state, in order to devote himself entirely to study and writing; henceforth he divided his time between Paris and the country estates of a few aristocratic patrons. By the time of his death in 1785 he had published some fifteen works; the editions of his *oeuvres complètes* that appeared during the Revolution fill fifteen volumes, including three of writings that had previously circulated in manuscript.

What sort of works were these? Even the briefest inspection of Mably's writing reveals two outstanding traits. On the one hand, his thought was exclusively political in orientation—government and society were virtually the only topics Mably found worthy of serious consideration, in a career that spanned more than half a century.[3] "Men were made to live in society," he wrote in a characteristically laconic formula, "and their happiness was left in their own hands; it is thus the study of society, politics, which ought to occupy their attention."[4] The consistency and direction of his intellectual career plainly sprang from a deep conviction about the place of politics in human life. Yet this intense focus should not suggest a narrowness or confinement of vision. For Mably's writing was also characterized by an impressive variety of genre and topic, within the limits of the political. His thirty or so works can be roughly sorted into three main categories. Mably's chief early writings belong largely to the genre of philosophical history, inspired by the model of Montesquieu's *Considérations* on the Romans: he published *Parallèle des romains et des français* in 1740, *Observations sur les Grecs* in 1749 (later revised and published as *Observations sur l'histoire de la Grèce* in 1764), *Observations sur les Romains* in 1751, and *Observations sur l'histoire de France* in 1765. In mid-career, however, his preference shifted toward the philosophical dialogue as a vehicle of self-expression. His first exercise in this genre was written in 1758, but appeared in print only posthumously: *Des droits et des devoirs du citoyen.* Over the next twenty-five years Mably published a series of book-length dialogues—*Entretiens de Phocion, De la législation, Principes de morale, De la manière d'écrire l'histoire*—and wrote more than a dozen others, of an impressive variety of length and form, extending over a wide range of sociopolitical topics. A third category, finally, is formed by the large number of specialized, polemical, or occasional works Mably wrote throughout his career. Among these were his guide to international law and treaties, *Le droit public de l'Europe* (1746, revised in 1748 and 1764), to which he added a long introduction, *Principes des Négociations,* in 1757; *De l'étude de l'histoire,* his contribution to the course of study assembled by his brother Condillac for the Prince of Parma (1774, but written earlier); a long and passionate attack on physiocracy, *Doutes proposées aux philosophes économistes sur l'ordre naturel et essentiel des sociétés politiques* (1768); and, in Mably's final years, two works that examined the prospects for reform in two very different regions of the eighteenth-century world, *Du gouvernement et des lois de la Pologne* (1781) and *Observations sur le gouvernement et les lois des Etats Unis d'Amérique* (1784).

All in all, there was hardly a more varied or copious body of political thought produced in eighteenth-century France. Moreover, Mably's *oeuvre* forms something like an intermittent commentary on the French political scene over a very long period, from the epoch of Fleury to that of Necker—an exceptional resource, it might be thought, for the study of the political culture of the *ancien régime.* How were these writings received by his contemporaries? By any reckoning, Mably's literary career was a successful one: nearly every one of his published works attained a wide readership, as attested by their multiple editions and translations, and most were favorably received by the contemporary press.[5] A closer look at his "reception," however, reveals one striking anomaly. It was long assumed, largely on the strength of the prestige he enjoyed during the revolutionary period, that Mably had been a typical radical *philosophe,* his thought a characteristic expression of the most progressive wing of the French Enlightenment. His first book, *Parallèle des romains et des français,* was indeed in many ways a representative product of the early Enlightenment, and won the warm approval of Voltaire, among others. Yet it was soon violently repudiated by its own author—the result of a striking reversal of political conviction, coinciding with the abandonment of his brief diplomatic career, which saw Mably move from the enthusiastic royalism of the *Parallèle* to the intransigent republicanism of his subsequent writings. The paradox of this change was that it was accompanied by a growing hostility toward the later Enlightenment, as it moved toward its triumphant maturity in France. No subgroup of the *mouvement philosophique,* from Voltaire to the *Encyclopédistes* to the *côterie d'Holbach,* was spared the criticisms of Mably. *Entretiens de Phocion* was in part a critique of Helvétius; *Principes de morale* was a rejoinder to Holbach; *Doutes proposées aux philosophes économistes* was one of the major attacks launched against physiocratic social thought; and *De la manière d'écrire l'histoire* contained a brusque dismissal of the great quartet of Enlightenment historiography, Voltaire, Hume, Robertson, and Gibbon.[6] Mably's antipathy for Voltaire was particularly intense, and it repeatedly thrust him into the sort of public polemic he otherwise scrupulously avoided.[7] Not surprisingly, the causes and meaning of this estrangement have come to form one of the central points of controversy in the recent scholarly discussion of Mably. Some historians have minimized the importance of his personal skirmishes with the *philosophes*, continuing to see him as part of the Enlightenment understood in the broadest sense; others have unhesitatingly assigned him to the antiphilosophic camp *tout court*. But whatever final judgment is made in this regard, the price of his self-imposed exclusion from the dominant philosophical-cultural movement of his epoch was evidently a heavy one. The possessor of a continent-wide reputation at mid-century, Mably spent the last decades of his life in increasing intellectual isolation. By the time of his death in 1785 he had become virtually a forgotten figure in France.[8]

A year later, Calonne, the controller-general of royal finances, reported the impending bankruptcy of the monarchy to Louis XVI, thus setting in motion the chain of events that was to culminate in the Revolution. It was in this altered ideological universe that Mably unexpectedly acquired a celebrity and respect that surpassed anything he had known in his lifetime. At the height of the propaganda wars of the "pre-Revolution," his literary executors published two works that Mably himself, always wary of absolutist censorship, had prudently withheld from print. The first was the completed text of *Observations sur l'histoire de France* (its first two volumes had appeared in 1765), which contained a stirring evocation of the original freedom of the French nation before the long night of feudal "anarchy" and monarchical "despotism" had descended on it, and which concluded with a passionate call for the restoration of the Estates-General. It quickly became by far the most frequently cited historical work in the flood of pamphlet literature of 1788–89, hailed as the "the catechism of the French" and the "national code": "This masterpiece of patriotism, erudition, of criticism and philosophy . . . was in the hands of every citizen: it was there that they found the precious traces of the heritage of their fathers."[9] The second was *Des droits et des devoirs du citoyen*, which had outlined—thirty years earlier—a detailed scenario for a transition from absolute to constitutional monarchy in France, one that proved to be an astonishingly clairvoyant prediction of the actual course of events of the "pre-Revolution." It too had a tremendous impact, prompting no less an observer-participant than Mounier to describe Mably thus: "Only one among all our writers had no other goal than to trace the path that we would have to follow in order to overcome the opposition and to achieve the happiness of which men are capable: would I be accused of exaggeration in calling him the legislator of the nation?"[10]

These two works laid the foundations for a revolutionary cult—with the usual trappings of busts, portraits, street-names, museums, and public commemorations in the great festivals—that seems to have been fully the equal of those enjoyed by figures such as Montesquieu, Voltaire, Rousseau, and Raynal.[11] Indeed, Mably's writings, which thereafter became available in more than one *oeuvres complètes*, proved useful to each succeeding levy of revolutionary leaders and publicists down to Thermidor, owing to their striking political and thematic diversity. Where the "pre-Revolution" had prized him chiefly for his historical and strategic writings, it was his constructive political and constitutional theory—his pointed insistence on the supremacy of legislative over executive power in particular—that received special attention during the Constitutional Monarchy. The leaders of the First Republic could in turn take up his more overtly egalitarian and republican works, with their characteristic emphasis on the seamless identity of "politics" and "morality," and their celebration of the politics of "virtue." Last, but not least important for his subsequent reputation, Mably was hailed by Babeuf and his co-conspirators, both in the *Tribun du peuple* and at their trial, as a key inspiration for their plans to institute the *communauté des biens*—a fact that still did not prevent conservative admirers of Mably from appealing to his authority in regard to the *exclusion* of the propertyless from politics, during the Directory.

Forgotten or reviled only a few years earlier, Mably was thus elevated to the ranks of the *pères de la nation* in the early years of the French Revolution, his authority put to a greater variety of political uses than perhaps that of any other eighteenth-century thinker. From this high point, however, his reputation gradually ebbed away. Its history from the Empire onward was one of slow decline, as Mably's works ceased to be read and his name gradually disappeared from public discourse. What proved durable throughout this long process was his intimate association with the Revolution itself: until very recently it has been all but impossible to view Mably except through its distorting lens. The reputations of other eighteenth-century thinkers have of course often been held hostage to this sort of anachronism—interpretations of Rousseau have notoriously been skewed by legends about his "influence" on the Revolution. But few have been so thoroughly stereotyped as Mably, not least because of his lack of any certain or unambiguous prerevolutionary reputation to serve as a counterweight. In fact, the record of his own hostility to the Enlightenment was forgotten to the extent that he came to be seen as the quintessential radical *philosophe*, whose "abstract" and "irresponsible" speculations had wittingly or unwittingly produced the Revolution.[12] It is possible, in any case, to discern two distinct phases in nineteenth-century commentary on Mably. We have already glimpsed something of the first. In the initial decades of the century, Mably's name was associated above all with the cult of Graeco-Roman antiquity that was so prominent a component of revolutionary political culture. It is often forgotten that it was Mably, not Rousseau, who was the real target of Constant's famous polemic:

> Besides, it is not to Rousseau, as we shall see, that we must principally ascribe the error against which I shall argue: it belongs much more to one of his successors, less eloquent, but not less austere, and a thousand times more exaggerated. The latter, the abbé de Mably, may be regarded as the representative of the system which, in conformity with the maxims of ancient liberty, aims at the complete subjection of the citizenry so that the nation may be sovereign, and the enslavement of the individual so that the people may be free.[13]

Nor was this judgment merely a personal foible or idiosyncrasy in Constant. A belief in Mably's culpability for the Jacobin cult of antiquity was shared by a large number of fellow liberals in the first decades of the nineteenth century. For Augustin Thierry, Mably was "the first of those advocates of ancient society against the modern world."[14] And Jean-Louis Lerminier, from his chair in the Collège de France, described Mably in these terms:

> This writer filled the public with false ideas about antiquity, together with the desire one day to imitate these mendacious representations. If later, at the epoch of the Convention, we encounter men who wished to bring Sparta back to life, and who believed that liberty is incompatible with wealth, luxury, and commerce, these were the pupils of Mably and not of Jean-Jacques. Mably confounded epochs and civilizations, and unsettled a great many minds.[15]

By mid-century, however, the echoes of revolutionary neoclassicism had begun to die out, and a quite different interest in Mably sprang up, which more closely reflected contemporary hopes and anxieties. The gathering momentum of the early socialist movement, now poised to make its political debut, naturally raised the question of its intellectual ancestry. Socialism's proponents and adversaries alike agreed in tracing its proximate origins to the left wing of the French Enlightenment—not only to Rousseau, but also to more explicitly "communist" utopians such as Meslier, Morelly, and Dom Deschamps. As we shall see, the cornerstone of Mably's mature thought was a critique of social inequality fully as stringent as that of Rousseau; to which was added a preoccupation with the notion of a *communauté des biens* that went well beyond anything in the latter, suggesting the direct influence of the *philosophes utopistes.*

Given the very tangible link provided by the testimony of Babeuf, it is thus not surprising to find that by mid-century Mably had become widely known as an early "socialist" or "communist" thinker. Already in 1848, with the shock of the June Days fresh in mind, the liberal professor Adolphe Franck identified one of the intellectual culprits behind the new doctrine: "Mably had the glory, if it can be called that, of having completed, in the eighteenth century, the theory of communism in its most precise and most logical form."[16] Franck's socialist opponents entirely agreed with the attribution. In 1849 Paul Rochery published a selection of Mably's works, introduced in this fashion:

> In fact, of all the philosophers of his time, it was Mably who best personified, in his books and his character, the democratic tendency. At once a socialist, a republican, and a revolutionary, no aspect of the great problem eluded him. He saw the moral solution in revolution, the political solution in republican government, and the final goal and salvation in social equality. Are there many socialists of our own time who can claim to have been so thorough and so logical as this?[17]

Eventually, the designation of Mably as an ancestor of the communist movement was acknowledged, in passing, by Marx and Engels themselves.[18] By the end of the century the label was firmly fixed in the great works of secondary literature of the epoch, bringing to a conclusion the process of stereotyping begun after the Revolution.[19] By this time, interest in Mably as a *political* thinker—as a contributor to the rich political culture of the Old Regime, or even as a source of constitutional theory during the Revolution—had largely evaporated. Awareness of the extraordinary variety of his writings, his *Observations* on French and classical history, his works on diplomacy and physiocracy, proposals for constitutional reform, was lost—all these disappeared behind the simple tab of "utopian socialist." Outside of a fairly narrow scholarly discussion, this is where his reputation has remained to this day. To cite just one example among many, in the standard English account of eighteenth-century thought, Gay's *The Enlightenment*, Mably hardly figures at all; but where he does, it is merely as one of the radical "lieutenants" of the Enlightenment and "precursor of socialism."[20]

The Scholarly Balance Sheet

Despite some isolated pleas—in M. W. Guerrier's *L'abbé de Mably, moraliste et politique* (1886) and Ernest Whitfield's *Gabriel Bonnot de Mably* (1930)—it was not until after World War II that any sustained scholarly discussion of Mably got under way.[21] Within two decades it was possible for an observer, referring to the recent publication of Aldo Maffey's monograph *Il pensiero politico del Mably*, as well as to a growing number of shorter articles and essays, to declare that Mably was no longer a "forgotten author."[22] Since then, the literature on his life and works has continued to expand, slowly but steadily. What has been the shape of this scholarly discussion? It has been marked by very sharp disagreement over the basic character of Mably's political thought. In effect, as Galliani accurately noted in his review article in 1972, scholarly opinion has divided, largely along political lines, into two opposing camps: "one that, insisting on the moderate or conservative character of the thought of Mably, seems at the same time to feel little sympathy for him; and another, interpreting his thought in a progressive sense, that pays homage to him with gratitude."[23] Given the history briefly recounted above, it was to be expected that the initial thrust of the discussion would be an attempt to move Mably out from under the shadows of the Revolution and of socialism. The first important post–World War II examination, a long revisionist essay by Giuliano Procacci, was in many ways the most sweeping effort along these lines, for it not only tried to refute the notion of a revolutionary or socialist Mably, but even argued strongly for his exclusion from the Enlightenment itself. Procacci began by introducing much of the evidence alluded to above: the fact that Mably's personal relations with the *philosophes* were either nonexistent or, more frequently, hostile; and that his own writings were filled with polemical attacks on a wide variety of "enlightened" positions. To explain this, Procacci pointed to Mably's Jesuit education—about which little is known—and to his lifelong attachment to the Church. Mably, he concluded, was essentially a "conservative Catholic" thinker, whose conception of human nature was an orthodox Christian dualism, and whose political naturalism was consequently wholly "medieval" in character, fundamentally at odds with the scientific, materialistic temper of the bourgeois Enlightenment. Where Rousseau's revolt against the Enlightenment pointed beyond it to the progressive movements that developed its legacy, Mably's rejection of it was merely the reflex of an archaic and reactionary moralism: "While the Genevan moved forward, elaborating and surpassing the philosophy of the Enlightenment, Mably remained irremediably behind, fixed in an obstinate polemic against a mode of thought that was wholly alien to him."[24] It is noticeable, however, that Procacci's case for the exclusion of Mably from the Enlightenment was primarily circumstantial: he was in fact unable to provide much textual warrant for the use of epithets such as "Thomist," "Scholastic," or "Jesuit" for Mably. There are certain difficulties with any attempt to set him outside the perimeter of the *lumières* altogether, not least his frequent declarations of allegiance to the philosophy of Locke and to the sensationalism of his brother Condillac, and the marked lack in his writings of any religious sentiments that might be termed "Catholic" or even "Christian"—aspects of his thought that were largely overlooked or brushed aside in Procacci's account.

Few of Procacci's immediate successors, in any case, were willing to place quite so much emphasis on Mably's polemics with the *philosophes*, or so confidently to describe his political thought as "conservative."[25] On the contrary, the predominant tendency, in the initial search for an alternative to a revolutionary or socialist interpretation of Mably, was to insist on the fundamental *continuity* of his thought with the moderate reformism of the French Enlightenment. Thus Ephraim Harpaz, in a series of articles, argued that notwithstanding his disputes with certain *philosophes* or his attack on physiocracy—in which he was in any case joined by more than one thinker whose "enlightened" credentials were impeccable—Mably's political thought was otherwise not very distant from that of the *Encyclopédistes*, being founded on similar conceptions of empiricism and natural law, and advancing political recommendations of a like kind.[26] These views then received their fullest presentation in the first book-length study since Whitfield's, Aldo Maffey's *Il pensiero politico del Mably*. This work marked a great advance in scholarship, with its painstaking compilation of facts about Mably's life and works. At the same time, it was sharply polemical, launching a full-scale critique of the claim that his thought could in any way be described as "utopian." Mably was perfectly aware, Maffey argued, that his ruminations on the *communauté des biens* were only "agreeable daydreams," with utterly no chance of realization. Similar reveries could be found in the works of every major Enlightenment thinker, even the most moderate. For a genuine example of eighteenth-century utopianism, it was necessary to turn to the works of Mably's contemporary Morelly, whose *Code de la nature* was indeed an abstract blueprint for a communist society, making him a true descendant of Plato, More, and Campanella. But no equivalent utopian sketch was to be found anywhere in Mably's works, which instead revealed a constant preoccupation with a wide range of modest, realizable measures, tailored for a variety of different political circumstances—in France, England, Sweden, Poland, and the

United States—of whose practical realities Mably possessed an admirably detailed knowledge.[27] For Maffey, then, the hallmark of Mably's political thought was its *realism*, based on a sober awareness of the possible: "He was neither a utopian, nor a communist, nor a revolutionary, but rather a student of man and society who, applying the results of his research—psychological, social, and historical—attempted to sketch a political system that seemed to him the best to which his contemporaries could aspire. At times he praised men and societies of the past, or looked ahead, hopefully or pessimistically, to a distant future, without, however, abandoning himself recklessly to utopian dreams and aspirations."[28] Mably thus emerged from Maffey's study as an eminently practical, level-headed, and even somewhat pessimistic politician—a depiction to which much detail has subsequently been added, as scholars have demonstrated his close knowledge of the history and practice of European diplomacy and explored his contributions to the intense disputes over physiocracy and the experimentation with the grain trade inspired by it, his constitutional proposals for Poland and the state governments of America, and, above all, his decisive intervention in what was perhaps the key ideological contest of the epoch, the debate over the history of the French monarchy.[29]

No less than Procacci, Maffey dismissed "revolutionary" or "socialist" interpretations of Mably, whether celebratory or censorious, as self-serving anachronisms, based on a limited acquaintance with his actual works. This was the judgment of perhaps the majority of commentators in the 1950s and 1960s, at any rate in Western Europe. But as Galliani later noted, other historians were far more reluctant to part with what might be termed the "traditional" picture of Mably. Nor should this be surprising. For whatever the merits of the "conservative" or the "moderate" interpretations of Procacci and Maffey, the manifest weakness of both was their common inability or unwillingness to account for those elements of his thought that had made his revolutionary cult or "socialist" reputation possible in the first place. It is clear enough, in the first instance, that the dominant political concern of Mably's career, from mid-century onward, was the overthrow of French absolutism and its replacement with a constitutional monarchy (at the least)—a desire expressed on more than one occasion in terms for which "revolutionary" is the only possible description.[30] But above all, there was the critique of inequality around which all of his later thought revolved—Mably's belief that private property was the "principal source of all the misfortunes that afflict humanity" and his apparent advocacy of what he termed the

"the agreeable idea of the community of property (*communauté des biens*)." "Nature destined men to be equal," he could thus write, in a typical formulation. "It seems to me that it is to equality that she has attached the conservation of social qualities and happiness; and I conclude from this that the legislator's work will be in vain, if he does not devote all his attention from the outset to establishing equality in the fortune and condition of the citizenry."[31]

While these central elements of Mably's thought were minimized or simply ignored in the accounts of Procacci and Maffey, they were of course precisely what enabled Eastern European scholars after World War II to continue to insist on its protocommunist character, in more or less direct continuity with nineteenth-century conceptions. Editions or selections of his works were translated into Russian in 1950 and Polish in 1952 and 1956, with prefaces that depicted Mably as a radical democrat whose principles, if they fell short of genuine communism, were nevertheless the authentic expression of the revolutionary aspirations that were to inspire sans-culottism and Babeuvism.[32] These views were not confined to Eastern Europe. An article by Composto sought to reestablish Mably's revolutionary and egalitarian intentions, suggesting that attempts to deny these had been politically motivated. J.-L. Lecercle admitted that there was a genuine vacillation in Mably's thought concerning the possibilities of political change, but insisted that it was still necessary to "take Mably's communism as seriously as he himself did." Galliani's own opinions, in his review of the current literature, came down firmly on the side of the "radical" interpretation of Mably.[33]

Since then, these views have plainly become predominant in West European scholarship as well. For the 1970s saw the publication of a series of monographs on Mably, all of which, to varying degrees, sought to reaffirm his connection with the traditions of utopian socialism. The most substantial of these was Giovanni Stiffoni's *Utopia e ragione in G. Bonnot de Mably*, published in 1975, which remains the most comprehensive and cogent account of Mably's life and thought. Stiffoni echoed a great many of Maffey's own arguments. Mably's writing, he argued, was indeed marked by a strain of political realism—in particular a very remarkable *tactical* sense, which doubtless owed a great deal to his youthful diplomatic service at Versailles—which made any assimilation of it to the utopianism of a Morelly or a Meslier impossible. At the same time, Mably's commitment to philosophical history as a foundational discipline for political thought also served to distinguish his thought sharply from that of Rousseau. But, in contradistinction to Maffey, Stiffoni also argued that Mably's proposals for political reform, even the most modest, were incomprehensible unless one grasped the egalitarian social ideal informing them. Mably correctly saw that there was little prospect for the establishment of a regime of common property anywhere in contemporary Europe. Nevertheless, the notion that the *communauté des biens* was the "natural" order of human society still served as a regulative goal for him. Even the most minor political reform was conceived as a remedial substitution for the absence of communism in the present, and as a possible step toward its eventual reestablishment in the distant future. For Stiffoni, this utopian "moment" was the key to every aspect of Mably's political thought, and he concluded by insisting that neither Babeuf nor the later utopian socialists were wrong to look back to Mably as an ancestor.[34] A similar portrait of Mably was offered in Brigitte Coste's more slender study, *Mably: pour une utopie de bon sens* (1975), as well as in two illuminating comparative treatments by German scholars, Hans-Ulrich Thamer's *Revolution und Reaktion in der französischen Sozialkritik des 18. Jahrhunderts: Linguet, Mably, Babeuf* (1973), and Lutz Lehmann's *Mably und Rousseau: Eine Studie über die Grenzen der Emanzipation im Ancien Régime* (1975). Thamer's conclusion was particularly categorical: "It has become clear in the course of this study that the socialist theory of Mably, far from being a peripheral intellectual sport, must instead be seen as the true centerpiece of his theory; this is confirmed by the self-understanding of the author, who repeatedly refers to 'my system' whenever he wishes to counterpose a more positive image of society to the atomized and alienated world. His communist system is in fact presented as the realization of natural law itself."[35] Lehmann, for his part, depicted Mably and Rousseau as both contributing to the creation of an "emancipation philosophy" that, if it was limited by its preindustrial horizons, nevertheless formed the initial step in the evolution of thought that culminated in the modern communist movement.[36]

Thus, after some initial and discrepant attempts to establish an altogether different portrait of Mably—reactionary Catholic or moderate political reformer—a rough consensus has now emerged, which has restored and reemphasized his credentials as a revolutionary and protosocialist thinker. Agreement has not been unanimous, however, since the most distinctive recent contribution to the study of Mably, Thomas Schleich's *Aufklärung und Revolution* (1981), points in the opposite direction entirely, suggesting nothing so much as a return to the position outlined by Procacci. In Schleich's view, Mably belonged, by birth and predilection, to a specific sociocultural milieu:

that of the politically active *noblesse de robe* and *haute bourgeoisie*, whose intellectual world was dominated by a refined cultural elite, politically conservative and respectful of religious tradition, formed in the late seventeenth and early eighteenth centuries. It was this older "republic of letters" that was brusquely displaced around mid-century, as the politically radical and militantly irreligious Enlightenment proper began to conquer the institutional strongholds of French cultural life. In reaction, Mably emerged as an embittered spokesman for the old intellectual order, devoting the last decades of his life to a losing battle against the venality, secularism, and intellectual iconoclasm of the *mouvement philosophique*. Even more emphatically than Procacci or Maffey, Schleich dismisses the radical Mably of the Revolution as a purely ideological confection, having nothing to do with—indeed wholly contrary to—his own intentions and the actual role he assumed in his lifetime. Again, however, it is significant that Schleich dispenses almost entirely with sustained analysis of Mably's writings themselves: Mably's political "intentions" in fact receive almost no attention at all in his study. The reason, one is led to suspect, is that this would almost certainly have cast doubt on his peremptory exclusion of Mably from the Enlightenment—his characterization of which is manifestly reductive and monotonal—which in turn would have canceled the pretensions of his larger polemical goal, an effort to establish that "the Enlightenment did not cause the Revolution, but rather the Revolution the Enlightenment."[37] The result is that Schleich offers no explanation for the paradox that his own *Rezeptionsgeschichte* highlights so eloquently—that of an intellectual whose attitude toward the Enlightenment and the political and social modernity it championed was so ambiguous, yet whose writings could inspire the astonishing diversity of appeals which were made to them during the Revolution.

Mably and Classical Republicanism

Such then has been the approximate course of the scholarly discussion of Mably over the past several decades. On the one hand, the majority of commentators have continued to see him as fundamentally a progressive thinker, a contributor to the Enlightenment and a recognizable ancestor of both the radical democrats of the French Revolution and the utopian socialists of the nineteenth century. On the other hand, a significant minority have demurred, portraying him instead as either a conservative and sober realist, or as a philosophic reactionary and "anti-Enlightenment" thinker *tout court*. But whatever the separate merits of these views, their combined effect has probably been to reinforce a more widespread suspicion that Mably's thought possesses *no* fundamental unity, but is simply a grab-bag of various themes and positions that were never fused into a coherent whole—thereby confirming the conclusion that his life and work deserve no wider attention than they have thus far received. Matters are unlikely to rest there, however. For Mably remains in many ways an unknown author to us. We are still some distance away from assembling the sources necessary for an adequate biography; and even so crucial a task as the precise dating of his writings has yet to be undertaken in a definitive way. Moreover, there are certain important aspects of his thought that have been largely ignored in the course of recent scholarly discussion.

One of these is particularly conspicuous for its absence. As we have seen, for Constant and other early liberals who portrayed him as a key inspirer of the Revolution, the central feature of Mably's thought was his veneration for classical antiquity—his sponsorship of "ancient liberty" as a living political ideal. In fact, nothing is more obvious to any reader than the absolute centrality of the reference to Graeco-Roman antiquity in his writings, from beginning to end. His first work, *Parallèle des romains et des français*, was an extended comparison of French and Roman history: its immediate model was Montesquieu, but the *Considérations* on the Romans itself clearly belongs to a tradition of philosophical history whose ultimate inspiration was the *Discorsi* of Machiavelli. This comparative optic, contrasting classical antiquity with European modernity, provided the framework for all of Mably's subsequent historical writing, whose major change afterwards was to abandon the residual royalism of the *Parallèle* for the overt republicanism of *Observations sur les romains* and *Observations sur l'histoire de la Grèce*, with their intense celebration of the "mixed governments" of Rome and Sparta. Meanwhile, the philosophical dialogues that Mably began to write in the 1750s and 1760s were conceived in self-conscious imitation (however imperfectly) of Plato and Cicero. In them, he became without any doubt the leading "laconomaniac" of the epoch.[38] To the extent that Mably's thought was dominated by a "utopian" model, it was neither a prelapsarian Christian paradise nor More's communal island, but rather the martial, egalitarian city-states of Lycurgus, Romulus, and Numa Pompilius. Every element of the package of reforms he advocated—essentially a "mixed government," supported by agrarian and sumptuary laws below, and various forms of public cult and censorship from above—was inspired by classical precedent. Finally, the far more pessimistic works of the last decade of Mably's life, most of them withheld from print, together form an extended meditation on themes derived directly from ancient moral thought: their common goal, in Mably's terms, was to search out an Aristotelian middle ground between the two extremes of "Stoicism" and "Epicureanism." There is hardly a single page of his writing, start to finish, without some reference to the history, politics, or philosophy of classical civilization.

Yet if no subject is more obvious in Mably's works, none has been more neglected in the recent scholarly discussion of them. His preoccupation with classical politics and history is so omnipresent that it cannot be ignored altogether. But with one exception—to which we will return in a moment—the universal consensus has been that this is merely an optional ornamentation in Mably's works, the expression of his conformity to the classical or humanist conventions of the epoch, with no bearing on the fundamental character of his thought, whether the latter is conceived as "progressive" or "conservative." Even where the subject is explicitly addressed, as in Schleich's article on the "second-best state," it does not affect the ultimate classification of Mably's politics, nor lead to any attempt to connect his attitudes with larger currents of French or European political thought.[39] Elsewhere, we are explicitly warned against exaggerating the role of classical antiquity in his writing.[40]

Such indifference to so central a feature of Mably's thought might seem surprising. In fact, it undoubtedly reflects certain larger changes in scholarly judgment and fashion. For nothing is so striking as the extent to which the entire subject of classical antiquity in the political thought of the Enlightenment and in the politics of the Revolution—so central a concern for such diverse thinkers as Constant or Marx—has disappeared from the agenda of twentieth-century historiography. There is, to all appearances, only one recent study of this topic in the epoch of the Enlightenment, Guerci's *Libertà degli antichi e libertà dei moderni* (1979)—an extremely valuable essay, which is, however, limited to a single question, that of the changing estimations of the Spartan and Athenian city-states, from Rousseau to the eve of the Revolution. As for the revolutionary period itself, the last look at the place of Graeco-Roman antiquity within its political culture, astonishingly, is Parker's *The Cult of Antiquity and the French Revolutionaries*, now sixty years old.[41] Again, the common assumption seems to be that the intense disputes between "Ancients" and "Moderns" in the Enlightenment, as well as the perfervid imitation of Graeco-Roman politics in the Revolution, were essentially facultative facades, masking more genuine or "real" problems—side issues, that is, without profound significance for an historical grasp of the era. It is this wider indifference to the topic that doubtless has made it difficult to see Mably's own obsessive concern with classical politics and history as an important or exceptional feature of his thought.

This indifference is unlikely to last, however. Indeed, developments outside French historiography proper now make it possible to return to the eighteenth-century cult of antiquity with a renewed sense of its importance and meaning. For in the same period that French historians lost interest in the whole phenomenon of political classicism, it was being rediscovered with a remarkable intensity elsewhere, in ways that have fundamentally and permanently redrawn our map of early modern political thought as a whole. The recovery and reconstruction of the classical republican tradition, in the series of texts that runs from Fink's *The Classical Republicans* to Pocock's great synthesis, *The Machiavellian Moment*, have formed one of the major cumulative achievements of postwar historiography. The central themes of the Renaissance re-creation of classical republicanism—the celebration of the self-governing and self-defending citizenries of ancient Sparta and Rome, the fixation on the problem of the stability and durability of political communities, the deployment of the vocabulary of "virtue," "fortune," and "corruption"—are too familiar by now to require any rehearsal here. The key achievement of the scholarship on classical republicanism has been to suggest the existence of a *unitary* tradition of political discourse: the way in which a Renaissance political idiom enjoyed a prolonged and politically potent afterlife in early modern Europe in a variety of distinct political and national settings, among them the Dutch Republic of the seventeenth century, Stuart and Hanoverian England, and Colonial America.

But if this picture can be accepted, then there is no justification whatever for the continuing exclusion of eighteenth-century France from its purview. Pocock himself was perfectly aware of the possibilities here. Montesquieu, author of the greatest summa of European political thought, is a central figure in the later chapters of *The Machiavellian Moment*, which also contain numerous gestures in the direction of Rousseau, the "Machiavelli of the eighteenth century."[42] In point of fact, the whole structure and chronology of *The Machiavellian Moment*—if not its actual bulk—could easily have accommodated the case of eighteenth-century France in its synoptic account of European republicanism.[43] Even before Pocock's synthesis,

Franco Venturi suggested, in his lectures on *Utopia and Reform in the Enlightenment*, that the English Commonwealthmen performed the vital function of having *preserved* republican idioms and values, in an epoch that saw their senescence and eclipse elsewhere in Europe.[44] Yet as Venturi insisted, the American colonists were obviously not the only beneficiaries of this heritage. No one familiar with French political thought of the eighteenth century and the recent historiography on classical republicanism will doubt that a dialect of precisely the same political "language" appeared there as well, itself crucially dependent, as the example of Montesquieu shows, on the English example and experience. As for its later fortunes, these were surely as explosive and significant in France as in America. If the notion of an "Atlantic republican tradition" is to be taken seriously at all, it is difficult not to see the First French Republic as one of its most astonishing fruits—perhaps the climactic chapter in its long history.[45]

It thus seems reasonable to expect, in the near future, a cumulative process of historical revision bringing these perspectives to bear on the French case: new efforts to explore the "cult of Antiquity" in the Revolution and to align the experience of the First Republic with the earlier "Atlantic republican tradition," as well as a renewed study of classical republicanism in the epoch of the Enlightenment, bringing the thought of Montesquieu, Rousseau, and many others into a single focus.[46] Signs that such a process is already under way include the recent volume of essays edited by François Furet and Mona Ozouf, *Le siècle de l'avènement républicain*, as well as Martin Thom's brilliant exploration of the fate of classical republicanism in the first half of the nineteenth century in his *Republics, Nations and Tribes*. As for Mably, what is most important about the current literature on classical republicanism is that it has already pointed the way toward a novel reading of the basic character of his political thought. For the exception to the rule referred to above is to be found in what has been virtually the only writing on Mably in English for over sixty years, two articles by Keith Baker recently collected in *Inventing the French Revolution*.[47] In his reconstruction of the "political consciousness" of Mably through the prism of *Des droits et des devoirs du citoyen*, Baker not only drew attention to the central place of classical history and politics in his *oeuvre* as a whole, but suggested that Mably's text seemed to owe a specific debt to the English "Commonwealth" tradition. In fact, *Des droits et des devoirs du citoyen* could be read precisely as a plea for the application of a classical republican perspective to the French political conjuncture of the 1750s, to which Mably himself amply responded a few years later in his *Observations sur l'histoire de France.*

The interpretation of Mably briefly sketched in Baker's essays formed the initial inspiration for the study at hand, whose particular aims can now be reemphasized. The chief purpose of this book is to provide an accurate portrait of Mably as a political thinker, recovering his intentions and restoring his works to the multiple contexts—biographical and ideological—in which they were written. At the same time, this study will also attempt to shift the terms of the present discussion of Mably away from the "progressive" and "conservative" interpretations that have hitherto dominated the field, in the direction indicated by Baker's articles. It will try, in other words, to restore Mably's credentials as perhaps the leading classical republican thinker of his epoch—"the first of those advocates of ancient society against the modern world," in Thierry's words. To read his thought in this way is by no means to foreclose consideration of the various alternate descriptions that have emerged in the course of recent scholarship—"Conservative Catholic," "Enlightened reformer," "utopian communist"—each of which will find its place in the analyses that follow. In fact, by drawing attention to a central aspect of Mably's work that has been largely ignored up to now, it may well be possible to reconcile some of the more contrary descriptions that have been applied to it—if not to resolve all of the antinomies noted above, at least to place them in a novel context. Above all, no attempt will be made to deny the real historical importance of Mably's contribution to the currents of thought that flowed into utopian socialism. On the contrary, it is precisely in light of these connections that a reading of Mably as a republican thinker takes on its greatest significance. For one of the more intriguing aspects of Pocock's own writings is his hints of a still undiscovered linkage between the later incarnations of classical republicanism and the earliest versions of socialist thought, in a complex succession of protest against political and economic modernity. As we shall see, Mably's thought provides a particularly apposite terrain for searching out such interconnections.

These goals, finally, have determined the procedure adopted in this essay. The size of Mably's *oeuvre*—well over thirty separate works, most of book length—and the diversity of the subjects and genres taken up over so long an intellectual career, pose formidable problems of exposition and analysis. Rather than attempt an exhaustive accounting of each of these works, this study will instead divide them into several clusters, focusing on certain key texts within each; these will be considered in chronological order, in order to suggest something of the overall dynamic of Mably's thought, within its changing political context. The relative paucity of background material—manuscripts, correspondence, anecdotal evidence—that he left behind naturally makes it difficult to establish the main phases and chronology of his intellectual career with any precision. It is clear, for example, that there were often long intervals between the initial composition of many of his works and their ultimate publication, permitting extensive rewriting in the interim: the actual date of any given piece of writing is thus often a matter of considerable guesswork. Nevertheless, certain major hinges in Mably's intellectual evolution seem evident enough. One is the break that is marked by *Des droits et des devoirs du citoyen*, apparently written in 1758 or shortly thereafter, and *Entretiens de Phocion*, published in 1763. Not only were these works Mably's first exercises in the philosophical dialogue, his genre of preference thereafter, but they also contain his earliest appeals to natural law and to the psychology of the "passions," which provided the conceptual foundations for all of his later writings. Yet if these two dialogues can thus be said to have inaugurated the "mature" phase of Mably's thought—providing us with the main periodization used in this study—it is important to recognize that he arrived at this point relatively late in life. *Des droits et des devoirs du citoyen* and *Entretiens de Phocion* were written as Mably entered his sixth decade, at mid-point in a literary career that had begun some twenty years earlier, and had already won him an international reputation. His "mature" thought, in other words, was the product of a very long intellectual apprenticeship, which was far more interesting and complex than is often recognized. It is to this process of development, the subject of the following two chapters, that we need to turn first.

CHAPTER 2

A Royalist Debut

Mably's first book, *Parallèle des romains et des français, par rapport au gouvernement*, was published in two volumes in 1740. It occupies a peculiar place among his writings, not merely for its priority. A decade after its appearance, its author described it in these terms: "Neither order nor connection in its ideas, numberless repetitions, objects presented in a false light—nor were these the only faults that the mania for parallels prompted in me. I found myself forced to pass over in silence many things that are necessary for understanding the peoples whose history I was studying, and, what is far worse, to say many things that I should never even have thought."[1] Mably's self-criticism apparently had its histrionic side as well. His friend and eulogist, the abbé Gabriel Brizard, reports that on one occasion Mably came across a copy of the *Parallèle* in the library of the Comte d'Egmont: to the shock of his onlooking friends, he took up the two volumes and tore them to pieces.[2] Not surprisingly, the book was proscribed from Mably's body of works: it is the only one of his major writings to appear in none of the *oeuvres complètes.*

The reasons for Mably's wholesale repudiation of his first intellectual effort are not difficult to discern. For *Parallèle des romains et des français* was a sustained statement of everything he opposed in his mature thought: it offered an enthusiastic apology for the Bourbon monarchy, as well as a breathless recommendation on behalf of the commercial civilization of contemporary Europe. Yet within a decade of its publication, Mably had become the proponent of a republicanism whose chief models were ancient Sparta and Rome, and a harsh critic of the European economic order. By 1758, he was able to contemplate the prospect of a violent "revolution" in France with sanguine approval. What brought about this profound reversal of political conviction? It can hardly be an accident that it coincided with a critical juncture in French political history. These were the years when the Enlightenment emerged as a powerful movement of social criticism for the first time, headquartered thereafter in Paris; the years when the precarious equilibrium between the French monarchy and its ruling elites, sustained for half a century, began to collapse in the face of fiscal revolt and reformation-style religious controversy; the years when the martial infirmity of Bourbon absolutism received its most spectacular and fatal confirmations abroad—the years, in other words, when the specter of the Revolution could first be glimpsed on the distant horizon. It was during this ominous political conjuncture that Mably matured as a thinker, and, as we shall see in later chapters, its effects are amply recorded in his writing. At the same time, however, it would be a mistake to portray his intellectual evolution as simply a series of responses to a changing external environment. For his development also followed an internal logic of its own, dictated in large part by the starting point of his earliest works, which established the permanent agenda for much of his later thought. Mably's dramatic shift of political allegiance in fact concealed what turned out to be a considerable degree of intellectual continuity, from *Parallèle des romains et des français* onwards.

At all events, little is known of his life prior to 1740. Mably was born at Grenoble on 14 March 1709. His family had only recently, within the previous generation, accomplished a transition from the upper legal bourgeoisie to the provincial *noblesse de robe.* His father, Gabriel Bonnot, arrived at the considerable position of *Secrétaire du Roi* in the local Parlement by the end of his career, and was prosperous enough to purchase several seigneuries in the region; among these was Mably-en-Forenz, from which his second son drew his name. Mably's elder brother Jean naturally inherited his father's estate, and eventually became *Grand Prévot* of Lyon; it was there, in 1740, that he engaged the services of Jean-Jacques Rousseau as a tutor for his children.[3] Mably's younger brother, Etienne Bonnot de Condillac, of course went on to become the preeminent philosopher of the French Enlightenment. As second and third sons, both Gabriel and Etienne were groomed for ecclesiastical careers. The former attended the Jesuit Collège de la Marche at Lyon, and then the Jesuit seminary of Saint-Sulpice in Paris, from which he emerged as a subdeacon in 1635. But Mably advanced no further than this in the Church. Never ordained, he joined the ranks of the worldly and often irreligious *abbés commendataires* who were so prominent in eighteenth-century social and intellectual life.[4] As we shall see, the precise character of Mably's religious convictions remains somewhat mysterious. Here it will be enough to note that the balance of the evidence suggests his consistent adherence to a fairly conventional form of deism; at no point do his writings betray any hint of a specifically *Christian* devotion. If he lacked the conviction or ambition to pursue a career in the Church, it was evidently because his interest had instead been captured from an early age by politics and history. In his brief pamphlet "La vie privée de M. l'abbé de Mably," his friend Jean-Jacques Barthélemy, author of *Voyage de jeune Anacharsis en Grèce*, reports that Mably had already written a long "Essai historique" by age seventeen. The fragments Barthélemy cites—whose authenticity is not verified elsewhere—suggest something like an early sketch for what eventually became his first published book.[5]

'Parallèle des romains et des français'

Our first real glimpse of Mably, in any case, comes only with his remarkable debut in *Parallèle des romains et des français*. As the title suggests, the book consists of alternating treatments of episodes in Roman and French history: the first volume examines the internal political development of the two nations, the second their foreign relations and imperial expansion. Mably's preface opens with a spirited attack on conventional antiquarian history, which is insufficiently "philosophical" in his eyes. Instead of uncovering "the springs that move society, and sustain its life," most historians are content merely to offer a "useless parade" of names, dates, and events, devoid of any genuine explanation. The young author announces his intention to "make reasons and facts march hand in hand, so that they can provide support to one another." On the one hand, he will try to avoid the mistakes of Plato, whose *Republic* is merely a "political novel," with no mooring in historical reality. On the other, he will shun the faults of those historians whose works, like those of Machiavelli, are marred by "half-truths, for having neglected to examine the facts from all sides and in all their circumstances"—or what is worse, historians who do not even attempt to provide genuine explanations for the events they recount.[6] Given these declarations of intent, it comes as no surprise when Mably concludes his preface with an acknowledgment of his debt to the "great book" that Montesquieu had published six years earlier, *Considérations sur les causes de la grandeur des Romains et de leur décadence*. It is clear that the latter provided the basic paradigm of historical discourse, not only for *Parallèle des romains et des français*, but indeed for all of Mably's subsequent historical writing: essentially, an episodic narrative, invoking a schedule of heterogeneous "causes" in order to account for the rise and decline of forms of government.[7] In fact, it becomes obvious, as the *Parallèle* proceeds, that Mably's narrative of Roman history itself depends very directly on that of Montesquieu. There is no sign of much more than a superficial acquaintance with ancient historians or sources; Livy is hardly mentioned, Polybius cited once, and Tacitus twice.[8] Nor is the French half of the narrative any less derivative. In it, Mably relies on an unsurprising array of secondary works, above all the two works that dominated the field of French history at the time, the great narratives of Mézeray and Daniel.[9]

In other words, there is little trace of the sort of historical erudition that Mably was to deploy so effectively twenty years later in *Observations sur l'histoire de France*. But the great interest of the book lies not in its negligible scholarly achievement, but in its character as a *political* statement. *Parallèle des romains et des français* was in fact a highly polemical—and unorthodox—intervention in an ideological contest that had a long prior history. This was the great debate over the history of the French monarchy, whose roots lay in the sixteenth century, but which had entered an entirely new phase with the passing of Louis XIV. It is clear that this dispute, which was central to the political culture of eighteenth-century France, was the crucible in which the political thought of Mably, along with that of many others, was formed. It was a French variant of a type of ideological struggle that was widespread in early modern Europe. For the legitimacy of absolute monarchy was everywhere particularly vulnerable to attack on historical grounds. Advances in centralized authority could nearly always be portrayed by its opponents as violations of an "ancient constitution" or "fundamental laws," normally understood to be an ensemble of inherited rights and prerogatives dating back to the medieval estates-monarchies. The great political upheavals of the sixteenth and seventeenth centuries in Europe, from the French Religious Wars and the Dutch Revolt to the English Revolution itself, were thus invariably accompanied by ideological battles fought on the terrain of history. For all of their propagandistic character, the resulting debates were often of central importance in the evolution of the local political culture: J. G. A. Pocock's careful reconstruction of a version of such an ideological controversy in seventeenth-century England, *The Ancient Constitution and the Feudal Law*, is a classic in the history of ideas. In France, the sixteenth century had seen a memorable discourse on the "ancient constitution," beginning with the *Mémoires* of Commynes and the *Monarchie de France* of Seyssel; this reached its climax during the ordeal of the Religious Wars, in works such as Hotman's *Francogallia* and Bodin's *Six livres de la République*, to name only two major texts.[10] Yet if historical reference was central to the political thought of the sixteenth century, it tended to be eclipsed as French absolutism moved toward its maturity in the seventeenth. Nothing is more striking than the near-total neglect of history as a means of legitimation in the major work of the Bourbon monarchy's official apologist, Bossuet's *Politique tirée des paroles de l'Ecriture sainte*.

Once French absolutism had passed its zenith, however, and the reaction to the iron discipline of Versailles and its record of defeat in the international arena began to form, it was only natural that its opponents would again attempt to vindicate themselves by means of an appeal to history.[11] The inaugural figure in the eighteenth-century debate was thus the enigmatic comte Henri de Boulainvilliers, who gave memorable expression to aristocratic resentment against absolutism in a number of writings, the most influential of which was certainly his *Lettres sur les anciens parlements de France*.[12] He echoed the earlier protests of a Hotman or Jurieu, but the eloquent candor of his class commitments, shorn of any appeals to Protestantism, conferred a sociological insight on his work that surpassed that of any of his predecessors. For Boulainvilliers, the founding moment of French history was the conquest of Gaul by the Frankish warriors from whom the present-day nobility was descended. The aristocratic republic they established, in which an elective monarch was subject to the authority of a sovereign assembly, was the primordial and sole legitimate government of France. But the prerogatives of the nobility were gradually usurped by a succession of adroit monarchs, who freed the dependent population of Gaul captured in the conquest, seized the great fiefs from which the feudal lords drew their sustenance, and finally destroyed the assembly of the realm. An untrammeled despotism was thus erected over the ruins of the "ancient constitution."

This rendering of French history, a masterpiece of political provocation, was to know an astonishing success in the eighteenth century: Boulainvilliers was discussed continuously down to the Revolution. Unsurprisingly, it immediately elicited a number of royalist responses, of which the most authoritative was that of Jean-Baptiste Dubos, permanent secretary of the Académie Française. The central claim of his *Histoire critique de l'établissement de la monarchie française dans les Gaules*, published in 1734, was that the entire notion of a "conquest" of Gaul was a mirage: no such event had ever taken place. The Merovingian kings were the legitimate heirs of Roman imperial authority in the region, their government a monarchy pure and simple. A rapacious nobility subsequently arrogated sovereignty to themselves, reduced the majority of the population to a state of servitude, and instigated the decline into the anarchy and brigandage of the feudal period. The gradual resumption of absolute authority by the French kings—together with the enfranchisement of the Third Estate—was, for Dubos, merely the restoration of the original and only legitimate constitution of the realm.

Such were the inaugural versions of the *thèse nobiliaire* and the *thèse royale*: virtually antithetical accounts of the national past. The works of Boulainvilliers and Dubos were in any case only the opening salvos in a contest that was to undergo a fascinating evolution over the course of the century.[13] Mably himself was to make a major contribution to a later phase of the controversy, to which we will return in Chapter Six. It was this debate, with its strange combination of antiquarian erudition and passionate political commitment, that provided the matrix for the intellectual development of the young Mably, and into which he entered as a participant with his first book. There is no uncertainty as to which side he took in the controversy. *Parallèle des romains et des français* was clearly conceived as a contribution to the royalist cause: as such, it contains the expected criticisms of Boulainvilliers and recommendations on behalf of Dubos.[14] At the same time, what is most striking about the book is what separates it from any orthodox statement of the *thèse royale.* For in effect, Mably dispensed entirely with the concept that served as the central token in the debate for both the royalist and aristocratic camps: the notion of an "ancient constitution" of the monarchy, legitimate by reason of its *priority* in French history. Instead, in a move that was both naïve and daring, he attempted a historical vindication of the monarchy by means of a systematic comparison of it with the greatest "monarchy" of classical antiquity, the Roman Empire. Of course, the use of "parallels" of this sort for apologetic purposes already had a long history in France, first emerging with the consolidation of absolutism itself in the sixteenth century, and reaching a monotonous climax during the reign of Louis XIV, when the identification or favorable contrasting of the king and his epoch with the Augustan age was an omnipresent element of royal ideology.[15] In fact, by 1673 usages of this kind had helped to give rise to an acrimonious and protracted cultural dispute, which in a sense was to provide the basic framework for French social thought from Fénelon to Montesquieu and beyond: the famous *Querelle des Anciens et des Modernes*. From the start, it was clear that a great deal more was at stake than the purely literary questions that were the official objects of the "Quarrel." In a sense, the whole attack on civilization characteristic of the most radical social criticism of the mid-eighteenth century was already prefigured in the apparently innocuous nostalgia of La Bruyère's evocation of Athenian "liberty";[16] while Perrault, Fontenelle, and other "moderns" understood themselves to be defending, not merely contemporary literary performances, but the entire political, martial, and economic program sponsored by the Sun King.[17] The "Quarrel" is conventionally thought to have ended around 1716, with the close of the final duel between Madame Dacier and La Motte. In fact, its central themes were resumed almost immediately in the debates that followed in the wake of the "Law System" and its debacle, which in turn provided the foundations for the great defenses of "luxury" and "commerce" of the 1730s, introducing Mandevillian thought into France for the first time: Melon's *Essai politique sur le commerce* (1734) and the abbé Cartaud de la Villate's *Essai historique et philosophique sur le goût* (1736).[18]

Against this background, the novelty of Mably's *Parallèle des romains et des français* emerges very clearly. It presents what can accurately be described as a *politicization* of the "Quarrel between the Ancients and the Moderns," in the service of royalism. Its title itself is a remembrance of some of the key texts of the "modernist" camp in the dispute: Perrault's famous *Parallèle des Anciens et des Modernes, en ce qui concerne les arts et les sciences* (1687–92), and Vertron's *Parallèle poétique de Louis le Grand avec les princes surnommés Grands* (1686), among others.[19] For obvious reasons, neither the participants in the "Quarrel" nor in the debates over "luxury" of the 1720s and 1730s had broached political issues explicitly. But this is what Mably now proceeded to do, in the context of the ongoing dispute over the history of the French monarchy. A closer look at the structure of his argument in the *Parallèle* brings this out very clearly. Its founding premise is the claim that the histories of both Rome and France reveal, at the highest level of generality, a slow evolution from a form of "mixed" government to a form of monarchy. Mably expends considerable energy in establishing the basis for this comparison. The Roman Republic and the French monarchy, he argues, both sprang from modest origins, in rude but fiercely independent warrior bands; the original government of both, formed without a legislator as the unintended consequence of domestic strife, was a "mixture" of two pure types; the decisive test for each nation came in an epochal struggle for survival with the "commercial" powers of Carthage and England; and the transition toward monarchy in both was assured by an episode of civil war. The Religious Wars thus become a reprise of the Roman Revolution, and the absolutist state of Richelieu and Louis XIV the modern counterpart of the Augustan settlement.

Of course, the real center of gravity of Mably's argument, once these somewhat strained "parallels" are established, lies in his account of the *divergences* between Rome and France. For the Roman Republic and the medieval French monarchy represented two very different forms of the "mixed government," in Mably's view. The former emerged unwittingly out of the struggle between the senatorial nobility and its plebeian antagonists.[20] The resulting regime was a "mélange" of democracy and aristocracy, in which the people possessed "supreme power," but were tempered in its application by the senate and the consuls. In France, on the other hand, the invading Germanic warriors had imported "a Military Government, difficult to define, which occupied an ambiguous middle ground between Aristocracy and Monarchy, preserving the abuses of both without any of their advantages."[21] The resulting tug-of-war—between nobles and ruling dynasties in this case—was then institutionalized by the remarkable figure of Charlemagne, who created a "*Gouvernement Aristo-Monarchique*," an act that determined the course of French history for centuries to come.[22] As to which of the two variants of "mixed government" was the better, Mably leaves little doubt. The Roman Republic, a predominantly popular state tempered by an aristocratic senate, was marvelously adapted for expansion. The result was its breathtaking ascent to a position of world domination. The French, on the contrary, "did not understand the mechanisms of a mixture of governments and, like the other peoples who established themselves within the Empire, believed that the more perfect the equality they established between Prince and Nobility, the more perfect their government would be."[23] This was a fatal error, for the "aristo-monarchical Government of Charlemagne gave rise to the cruelest divisions. A poison can be made from the mixture of two salutary liqueurs; there are such antipathies in the moral world as well, and the union of monarchy and aristocratic government produced a form of regime that was long the source of all the evils from which France was to suffer."[24] The lethal stalemate formalized by Charlemagne almost immediately collapsed into the anarchy of the "feudal government," in which sovereignty was hopelessly fragmented into a thousand parts, all at war with one another: "It is impossible, I believe, to imagine a more vicious government than that established in France under the second dynasty of our kings. Despite the order aimed at in feudal law, the laws themselves reduced everything to an equal anarchy . . . from which emerged an uncertainty of the citizen in regard to his fate, a confusion of laws, the oppression of the weak, and all the disorders of civil war."[25] In Rome, one version of mixed government produced a rise to world empire; in France, another yielded a descent into barbarism.

The key to this argument lies in Mably's deployment of the concept of "mixed government." No complete historical account of this notion, so crucial in Western political philosophy, exists, but the main lines of its development are well enough known.[26] The idea first emerged with the classical taxonomy of governments itself, in the earliest Greek political thought, where its initial function was perhaps to signal some of the empirical limitations of the simple tripartite schema of "monarchy," "aristocracy," and "democracy." By the time of Aristotle, however, the notion had been elevated to a far more important position, and taken on a normative role: the *politeia* of the fourth book of the *Politics* is described as a blend of democracy and aristocracy. The tripartite version of the idea, in which mixed government is supposed to unite all three forms of government, seems to have been a post-Classical development, a product of Hellenistic, particularly Stoic, writers. Finally, it was the explanatory problems posed by the Roman conquest of the Mediterranean that brought the doctrine to its fullest development in antiquity. The sixth book of Polybius's *Histories* fixed the theory of mixed government in its canonical form: the success of the two most celebrated city-states of antiquity was expressly attributed to their perfect blending of the three forms of government, producing both the tranquil durability of Sparta and the triumphant expansionism of Rome. It was in this fruitfully reductive form that the theory was bequeathed to medieval and early modern Europe, through the mediation of Machiavelli above all. Soon enough Mably himself would take up the Polybian-Machiavellian doctrine of mixed government, making it a central token of his own thought. In the *Parallèle*, however, he avoids the tripartite version, for reasons that seem clear enough. The purpose of the latter, after all, was to account for the *stability* of the governments it describes: Mably instead wished to emphasize the *instability* of the two forms of "mixed government" of Rome and France, which finally capsized into two different forms of monarchy, leading ultimately to a spectacular reversal of fortune for the two nations.

Neither of the two authorities that Mably follows on Rome makes use of the notion of "mixed government," Polybian or otherwise. But both Montesquieu and Vertot do, in fact, tend to portray the history of the Republic as a change from an aristocratic to a democratic state. For Montesquieu, the government of Rome became purely "aristocratic" with the expulsion of the Tarquins; then, starting with the creation of the tribunate, "Power was bound to revert to the greatest number, and an aristocracy changed, little by little, into a popular state."[27] Vertot's analysis is nearly identical: "With the establishment of the tribunate, Rome changed the form of its government for a second time. As we have seen, it had evolved from a monarchical state into a kind of aristocracy, in which all authority was in the hands of the senate and the grandees. But the creation of the tribunate saw the emergence, imperceptibly and by degrees, of a new democracy, in which the people, under different pretexts, took possession of the greater part of the government."[28] In practice, Mably's version of late Republican history remains very close to this conception. He provides a conventional account of the fall of the Republic, relying heavily on Vertot and Montesquieu. The Republic, in essence, was corrupted by the wealth and civilization of its new Eastern possessions, and finally was crushed under the weight of its imperial responsibilities.[29] The only result of a half century of civil war was to determine which military commander would make himself king. The establishment of the Roman monarchy then revealed the disadvantages of the mixture of democracy and aristocracy that had been the glory of the Republic. It had secured an empire for Rome, but had done nothing to prepare its people for monarchical rule. The basis for imperial authority, the *lex regia*, simply deposited the power of the people and the nobility alike into the hands of a single man. There were no barriers against despotism, nothing to prevent the empire from sinking into the sheerest tyranny, which it promptly did.[30] The Roman people were thus doomed to centuries of bleak oppression and the eventual dissolution of their empire. Loyal to Montesquieu's picture in the *Considérations*, Mably can summon up no enthusiasm for the rule even of the Antonines.[31]

The outcome in France, on the other hand, was very different. For all the miseries of the "feudal government," it paradoxically prepared the way for its own superscession: "The government founded on the law of fiefs carried within itself the cause of its ruin. Flawed by nature and contrary to all order, it was consequently unstable, for the two things are tied together as cause and effect. This government exposed the French to so many foreign perils, and placed them in a situation so unbearable, that the result would have to be either a final poison that would destroy the monarchy, or some general remedy for its vices."[32] The remedy was found in the basic premise of feudal law, the notion that all fiefs were ultimately held from the king. Over the course of many centuries, using a variety of skillful expedients, the Capetian kings—who thus merit the title of "fathers of the nation" in Mably's eyes—progressively made good their claims to sovereign authority in France, reducing the arrogant feudal nobility and freeing the dependent population of the countryside from its servitude. Moreover, the gradual and largely pacific nature of this process produced a *perfected* form of monarchy in France, immune to the defects of the ancient form:

> It was without shock and without convulsion that the kings took possession of their rightful authority. Philippe-Auguste launched the enterprise; after many vicissitudes, Louis XIV carried it to its conclusion. . . . The French never felt themselves to be oppressed, nor did their kings ever have occasion to regard themselves as usurpers. Manners (*moeurs*) prepared the way for the events that followed; thus the manner in which the kings acquired their authority is the guarantee that they will never exceed it. . . . The continual security in which the French nation found itself in not passing from one government to an entirely different one, established there the confidence that makes for the strength and happiness of peoples. Since there had never been a complete and sudden abrogation of all laws in France, as there had been in Rome, there emerged, if one can put it this way, a mixture of ancient laws and novel usages. The latter served to correct the former, and the former as a barrier against despotism.[33]

The mixed government of medieval France, for all of its faults, thus yielded the most perfect of governments. European monarchy, Mably insists, is so constituted that it is incapable of degenerating into despotism: "Although the prince is the supreme legislator and possesses all authority, the liberty and the privileges that he has accorded to the different orders of his state are never disturbed. He has every right to take them away, but this liberty and these privileges are such that they prevent him from actually doing so."[34] By contrast with the mixed governments of antiquity, not to speak of ancient monarchy, the absolutist state of modern Europe engages in a continual process of self-correction which makes it immune to any fatal corruption: "Monarchy, and here I speak of that which admits of no mixture with other forms of government and which nevertheless carries within it a barrier against despotism . . . is of such a nature that it is subject only to temporary maladies."[35] Mably can thus conclude with a rather unguarded prediction as to the future of the Bourbon dynasty: "The more one meditates upon the fall of the Roman Empire, and on the other great monarchies that have preceded it, the more one is tempted to predict an eternal duration for the French Monarchy."[36]

Mably's first book thus ends with an unabashed apology, not merely for the Bourbon monarchy, but for modern civilization itself. In effect, the juxtaposition of its parallel histories, both recounting a slow transition from a form of mixed government to a form of monarchy, produces a *third* narrative, covering the whole change from the ancient to the modern world. This makes possible a passage from what Mably calls a "*bonté relative*" to a "*bonté absolue.*" In absolute terms, he declares early in the book, there is no doubt that monarchy is the best and most suitable form of government for mankind—as most authorities agree, it occupies the middle ground between the anarchy of democracy and the despotism of aristocracy.[37] But the best and most perfect form of monarchy was simply unavailable to the Romans, and to ancient peoples in general. In essence, the material equality, poverty, and spirit of independence of the citizens of the early Republic were incompatible with monarchy: "Mores (*moeurs*) were in contradiction with the subordination that monarchy requires. The latter form of government permits true obedience, while the character of the Roman people could only be reconciled to the laws of democracy."[38] Later, once the transition to monarchy unwittingly had been assured, the Romans proved woefully ignorant of the means of erecting "barriers" against despotism—that is, of ensuring that the interests of the monarch and those of the nation would coincide. In those circumstances, the "mixed" government that united democracy and aristocracy was by far the best available form of government: it was responsible for all the achievements of the Spartan and Roman Republics. But the world of antiquity passed irrevocably away with the fall of the Empire. Mably provides no precise causal account for this deep change, nor even any clear description of its exact provenance. His language shifts constantly from elements that are roughly material—changes in social stratification and kinds of economic activities—to those that are "ideal" or normative, which he typically designates as "*moeurs*" or "customs." But it is clear that the heart of this transformation concerned the status of commerce and "luxury" in the ancient and modern worlds:

> Luxury destroyed equality in Sparta and Rome, while in France it did the contrary, distributing to the people the superfluity of the rich; it united social echelons, and promoted a circulation among them that was as useful under a monarchical government as it had once been pernicious under a democracy. . . . Wealth, abundance, the arts and industry, are real

goods for men; it is by means of the patient uncovering of the new ties and new relations that these create in society, that modern politics has found the secret of rendering itself superior to that of antiquity.[39]

Not only did this change preclude the possibility of reproducing the balance of Democracy and Aristocracy found in the ancient republics—"it is impossible for men to assume again the character of the Spartans and the earliest Romans"[40]—but it ultimately paved the way for the development of the *bonté absolue* of modern monarchy, shorn of the defects that characterized ancient despotism: "It is among the modern peoples, and in particular from the French government, that one can learn to unite warfare, commerce, and the arts so as to create a truly flourishing state."[41] In these lines we hear very clearly the echoes of the defense of economic modernity that was the work of so many writers of the early Enlightenment.[42]

We have already glimpsed something of Mably's own later estimation of the merits of his first book. How in fact should *Parallèle des romains et des français* be judged? A sense of both its achievements and its limitations can perhaps be obtained by briefly comparing it with another book, published a few years later, which also constituted, in part, an oblique contribution to the debate over the history of the French monarchy: *De l'Esprit des lois.* For Mably's volumes might well seem, at first glance, to anticipate many of the themes that were to receive a rather more poised and authoritative treatment in Montesquieu's masterpiece. After all, the historical thought of the latter was itself dominated by an awareness of the gulf that separated modern Europe from classical antiquity, whether expressed in the terms of the "theory of governments" of the opening books of *De l'Esprit des lois,* or of the "history of commerce" presented in Books XX and XXI. Mably's construal of the virtues of the French monarchy might thus be seen as a cruder anticipation of Montesquieu's mature theorization of European monarchy, in which a king "rules by fixed and established laws"—a form of government that Montesquieu insisted was wholly unknown to antiquity. At the same time, of course, whatever their surface similarity, an enormous distance separates the *Parallèle* from Montesquieu's great treatise. It concerns not so much the overall conception of historical progression assumed by both, as their differing conceptions of the particular character of the modern world. One clue to the difference is the handling of England within their respective theoretical schemes. By and large, the English constitution appears in Mably's text only as a test case for "mixed" government in the modern world. His judgment is uniformly negative: its unworkable combination of aristocracy and monarchy is what condemned it to ultimate defeat in the Hundred Years' War and then to an experience of domestic strife unique in Europe.[43] It hardly needs to be pointed out how far Mably's dismissal of the case of England lies from Montesquieu's grasp of its absolute centrality for any assessment of European political modernity.

But the most important divergence between the two concerns simply the nature of monarchy itself, specifically in regard to the precise *limits* on royal authority envisioned by each writer—always the most sensitive point for any theorization of absolute monarchy. Montesquieu's conception of the "nature" of monarchy is famous: "The intermediate, subordinate, and dependent powers constitute the nature of monarchical government, that is, that in which one man alone governs by means of fundamental laws. I said the intermediate, subordinate, and dependent powers: in fact, in monarchy the prince is the source of all civil and political power."[44] At first glance, this seems little different from the pronouncements of Mably noticed above. But Montesquieu goes on to provide his account of the limits of monarchy with a basis in social class ("The most natural intermediate and subordinate power is that of the nobility. It enters, in a sense, into the essence of monarchy, whose fundamental maxim is, *no monarchy, no nobility, no nobility, no monarch*") and an institutional structure (both in the clergy and in the *parlements*, the guardians of the "fundamental laws") wholly missing in that of Mably. The latter hardly mentions the *parlements*, which would later loom so large in his own explorations of French history.[45] Lacking the sociological insight of Montesquieu, Mably instead resorts to the most conventional shibboleths of absolutist apology, the notion that the guarantee against despotism in France lies not in positive laws but in the "manners and customs" of the French,[46] and appeals to the "Salic Law."[47] These comparisons reveal the limits of the *Parallèle des romains et des français* as an exercise in political and historical thought. In the end, the energy and ingenuity of its manipulation of political concepts and historical schemes are crushed under the weight of the rather conventional apologetic purposes to which they are subordinated, which were in fact soon enough repudiated by the young author.

A Career in Diplomacy and a Change of Direction

Still, Mably's first book met with some success among contemporary readers, receiving favorable notice in the *Mercure de France*, the *Mémoires de Trevoux*, the *Journal des Sçavans*, and the

Bibliothèque raisonnée.[48] Voltaire described it approvingly in a letter to his friend Hénault: "It is true that the comparison is a bit surprising, but the book is full of spirit: my guess is that it was written by a bastard of M. de Montesquieu, who wishes to be both a philosopher and a good citizen."[49] This first literary success coincided with Mably's definitive move to Paris. He had the great fortune to be related to Claudine-Alexandre Guérin de Tencin, one of the most redoubtable social figures of the first half of the century. Having left behind the scandals of her youth—which included the illegitimate birth and abandonment of the son who became d'Alembert—Madame de Tencin had settled into a life of novel-writing and literary patronage, presiding over one of the handful of great salons of the epoch.[50] Both Mably and Condillac were welcomed into a company that included, at different times, Fontenelle, Marivaux, Marmontel, Duclos, Prévost, Saint-Pierre, Montesquieu, Bolingbroke, and Chesterfield. The association also brought Mably more tangible benefits. For Madame de Tencin had managed to secure, in 1742, the elevation of her brother, the archbishop of Embrun, to the post of Minister of State in the administration of the aging Fleury. The archbishop, discomfited by the prospect of speaking before the Council, and impressed by the "profundity" of his young relative's political opinions, engaged Mably as a secretary, to aid in drafting written statements of his views. Mably thus began a career in the bureaucratic corps of the French monarchy that lasted only a few short years, yet left him with a knowledge of the machinery of absolutist diplomacy shared by few other writers of the epoch.[51]

This in turn gave him the opportunity to venture into print a second time. For the benefit of Cardinal Tencin, Mably had assembled summaries of the major international treaties and agreements of the past century. This was published, with his explanatory notes, in two volumes in 1746, as *Le droit public de l'Europe, fondé sur les traités.* It consists of résumés and citations, together with a considerable explanatory apparatus, of the chief international treaties and agreements among the major European powers, from Westphalia onwards. As such, the first edition of the *Droit public* is a virtual history of international relations from 1648 to 1740. Its originality need not be exaggerated. It was proceeded by works such as Amelot de la Houssaye's *Recueil des traités de paix* (6 vols., 1693), Barbeyrac's *Histoire des anciens traités* (10 vols., 1739), and Rousset de Missy's *Recueil historique d'actes, négociations, mémoires et traités, depuis la paix d'Utrecht jusqu'à présent* (19 vols., 1736). By comparison with these gigantic compendia, however, Mably's handbook was a model of clarity and rational exposition, and it met with instant success, not only in France but abroad as well. German translations appeared in 1749 and 1756; and an Italian edition in 1784; in England, the *Droit public* was used as a university text.[52] In the meantime, a new French edition was published in 1748; a final revision, adding a volume that took the story down to the Peace of Paris, was published in 1764.

What does the *Droit public* reveal about Mably's outlook on European politics? The work was undertaken in the service of the French monarchy, and no edition, in fact, strays very far from the posture of detached neutrality that might be expected from a low-ranking civil servant. Still, a certain amount of judgment and appraisal was inherent in the project. On the one hand, Mably's initial application for permission to publish the *Droit public* was refused, forcing him to have the book printed in Amsterdam instead of Paris. The offending passages were some mild criticisms of the foreign policy of Louis XIV, a denunciation of the Edict of Nantes, and an acerbic description of oriental despotism. On the other hand, Mably soon found himself under attack from the opposite direction. In 1748 the Huguenot Rousset, himself a stipendiary of the Dutch government, brought out an unauthorized edition of the *Droit public*, to which he added an enormous commentary of his own, highly critical of Mably. Rousset acknowledged the usefulness of the compilation, but constantly castigated its author for his biases against the Dutch and the Austrians. In his eyes, Mably was plainly an agent of Versailles, inspired by the *raison-d'état* principles of Richelieu and Colbert. Mably dismissed these charges disdainfully in a new preface to the 1764 edition of the *Droit public*.[53] Still, it is clear that he was stung by at least some of the criticisms, for the same edition incorporates changes in a number of the passages singled out by Rousset.[54]

In any case, as his fortieth year approached, Mably had not only established a certain literary reputation, in France and abroad, but was apparently well-placed to build a diplomatic career in the service of the Bourbon monarchy. Yet he abruptly abandoned his post in 1747 and severed all relations with Tencin. The occasion was the Cardinal's decision to authorize the annulment of a Protestant marriage, over Mably's objections. Brizard reports: "[Tencin] said that he wished to act as a Cardinal, a Bishop, and a priest. Mably argued that he should act as a statesman. The Cardinal responded that he would dishonor himself in following such advice; the Abbé, furious, took his leave abruptly, and never saw him again."[55] We know nothing more about the incident, but the principle involved is evident enough. Beyond these immediate circumstances, the rupture was surely also the expression of a deeper discontentment with his activities and surroundings, which ultimately disqualified Mably for any career in the service of either Church or State. Numerous passages in his later works testify to his profound revulsion for the injustices and irrationalities of court politics. Brizard adds that in breaking with Tencin, Mably sacrificed "his fortune for his liberty." This may indeed be taken in a literal sense. Peter Friedemann has assembled the sources regarding Mably's income at various points in his life, and they reveal quite modest resources, very nearly approximating the virtuous poverty so frequently extolled in his writings.[56] After the break with Tencin, his income consisted entirely of a small annuity from the estate of his parents and the rent from a minor ecclesiastical office he received in 1643. This revenue was nearly doubled some twenty years later, when Mably was granted an ecclesiastical pension through the intervention of the Duchesse d'Enville. Even after this, however, his total income never exceeded 6,100 *livres* a year.[57] This permitted him to devote himself entirely to study and writing, but on condition of an extremely frugal existence.

CHAPTER 3

About Face: From the 'Parti des Modernes' to the 'Parti des Anciens'

Whatever its precise role in his development, the breach with Tencin signaled the beginning of a sea change in Mably's political convictions. One result, as we have seen, was the repudiation of *Parallèle des romains et des français*. But Mably did not in fact simply discard his first book. Instead, he divided its volumes into their two component parts—the parallel histories of ancient Rome and modern France. These were then carefully revised, in a long process that neared completion only with the publication of *Observations sur l'histoire de France* in 1765, a quarter-century after the appearance of the *Parallèle*. However, the first important step in this process, marking a decisive departure from the outlook of *Parallèle des romains et des français*, was not long in coming. In 1749, shortly after the break with Tencin, Mably published *Observations sur les Grecs*—"observations" now became the preferred designation for his historical works, which were still conceived according to the model of Montesquieu's *Considérations*. This new book, Mably wrote in its dedication, "is merely a series of reflections on the manners, the government, and the politics of Greece, in which I examine the general and particular causes of its prosperity and its misfortunes."[1] Having established this interpretation of ancient Greece, Mably then returned to the account of Roman history provided in the *Parallèle*. His revision of this material, entitled *Observations sur les Romains*, was published two years later, in 1751. The importance of these two works for Mably's intellectual evolution can scarcely be overestimated, for this new appeal to classical antiquity was to form the cornerstone on which the whole structure of his mature political thought was erected.

It is no doubt a sign of some initial hesitation before this change that Mably soon became dissatisfied with his inaugural exploration of Greek history. He started to revise the work at some point during the next decade, and the final version of it appeared in print only in 1764, as *Observations sur l'histoire de la Grèce*. In a new preface, Mably writes: "When one has mishandled a worthy subject, is it possible to refrain from returning one's work? I could have left my Observations on the Greeks such as they were, had it been only a question of poor writing. But a dangerous doctrine should not be permitted to stand: false political maxims are too important for the happiness of men, for an author not to correct himself once he has glimpsed the truth."[2] In fact, the original and its revision are far more similar to one another than Mably's comments would indicate. Most of the themes and arguments of the first are faithfully reproduced in the second; the vast majority of alterations are indeed stylistic. What, then, was the "dangerous doctrine" to which Mably referred? As we shall see, the major substantive change from the *Observations sur les Grecs* to the *Observations sur l'histoire de la Grèce* appears in the section dealing with the career of Philip of Macedonia; unsurprisingly, it reflects Mably's changing estimation of monarchy as a political form. Aside from this, the two works on Greece can largely be treated within a single focus. On the other hand, Mably let *Observations sur les Romains* stand largely as it was published in 1751—a clear sign that the main lines of his new interpretation of ancient history were already fixed by that point.

Classical Antiquity According to Mably

For all the similarity of their overall approach to historical discourse, the two *Observations* on Greece and Rome differ from *Parallèle des romains et des français* in one immediately obvious respect—the quality of the erudition sustaining their arguments. Where Mably had relied largely on modern historians for his first book, the new accounts of Greek and Roman history are founded on a far more thorough knowledge of ancient sources.[3] This increasing command of classical history and political thought was certainly an essential element in his adoption of a republican outlook. But the most striking and most important change revealed in the two works is simply the total shift in Mably's conception of the *optimus status reipublicae,* announced in his enthusiastic portraits of the "mixed" governments of the Spartan and Roman republics. We can begin with Sparta. As with his earlier discussions of Rome and France, Mably's treatment of Greek history is episodic, divided into four parts: the first covers the early history of the Greek republics, down to the Persian War; the second, the period from the start of the Peloponnesian War to the battle of Leuctra; the third, the epoch of the Macedonian ascent and the conquests of Alexander; and the fourth, the Hellenistic period, from the Diadochi to Pydna. The centerpiece of the first section, indeed of the entire work, is the portrait of the government of Sparta. The key problem of early Greek history, in Mably's eyes, was political instability, whose ultimate source was to be found in the "distinctive character trait" of the Greeks, their "love of independence."[4] This had led to the overthrow of kings by local aristocracies all over Greece, who were in turn attacked by the impoverished citizens beneath them: "There arose on all sides quarrels between the nobility and the people, the rich and the poor, magistrates and citizens; their rights and their fortunes were continually placed in question."[5] In Sparta, where monarchy had not yet been overthrown, there was a perpetual contest between kings and the people: "each faction seized control of sovereign power in turn, and the government, given over to either tyranny or to anarchy, continued to pass violently from one extreme to the other."[6]

The reforms of Lycurgus were a response to this situation of endemic instability—their goal was the establishment of a stable and durable social order in Sparta.[7] To accomplish this, he estalished a government in which "sovereign authority"—specified as the right to pass laws, declare war and peace, and elect magistrates—was placed in the hands of an assembly of the whole body of citizens; this assembly elected a senate of twenty-eight members, who filled the magistracies, served as a council to the kings, and prepared the agenda of the public assemblies; the kings were given absolute power over the armies in the field, but were otherwise reduced to mere executives, unable to act except with the consent of the senate. Finally, "in order for the people to have a greater confidence in its situation, and that, under the pretext of conserving their liberty, they would not fall subject to a stormy and tumultuous mistrust," Lycurgus established the five-man ephorate: "they were specifically charged with preventing the kings and the senators from putting themselves above the laws, or even violating them, through an abuse of executive power."[8] What sort of government was thereby established? It is worth quoting Mably's answer at length:

> The republic of Lycurgus, in just the same way that Polybius described the Roman republic, united all the advantages that aristocracy, monarchy, and democracy possess only in small measure when not formed into one single government, yet lacked all the vices that are natural to them. . . . As a result of the equilibrium established between the different powers, once the democratic part of the government showed signs of abusing its authority, it found itself powerless, and constrained by the strength of the magistrates. Thus one never saw in Lacedaemonia those whims, extravagances, seizures of panic, those bouts of violence that shamed most of the republics of Greece. As a result of the same equilibrium of powers, the all-powerful magistrates in turn found themselves under the imperious hand of the people, once they departed from the path of the law. All orders of the state aided and enlightened the others, bringing each to perfection by means of the censure they exercised on one another. Great abuses were impossible, since even the small had been foreseen. The senate, which owed its moderation and wisdom in the exercise of executive power to the vigilance of the ephorate, in turn rendered the people capable of knowing and discussing its own interests, of keeping to its principles, and of conserving its spirit. The kings were powerless except as organs of the senate, and nevertheless gave the armies that prompt and diligent action which is the soul of military success, though hardly ever known among free peoples.[9]

Such is the portrait of the government of Sparta in *Observations sur l'histoire de la Grèce*. If we turn to the revised account of Roman history in *Observations sur les Romains*, we find that Mably has abandoned the claim of the *Parallèle*, that the Roman republic represented a mixture of democracy and aristocracy. Instead, it is now explicitly described as an exact replica of the Spartan republic, differing only in the fact that it evolved without the aid of a founding legislator. The key change in Rome was the introduction of the tribunate in response to the first secession of the plebs:

> The success of the tribunes changed the form of government, and once the people reclaimed the exercise of sovereignty they had enjoyed before the creation of the centuriate, Rome began to present the image of a perfect republic. I have attempted, in another work, to show the skill with which Lycurgus placed all political authority in the hands of the Spartan people, while at the same time purging democracy of its natural vices, indeed endowing it with characteristics that seem more natural to aristocratic and monarchical government. Here I must point out that chance [*le hasard*] produced in Rome what the wisest of legislators had created in his own country. Lycurgus intended that the people should be the arbiters of all the operations of the republic, in order to infuse them with the virtues that love of liberty and of the fatherland give to free men; yet the different branches of government, which the people as a whole are inca-

> pable of wisely administering, Lycurgus assigned to specific magistrates, and thus created a mixed government, whose parts tempered one another, permitting none to neglect its duties, nor abuse its authority. . . . Polybius remarked that if one examines the power of the consuls, or that of the senate, or the authority of the people, one will decide in turn that the Roman government is monarchical, aristocratic, and popular. In effect, it united the advantages of all three, and the republic found within itself at one and the same time that prompt and decisive action which characterizes monarchy, that durability of the same spirit which is only found in aristocracy, and that zeal, that fire, that enthusiasm which democracy alone produces.[10]

With this double portrait of ancient Sparta and Rome, Mably thus announced his conversion to what might well be termed a Polybian-Machiavellian account of ancient politics. The name of Polybius is continually invoked in the pages of the two *Observations*, but Mably was clearly no less dependent on the author of the *Discorsi* on Livy for his new views. This is nowhere more obvious than in the emphasis he places on the tribunate in his description of the Roman constitution. For while any central reference to the tribunes is conspicuously absent in the Sixth Book of Polybius's *Histories*, they are made the key lever of democracy in Machiavelli's account, which Mably virtually paraphrases.[11] The latter even echoes approvingly some of the more notorious antiaristocratic passages of the *Discorsi*: "Machiavelli has shown, in his political discourses on Livy, that liberty cannot long endure in a republic in which there are nobles. A nobility believes that it is destined to rule. It is a vermin, he writes, that cries liberty without meaning it."[12]

At the same time, Mably's account of "mixed government" also departs from that of Machiavelli in certain crucial respects. For one thing, the democratic tenor of Mably's portrait of Sparta and Rome is made even plainer by his use of a descriptive terminology that was unavailable to Machiavelli. This is the differential analysis of governmental functions or "powers," pioneered in seventeenth-century England. The exact relation between the doctrine of the separation of powers, or that of "checks and balances," and the theory of mixed government is one of the most vexed questions in the historiography of political thought. However logically and historically distinct they may have been, the affinity between the two notions was undeniably very great.[13] It happened, in any case, that the emergence of the terminology of governmental "powers" coincided with the triumph of the language of classical republicanism in a single locale, and this linked their fates together, at least for a historical period. What was rare down to the time of *De l'Esprit des lois*, was to find any version of the one untouched by the other. We shall return below to the question of whether Mably was able to fuse the two together coherently in his own constitutional theory. But whatever final judgment is made here, the effect of his adoption of this terminology was to make clear that the governments of ancient Sparta and Rome were essentially *democratic*: legislative power in both is lodged with a popular assembly, and the senates and kings/consuls are assigned only executive functions.

A more important departure from a strictly Machiavellian interpretation of ancient politics concerns the strikingly different historical fates experienced by Sparta and Rome. The latter was destined to accomplish the transition from city-state to empire in a spectacular fashion, and this was the main object of the attention of both Polybius and Machiavelli. Polybius did not address the question of why the *first* great exemplar of the mixed government undertook no similar program of imperial expansion. Machiavelli, on the other hand, was driven to attempt an explanation of this conundrum by the challenge posed by the contemporary "Venetian" paradigm of republican stability.[14] The *Discorsi* on Livy was an impassioned apology for Roman imperialism, and in the sixth chapter of Book I, Machiavelli deliberately counterposed the serene immutability enjoyed by the republics of Venice *and* Sparta to the tumultuous "grandeur" of the Roman conquest of the Mediterranean. The stability of the Venetian republic, Machiavelli suggested, was to be explained by the preponderance of the aristocratic element in its constitution; that of Sparta, conversely, was owing to the small population of the state and its exclusion of foreigners, combined with the egalitarian thrust of the laws of Lycurgus. In Rome, on the other hand, the struggle of the orders drove the republic inexorably into the endless wars that won them their empire. Given a choice, which was the better path? Machiavelli's option for the "more honorable" career of military dynamism is well known:

> Since it is impossible, as I believe, either to balance these things, or to maintain a middle position exactly, one ought, in establishing the republic, to plan to take the more honorable path, and to constitute it in such a way that if it becomes necessary for it to expand, it will be capable of holding on to what it has acquired. Thus, to return to our starting-point, I believe it is necessary to follow the Roman model, and not that of any other republic, because it is impossible to find a middle path between these two extremes; and the struggles between the people and the senate should thus be seen an inconvenience which made possible the greatness of Rome.[15]

Mably's *Observations* on Greece and Rome brought him face to face with the same question, and without directly confronting his republican ancestor, he forthrightly reverses Machiavelli's judgment. The chief alternative to Roman imperialism, in his eyes, was not the Venetian oligarchy that preoccupied Machiavelli, but rather the egalitarianism of Sparta. Going well beyond Machiavelli's fleeting comments about the latter, Mably explicitly appeals to those aspects of the classical tradition of "laconism" that were largely ignored by the ancient and modern proponents of "mixed government," including Machiavelli. Lycurgus realized, Mably explains in the *Observations sur l'histoire de la Grèce,* that a mixed government, for all of its virtues, still did not remove the ultimate sources of political instability: "What would the fruits of his efforts to render the laws alone strong and sovereign have been, if wealth and luxury, which always march hand in hand and are always followed by the corruption of manners, the inequality of citizens, and, finally, by tyranny and servitude, had once again led the Spartans to scorn or elude their new laws?"[16] The legislator's solution was not merely to make an absolutely equal division of landed property among the Spartan citizens, but also to ban the use of gold and silver, and to establish the celebrated collective institutions of Sparta, the public meals and the elaborate system of state education. "In a word, he limited their needs to those that are inexorably imposed by nature. From that point on, the arts of luxury deserted Laconia; useless wealth seemed contemptible, and Sparta became a fortress inaccessible to corruption."[17] The sources for Mably's descriptions of the egalitarian legislation of Lycurgus are familiar enough: they are near paraphrases of parts of Xenophon's *Constitution of the Lacedaemonians* and Plutarch's *Life* of Lycurgus. An emphasis on this separate tradition of "laconism" permits Mably to draw a far more explicit contrast between Sparta and Rome than had interested Machiavelli. For the situation in Roman history was very different. Mably remembers the legend of the Romulan distribution of equal property at the beginnings of Rome, but he makes clear that this egalitarianism had been irretrievably lost during the monarchy. In fact, he congratulates Brutus for having resisted the temptation to redistribute property with the establishment of the Republic, an impossible aim in any case.[18] The subsequent creation of the tribunate produced a mixed government on the Spartan model, but no attempt to impose an agrarian law in Rome ever succeeded.

This difference governed the fates of the two republics, in Mably's view. Although the Spartans were naturally invincible on the battlefield, the strict egalitarianism of the Lycurgan reforms removed any rationale for expansion:

> Their love of poverty made the Spartans indifferent to booty and tribute from their victims; living only off the produce of their own lands, using money that no one else recognized, and having no funds in reserve, it was impossible for them to make war far from their own territory. The law did not permit them to bestow citizenship on foreigners, and even prevented them from restoring the losses that resulted from victory; everything led them to regard peace as the most precious of human goods.[19]

Lycurgus sealed this pacifism with a law that absolutely forbade any offensive war. The Romans, on the other hand, were driven into expansion by the very success of the "equilibrium" established by the tribunate. No leveling of social classes in the Lycurgan fashion occurred. Instead, the energy unleashed by the struggle of the patricians and plebians was continually deflected onto external objects. Mably reproduces here a thoroughly Machiavellian explanation of the role of the struggles in Roman expansion: "These conflicts between the nobility and the people, which perfected the government of the republic, contributed no less to making it a conqueror."[20] He provides an enthusiastic exegesis of the descriptions of Roman military discipline in Polybius and Vegetius, but still concludes that the dissensions were the engine that drove Roman conquest forward: "As I have shown, the quarrels between nobility and people that dominated Rome, served to stimulate talents and to give the energy of passions to virtues; in a word, the Romans behaved with the energy of a people creating itself, and treated their enemies with the firmness that comes from following a path laid down for them long before."[21] The contrast between Spartan pacifism and Roman bellicism could hardly be greater. While the Spartans remained camped for centuries on the tiny Laconian plain, fighting a series of defensive wars that earned them little more than their independence, the Roman city-state gradually, but inexorably, conquered the entire Mediterranean basin, east and west.

Naturally, Mably never totally repudiates Roman imperialism, for he had too clear an idea of the irreplaceable function of warfare in the ancient world: "For the Romans, war took the place of the commerce, arts, and economy that are the sole sources of wealth among modern peoples."[22] But his overall preference for the Spartan renunciation of imperial expansion is unmistakable. It can be seen most clearly in a feature that sets *Observations sur l'histoire de la Grèce* somewhat apart from most treatments of Greek history in the eighteenth century, its continual—even exaggerated—celebration of Greek federalism.[23] The opening pages of the book are dominated by a discussion of the half-legendary "amphictyonic council" in these pregnant terms: "[T]he amphictyonic assemblies became, if I can put it this way, the Estates-Generals of Greece; a hundred free and independent cities formed a single federal republic, of that kind that today only the Swiss cantons suggest a reasonably similar picture."[24] The subsequent success of the Lycurgan reforms made Sparta the natural leader of a renewed Greek Confederacy, whose supreme achievement was to meet and throw back the massive Persian invasion mounted against it. Much later, there was a final renascence of federalism, thanks to the brief gap that opened between the initial Macedonian subjugation of the Greek peninsula and the final loss of liberty to the Romans. The last book of the *Observations sur l'histoire de la Grèce* is devoted to a detailed and celebratory discussion—plainly indebted to Polybius—of the Achean League, which is again congratulated for its lack of ambition: "The Acheans desired neither to acquire great wealth nor to make themselves famous for their exploits; they aspired to nothing more than an obscure happiness, the only sort for which men were created."[25] What Mably does here, in essence, is to reverse the hierarchy of republican value established by Machiavelli. For him, too, the record of antiquity offered *two* distinct examples of unequaled political achievement. The greatest of all was that of ancient Sparta, where the combination of a perfectly balanced "mixed government" and a wholly egalitarian social order produced an unmatched record of stability and harmony: "For what society has ever offered reason a more noble and sublime spectacle than Sparta? For nearly six hundred years the laws of Lycurgus, the wisest ever bestowed upon men, were observed with the most religious fidelity."[26] Second, in Mably's eyes, came Rome, where the relentless struggle of the nobles and the plebians deprived the city of any chance to enjoy the peace and repose of a Sparta. But there the same "mixture" of governments not only preserved the republic from self-destruction, but conferred on it an immeasurable superiority in its endless wars, as it advanced toward the conquest of the world.

It was only a consideration of the ultimate fates of the two republics that confirmed the superiority of the Spartan over the Roman model. There is no need to insist on the utopianism of the portraits that Mably drew of Sparta or Rome in his two *Observations*. Political recommendation of this sort was inscribed in the nature of the kind of history he was writing—*une école de morale et de politique*, as he repeatedly termed it. In this sense, Mably had merely replaced his earlier apology for European absolutism with a hardly less visionary celebration of the "mixed governments" of antiquity. Yet there was a difference. Where he had been able to end the *Parallèle* with a prediction of an "eternal duration" for the French monarchy, Mably had now joined a political tradition whose very real utopianism was at the same time tempered by a profound pessimism, of which Machiavelli provides only the most famous example. For Mably, Sparta and Rome represented the absolute zenith of political achievement. But they were no less mortal than any other human creation: indeed, they were doomed to what classical republicanism had always deemed the necessary "corruption" of even the best of governments. "Mixed government," in his account, was largely a victim of its own success, as it maneuvered through an environment that was ultimately beyond its control.

The pathology he provides for Sparta is the most revealing, in this respect. Lycurgus had bestowed a perfect government on Sparta, but it had to coexist with a set of imperfect partners, within the Greek confederation. Mably's scathing depiction of Athenian democracy, a thoroughly conventional one, forms a dystopian counterpart to the portrait of Sparta in the first part of the *Observations* on Greece. Solon, he writes, faced the same problems as did Lycurgus, but "in attempting to remedy the faults of the republic, this imprudent legislator merely palliated them, and ended in giving a new life to the old vices of its government." Instead of the Lycurgan social legislation, Solon gave the populace of Athens

> permission to scorn its laws and its magistrates. Thus to authorize the appeal of the sentences, decrees, and orders of all judges to the tumultuous public assemby—was this not to establish the ignorant and fickle multitude, jealous of the rich, always the dupe of some intriguer, and always governed by citizens who are both violent and adept at flattering their vices, as an all-powerful magistrate? Was this not to establish, in the name of democracy, a veritable anarchy?[27]

The turning point for the Greeks came with their defeat of the Persians. While the Spartans were naturally little tempted by the spoils, the Athenians were unable to resist the lure of oriental wealth.[28] By the time of Pericles, this had driven them into a full-scale bid for a Greek empire, which destroyed the confederacy built by Sparta, and dragged all of Greece into a fatal civil war. Sparta emerged victorious, but only with Persian assistance. Now, led by the unworthy Lysander ("never did a Spartan so lack the character of his country as did Lysander"), the Spartans themselves succumbed to the attractions of imperialism.[29] The final blow to the republic was the defeat at Leuctra. In its aftermath, the Spartans

> fell into the most shameful abasement, once the ephor Epitadeus had flung open the doors to avarice, by passing a law that permitted the sale of personal possessions and their inheritance by will. The greed of the wealthy overran all of Laconia, and the propertyless slavishly sought their favor, or incited sedition in order to recover the goods they had lost. The hands of the Spartans, which Lycurgus had intended to handle only the sword, the lance, and the shield, were dishonored by the instruments that luxury brought into an astonished Laconia.[30]

Deprived of the anchor of egalitarianism, Sparta joined the crowd of weak and vacillating city-states who were soon to succumb to Macedonian imperialism.

The mechanisms of corruption in the Roman republic were similar, but naturally operated on a far vaster and more destructive scale. Here Mably largely preserved intact the Montesquieuean account he had used in the *Parallèle*. The Romans, he argues, had never shared the Spartan reverence for poverty; their decline began the moment they started to conquer enemies richer than themselves. "Avarice having taken the place of the love of glory in the heart of the citizen, the ambition of the republic became an insatiable drive toward pillage and conquest."[31] The immediate domestic effect was to upset the delicate equilibrium of their government:

> Public power soon passed into the hands of the rich . . . and under the deceptive forms of the older government, the Romans fell under the control of a genuine aristocracy. . . . One reads the wisest regulations against luxury; but in fact, citizens wealthier than kings force the laws to fall silent, with an imposing display of pomp. The republic had once been made up of patricians and plebians; now it was made up of rich citizens and poor citizens.[32]

The end of social harmony in Rome was announced by the revolt of the Gracchi. Soon the loyalty of the armies was diverted onto their separate commanders; the municipal poor were driven into sedition; and the wealthiest strata of society fell into the epic series of civil wars that destroyed the Republic. Then the awful risks inherent in the option for imperialism taken by the Romans and endorsed by Machiavelli suddenly became visible. "We have seen free peoples lose the privileges of governing themselves," Mably wrote, obviously referring to the rise of monarchy in Europe, "while nevertheless escaping the ravages of despotism; this was because their loss of liberty was not the result of a sudden and stormy revolution, but was instead the work of many centuries."[33] Nothing of the sort occurred in Rome, where the end of the Republic was so sudden, and imposed with such violence, that the sheerest despotism was the only possible outcome. As he surveys the centuries of the Empire, with no more admiration than he had displayed in the *Parallèle*, Mably continually emphasizes that the *comble de malheur* of Roman despotism was that once installed, it was irretrievable and irreparable: "It is only during the convulsive movements of a revolution that a people can recover its courage and its liberty; yet despair alone can motivate them, and despair is a passion too blind and too temporary for us to expect very much from it. The tyrant is sometimes overthrown, but the tyranny subsists."[34] The fall of the Roman Republic spelled the irreversible end of ancient liberty for *all* the inhabitants of the Empire.

The "corruption" of the Greek republics, on the other hand, had not been characterized by the same enormity or finality. The decline of Sparta, Athens, Thebes, and the rest in the fourth and third centuries had been real enough, as they exhausted themselves internally in internecine warfare, and then were overwhelmed from without, first by Macedonian, and then Roman imperialism. But for Mably, post-Classical Greece still had to be seen as offering a vast field of possibility for conscious political maneuver, even for the reform or mitigation of "corruption" in some instances. The most memorable pages of his writing on antiquity, in fact, are not really his derivative descriptions of the republics of Lycurgus or Brutus, but rather his vignettes from Hellenistic Greece. Firstly, there is his judgment on the various responses by the Greek city-states to the Macedonian threat, particularly the contrast he draws between the policies of the two Athenian commanders, the orator Demosthenes and the general Phocion. Mably joins Polybius in a critique of the former, who tragically overestimated the prospects for a successful resistance to Philip II; and then provides a spirited defense of Phocion, whose cautious appeasement of Philip, superficially a far less attractive stance than the courageous intransigence of Demosthenes, was in fact the superior policy:

> I much prefer the admirable wisdom of Phocion, as great a commander as Demosthenes was a poor one, who placed himself on the same level as his fellow citizens and recommended peace, when a war would have brought him to the head of the republic. . . . Such was the policy of this great man, who did not judge the strengths and resources of the state by those momentary and destructive transports of courage and confidence, but by its ordinary character and the customs given to it by its laws. Phocion considered his republic, and all of Greece, to be so ill as to make a rapid return to health impossible; yet for whom it was necessary to prolong life and gradually to restore the constitution, by means of a wise and circumspect treatment.[35]

In later writings, Mably returned again and again to the figure of Phocion, careful diagnostician and cautious political healer, always his model for a true republican prudence.

The inevitable absorption of Greece by the Macedonian monarchy brings us to the one major change made by Mably between his first *Observations* on Greece and its final revision. In the original, a detailed narrative of Philip II's tactical and strategic success is followed by this celebration of his political skills:

> In Philip I see a politician superior to every event, and born to govern men. Fortune never presented him with obstacles that he had not foreseen, and he overcame them, adapting to their different nature, by means of his wisdom, his patience, his courage and his activity; I sense here a powerful mind, each of whose efforts were linked to the others, lending them a mutual force.[36]

The imprudence of Alexander alone is blamed for the disasters that subsequently befell the Macedonian Empire. In *Observations sur l'histoire de la Grèce*, on the other hand, Mably reproduces the examination of the rise of Macedonia, begins to repeat the same congratulation of Philip, and then stops, adding this passage:

> I doubt whether the ambition of a single man has ever presented so interesting a spectacle as the reign of Philip. What prudence and what courage in every detail of this prince's conduct! . . . and I would undertake to explain, to the extent that I could, the springs of this unhappy policy, if the object of it all had not been so petty, so contemptible, and even reprehensible in the eyes of that superior policy, whose purpose is not to serve the passions of the monarch, but to render states happy. In fact, what did Philip accomplish for the good of Macedonia and for his own family? Thinking only of satisfying his ambitions, he used the great talents and priceless resources of his genius to construct an edifice that was destined to collapse almost immediately.[37]

By this point, prudence in the service of monarchy had become a contradiction in terms for Mably. Philip II is now condemned in the strongest language, for he had wasted that rarest of opportunities, the chance to restore "liberty" to a state: "This prince could have equaled Lycurgus. A happy Macedonia could easily have defended itself against foreigners; combined with those of Greece, its forces could have turned back any assault, and perhaps even Roman grandeur would have been humbled in a collision with this mass of free and flourishing states."[38]

Philip's chances for the recovery of Greek freedom may have been the fairest, but they were not quite the last. As we noted above, Mably ends the *Observations* on Greece with a vivid discussion of the last epoch of Greek independence, in the heyday of the Achaean League. Here he singles out the Achaean commander Aratus, who led an epic campaign to expel tyranny from the Peloponnese, for the same kind of praise he had earlier bestowed on Phocion: "one might well have said that the peoples of Greece, seized by a new passion for liberty and instructed by their experience, now possessed a golden opportunity to form themselves into one single republic."[39] But, alas, not even Aratus could avoid a fatal accommodation with Macedonia, as the threat of Roman imperialism loomed on the horizon: "Aratus was one of the greatest figures of antiquity; but such is the fate of men that we often judge them without recalling that politics, subject to the fatality of interlocking events, is typically a matter of being surrounded by obstacles and confronted with a choice between evils."[40] At the end of the *Observations sur l'histoire de la Grèce,* Mably returns to the contrast between the Greek and the Roman models of republicanism:

> One might say that the grandeur of the Romans was the work of the whole republic, and that no single Roman citizen rose above his century and the wisdom of the state in order to effect a great change in the course of things. . . . In Greece, on the other hand, we often encounter powerful and creative minds who resist the torrents of custom and habit, who address themselves to all the different needs of the state, who open a new path, and who, glimpsing the future, render themselves the masters of events. Greece experienced no misfortune that was not foreseen long in advance by at least some of its rulers.[41]

Here the logic of Mably's dissension from the Roman paradigm of Machiavelli is plain to see. His greatest admiration was always reserved for those legislators and reformers who sought to exercise a genuine *self-determination,* whether in founding republics or in attempting to restore them to liberty. At the same time, this conclusion may serve to remind us why it was the Hellenistic world that seemed always to capture the imagination of Mably more than any other epoch of antiquity. It was the historical experience of that period, one of still reversible and reparable "corruption," and not the two great peaks of ancient liberty in classical Greece or republican Rome, that spoke most directly to the situation in which Mably's contemporaries found themselves.

A Critique of Modern Diplomacy

The revision of the parts of *Parallèle des romains et des français* that dealt with classical antiquity was thus completed, in its essentials, by 1751. Mably's reworking of the other half of the book took considerably longer, since the final additions to the text of *Observations sur l'histoire de France* were not made until after the "Maupeou coup" of 1771. Deeply colored by the bitter parliamentary oppositionism that dominated French politics after 1751, this later intervention in the debate over the history of the monarchy belongs to a distinct political conjuncture, and will be considered separately, in a later chapter. In order to view the interim development of Mably's thinking about modern Europe, it is necessary to turn instead to the works that grew out of his brief diplomatic career as secretary to Cardinal Tencin—Mably's summary of a century of international treaties in *Le droit public de l'Europe*, published in 1746 and revised in 1748 and 1764, and the long "introduction" he wrote for it, *Principes des Négociations*, which appeared in 1757.

As we have seen, even the first edition of *Le droit public*, published when Mably was still in his "royalist" phase, encountered difficulties with the censor. By the time he wrote the preface for the last edition in 1764, he had adopted a very critical tone indeed:

> I wish it were possible to look favorably upon everything that has occurred in Europe over the last two centuries. But when one sees the continent continually torn apart by the cruelest wars, under the grip of the most destructive passions, it is impossible for a man to approve the very faults that guarantee the misery of mankind; it is impossible to write about justice while overlooking injustice; in a word, it is impossible to be both a historian and a flatterer.[42]

Mably's writings on diplomacy were of course deeply marked by the record of French performance in the international arena, about which we need only state the obvious—the striking failure of the Bourbon monarchy, for over a century, to achieve any rational strategic goals, or even to maintain its position relative to its principal rivals in Europe.[43] No sooner had French absolutism reached its fullest development in the decades just after Westphalia, than it was faced with what was, in effect, a struggle on two fronts, indeed in two historical worlds—the traditional territorial rivalry between the continental monarchies, and the new worldwide competition for mercantile empire. The colossal war efforts of Louis XIV ended in impasse on both fronts. On the one hand, France's perennial dynastic opponent, Habsburg Austria, strengthened its domestic position and gained a firmer grip on its possessions in Italy and the Netherlands; on the other, the spoils of the Spanish colonial empire were seized by a new commercial competitor, England. Thereafter, as Fleury recognized, the chief strategic goal of France was simply to maintain its position against these antagonists. This policy barely survived the adventurism of the War of the Austrian Succession—the period of Mably's own involvement in French diplomacy—which produced minimal gains in Europe and ominous setbacks in the rest of the world.

The turning point in this holding operation came just after midcentury, when the sudden expansion of an energetic Prussian absolutism threatened to upset the balance of the continental powers. The Bourbon monarchy was heedlessly lured into the new anti-Prussian coalition, plunging it into a European war in 1756 that made any adequate defense against the simultaneous English assaults outside Europe impossible. Despite the diplomatic efforts of Choiseul, the first French colonial empire was dealt a death-blow in 1763. Moreover, the effects of this foreign disaster were immediately relayed to the heart of the domestic scene, in the form of an irretrievable fiscal crisis. The great financial achievement of the entire first half of the century had been to retire the enormous war debt inherited by the Regency in 1715. This work was now undone. The Seven Years' War became the first major war in France to be financed through loans: the debts accrued by 1763 may have surpassed those left by Louis XIV, with far less to show for them. In addition, the archaic structure of the French fiscal system, intricately linked to the general system of venal offices, now rendered impossible any moves in the direction of a rational program of debt management on the Dutch or English model.[44] All that remained to produce state bankruptcy was a further exacerbation of the deficit, duly provided in the next decade by the irresistible adventure of the American Revolution, which punished England without bringing any recompense to France—reminding us that the social agency that probably contributed most to the collapse of the absolutist state in France was not so much a rising bourgeoisie at home as an ascendant capitalist rival abroad.

These results all lay in the future, of course, when Mably drew up his balance sheet of the record of international relations in Europe in 1757, summarizing the lessons of his diplomatic work. *Principes des Négociations* prudently refrains from explicit discussion of the "diplomatic revolution" and the war it had produced the year before. Nevertheless, it is difficult to understand the book except in terms of this context. Far from being a mere handbook for diplomats, the work is a sustained critique of the whole practice of modern European warfare, of the type whose greatest example was to be the Seven Years' War. *Principes des Négociations* opens with this capsule history:

> For more than two centuries, Europe has been dominated by two rival powers, which believe themselves destined to rule over the others, and whose efforts, aimed less at enjoying their fortune than at making it grow, give movement to all other events. These miseries will not end soon. Concerned only with destroying the other, in order to subjugate other states more easily, the dominant powers seek alliances with smaller states that they otherwise scorn, dislike, and attempt to deceive. Such states as are powerful enough to dare to take part in the larger quarrels, put their assistance on the block, selling it to the highest bidder. Meanwhile, princes who form a third class of states, too weak to undertake projects of fortune and expansion, resign themselves to trying to steer clear of the storm, or at least exposing themselves to it only with the greatest caution.[45]

Of course, the participants in this giant struggle had changed over time. According to Mably's scheme, Spain had been the *puissance dominante* in the sixteenth century, France its rival; with the Treaty of Westphalia, the leading position passed definitively to France, with Austria emerging as its main adversary; the Treaty of Utrecht, finally, had marked the replacement of Austria by England as the new rival power. Could anything be done to alter the endless repetition of this destructive pattern? Mably takes great pains from the outset to distance himself from any utopian pacifism. He had known the abbé de Saint-Pierre and was certainly familiar with the *Projet pour rendre la paix perpétuelle en Europe*; it was Mably, in fact, who had recommended, in 1754, the recruitment of Rousseau to make an abridgement of the works of the late abbé. But in *Principes des Négociations* he disavows any attempt to follow in the footsteps of Plato or Saint-Pierre: "My moral system is so undemanding," writes Mably, "that I do not even require my readers to be honest men, but rather merely ambitious men who are prepared to use their heads."[46] His goal, in other words, is to try to found a rational *science* of diplomacy, making it into an effective tool of political agency—exactly what it had never been, in his eyes.[47]

Mably's historical works have already prepared us for the principles of this science—its key is to locate some deeper pattern of social determination, to which diplomatic activity must conform. He thus introduces a conception of "fundamental interests" with a distinctly Montesquieuean flavor: "The laws, manners, and topographical position of each state give rise to a distinctive mode of being, which alone determines its true interests. In conforming to it, the state expands, preserves itself, or staves off its ruin, according to whether it is built for expansion, self-preservation, or durability."[48] The success of any diplomatic effort depends on discovering these "interests": "It will be seen that a state's negotiations must be undertaken and conducted in accordance with its fundamental interest. . . . Without a just proportion between its proposed end and the principles of the government, all negotiation will be in vain."[49] It is no surprise that for Mably, the masters of this kind of diplomacy were the Romans. The creation of their empire was the last great feat of deliberate and concerted "will" in the history of international relations. By contrast, it was the profound ignorance of Europeans concerning their deepest interests that had produced the endless series of fruitless and destructive wars that littered their history and confounded all attempts to achieve a stable international system.

What, then, were the "fundamental interests" of the various states of Europe? The answer to this leads Mably to outline a theory of the historical development of Europe, from the feudal age onward. Medieval Europe was originally a fully militarized society, dominated by a ruling aristocracy for whom warfare was a profession and violence a way of life. A series of interconnected events then supervened, which together deprived war of any economic or social rationale. The conquest of the New World brought a vast influx of wealth into Europe, introducing its inhabitants to a wide range of novel commodities, which soon became "necessities"; many of those who had formerly earned their living through arms gradually became merchants or manufacturers, while most of the rest were forced to sell their labor on the market. The passage from military to "commercial" civilization, Mably concludes, thus completely altered the principles that ought to govern statecraft and diplomacy. The basic interest of the "dominant power" in Europe was henceforth to renounce any attempt at further expansion, and instead to bend all its efforts toward the *maintenance* of its position; equally, the goal of its rival should be not to replace the current dominant power, but to maintain its own position as well.[50] Mably allows a greater leeway to the lesser powers, who are advised to profit from the conflicts of the greater, if they can.[51] But, above all, it is pointless for any European power, of whatever rank, to undertake a project of purely *military* expansion. For one thing, no modern state is really capable of such a project:

> Great enterprises require deliberate planning, founded on careful preparation, which is beyond the powers of the forms of government known to us today. Let us face facts: with the exception of Venice and Switzerland, where the governing magistrates are themselves governed by the spirit and the laws of the nation, such that a policy can be expected to persist over time, no government is capable of executing a project of any importance—nor do I exempt even the free states of Europe.[52]

But the deepest reason was simply that there was no longer anything to be gained from war. Power in postfeudal Europe was the result of wealth, wealth was the result of commerce—and commerce depended on peace.

Why then had warfare in Europe not only continued after the medieval period, but even escalated in frequency and intensity? The answer lay in the *political* structure of the European states. "No doubt," Mably explains, "if the people had been their own legislators, their policies would have conformed to their new passions." But the dominant form of government in Europe was monarchy, led by princes who gravely misunderstood the character of commercial civilization: "They did not understand that luxury, which diminishes courage, debases the arts, and depopulates the countryside, had fatally weakened their military strength and resources; that their money furnished them with armies made up of men chosen by chance from the very dregs of society, soldiers who were incapable of foreign conquest. Their blind ambition drove them according to contradictory principles."[53] The mistake of absolutist princes was to make the commerce and wealth of their neighbors the objects of *martial* ambition, as if they were no different from the territories fought over by their feudal predecessors. The results of this grave illusion could be read in the history of the past two centuries, above all in the catastrophes that had befallen first Spain and then Austria. "In whatever conjuncture, let us always expand," was the motto of the emperor Leopold—and this was precisely how Austria had fallen out of the first rank of powers. It is fortunate for contemporary Europe, Mably comments, that England was now one of the two dominant powers of Europe:

> Commerce, which forms the principle object of their policy, necessarily inclines them toward peace, and the public will, in a free state, often succeeds in imposing itself on the government. Besides, must not the English know that their constitution, a good deal more precious than all the commerce of America, is secure only under conditions of peace, and that war furnishes their king with a thousand plausible pretexts for the extension of his prerogative and their subjection? The tastes of the English necessarily spread to its rival; and although I write at a time when these two powers are at war, I am willing to predict that we are now seeing the happy effects of this influence. So long as these conditions persist, Europe will be exposed to fewer and less violent convulsions.[54]

For all of this tentative optimism—soon to be belied by events—Mably's final assessment of relations between the nations of Europe was still a melancholy one: "Alone against all, such was the motto of Louis XIV. The phrase, which ought to have been understood as a revealing satire of the imprudence of his decisions, was instead taken by his subjects, and still is today, as a tribute to his courage—so little do dominant powers grasp their own interests, situation, and powers."[55]

Such is Mably's critique of mercantilist warfare, which, in the end, is not fundamentally dissimilar to that of many of his contemporaries. One form or another of just such an analysis had become a staple of Enlightenment social criticism by the middle years of the century.[56] Far more interesting for our purposes are the brief passages in which Mably moves to an attack on "commercial" civilization itself. We have seen above how *Parallèle des romains et des français* concludes with an enthusiastic celebration of the commerce and luxury of modern Europe. Given the role he had already assigned to these in his descriptions of the corruption of the Spartan and Roman republics, we may be sure that these beliefs had changed by 1751 at least. But it is only in *Principes des Négociations* and in the final revisions of the *Droit public* that Mably proceeds to a direct attack on commercial ideology, of the type that occurs again and again in his mature writings. The question first arises in Chapter XVII of the *Principes*, whose subject is commercial treaties between states. Mably begins with an argument for free trade, which follows directly from the critique of mercantilist intervention in the economy laid down earlier in the book. Then he announces: "I yield here to the temptation to insert a few reflections, perhaps marginal to my subject, but which seem important to me."[57] What follows is essentially a dialogue with David Hume, whose *Political Discourses* on the "vulgar subjects"—the phrase is Hume's—of commerce, money, and trade had appeared in a number of French editions after 1752.[58] In his choice of this opponent, Mably was bypassing the troop of French apologists for commercial modernity led by Melon and Voltaire, with whom he was undoubtedly familiar. Hume, however, was not only a weightier economic thinker than any of these, but was also, for precisely this reason, far more alive to the arguments to be made *against* commercial ideology. There was much for Mably to admire in Hume's essays. Not only was the latter willing to concede that "luxury" could sometimes be "vicious" for society, even as he praised its effects in general;[59] but he also displayed a certain sensitivity to the problems generated by an unequal distribution of wealth, nowhere more clearly than in the famous lines from "On Commerce":

> Every person, if possible, ought to enjoy the fruits of his labour, in a full possession of all the necessaries, and many of the conveniences of life. No

> one can doubt, but such an equality is most suitable to human nature, and diminishes much less from the *happiness* of the rich than it adds to that of the poor. . . . Add to this, where the riches are in few hands, these must enjoy all the power, and will readily conspire to lay the whole burthen on the poor, and oppress them still farther, to the discouragement of all industry.[60]

At the same time, *Political Discourses* remains a superbly argued brief on behalf of the "industry and arts and trade" that had been brought to perfection in contemporary Europe, through international trade above all. "In short," Hume concludes,

> a kingdom, that has a large import and export, must abound more with industry, and that employed upon delicacies and luxuries, than a kingdom which rests contented with its native commodities. It is, therefore, more powerful, as well as richer and happier.

It is against these views that Mably attempts to register his dissent in *Principes des Négociations*. "When one considers commerce from the standpoint of a merchant," Mably begins,

> I am not surprised to find a tribute to luxury. But how can Hume, philosopher and politician, fall prey to this fatal misconception? If the object of the government in promoting commerce is and must be to enhance the strength of the nation and to render it capable of defending its laws and its possessions against its enemies, how could one doubt that luxury is not absolutely contrary to this end?[61]

Mably's first move, however, differs somewhat from what we might expect, at least at the outset. Warning "let no one fear that I mean only to rehearse a few commonplaces of morality here," Mably introduces what he advertises as a purely *economic* argument against "luxury," referring for the first time to a writer whose name he would invoke constantly in later writings. This is Richard Cantillon, whose *Essai sur la nature du commerce en général* was one of the landmarks of economic thought prior to Smith.[62] A reading of this book, Mably assures us, will demonstrate that "luxury, far from being favorable to commerce, is, on the contrary, a symptom of its impending decline."[63] What Mably was seizing on here was Cantillon's definitive refutation of one of the core doctrines of mercantilist thought, the idea that a favorable balance of trade was the chief index of the economic well being of a nation. In its essentials, the argument said that an inflow of bullion in a nation would inevitably raise domestic prices and wages, eventually resulting in a reversal of its initial advantages; the goal of maintaining a surplus of exports was thus strictly self-defeating, since an equilibrium between imports and exports—and a "natural distribution of species" between world trading partners—would always be reestablished in the long run. Cantillon was by no means the only thinker to make this argument. Fragmentary versions of it were becoming widespread in this epoch, as all aspects of mercantilist theory came under increasing criticism.[64] As it happened, Hume's third essay in the *Political Discourses*, "On Money," itself contained a slightly different version of the argument, which eventually proved to be more influential than that of Cantillon.[65] What is clear, however, is that neither writer drew the same conclusions about the doctrine of the "specie-flow mechanism" as did Mably. Cantillon's presentation does place a disquieting emphasis on the *uneven* character of economic development in Europe, as the comparative advantage in trade seemed to shift perpetually from one nation to another.[66] But he also constantly raises the possibility of calculated intervention in the economy by governments, in order to reverse disadvantages imposed by the play of the market. As for Hume, he too was keenly aware of the mercurial nature of success in the world economy. But not only did Hume trust in the kind of corrective adjustments envisioned by Cantillon, he could also proclaim, citing the example of the Chinese, that a commercial nation could even "lose most of its foreign trade, and yet continue a great and powerful people."[67] Perfectly aware of the *instability* of commercial civilization, neither Cantillon nor Hume were ever led seriously to doubt its superiority to any possible alternatives.

Yet this is precisely what Mably means to do. His conclusion is that Hume's endorsement of foreign trade is self-contradictory. If his goal is really to augment the power and happiness of a state, it is wiser in fact to *discourage* a reliance on foreign trade and instead try to promote internal commerce, based on agriculture, "the form of commerce most likely to benefit the greatest number of citizens."[68] Mably does not take these arguments much further than this in the *Principes des Négociations*. But the direction in which they are heading can plainly be seen if we turn to the discussion on commerce that he added to the last edition of the *Droit public de l'Europe* a few years later. There the question is posed again: to what extent is the accumulation of wealth through foreign trade a reasonable and worthy goal of statecraft? Again the name of Cantillon is invoked. In this instance, Mably cites a passage from the *Essai* in which Cantillon points to means for correcting or regulating the pressures of the international market:

> In order to repair the damage caused by an abundance of money and to restore the state, it is necessary to try to establish annually and constantly

> a real balance of commerce, and to encourage, by navigation, those manufactures which are most capable of being sold on foreign markets. . . . But when money has become too abundant in the state a second time, excessive consumption and luxury will establish themselves, and the state will fall into decadence a second time. This then is the circle that can create a powerful state, when it possesses resources and industrious inhabitants; and an able minister will always be able to restart the circle.[69]

Now Mably enters a vigorous protest against Cantillon's own recommendations:

> I ask the reader to ponder at length this passage of Cantillon. Isn't it necessary to conclude that the ancients were better reasoners than ourselves, and that it is merely a false and mistaken policy that looks upon an instrument that procures wealth only to lead to poverty in turn, as the principle of the happiness of the state? A true policy will aim at a more durable happiness. The fact is that a state that regards wealth and the commerce that procures it as the keys of war and peace, is destined to pass through unending revolutions, from luxury to poverty, and from poverty to luxury—that is to say, to find itself always reduced to one of the extremities that announce the ruin of a people.[70]

The specter of "unending revolutions" that is raised here tells the whole story. The operation of the world market, whose mechanisms governed the rise and fall of the trading nations, had become for Mably that most disturbing of prospects: a Polybian *anacyclosis*, a cycle of unwilled and unstoppable change. To follow the path indicated by Cantillon or Hume was to stake the happiness of the nation on one's ability to master its economic fortunes—always a losing proposition in the long run, in Mably's view. The great thinkers of ancient Greece or Rome would never have made this mistake: "What would all the great men at the head of the most celebrated peoples of antiquity; what would Plato, Aristotle, Cicero, all the ancient philosophers who wrote on politics have thought, if they overheard us insisting that a state can be happy and flourishing only by means of its commerce, and that money must be the key to its armed forces? They would take us for madmen."[71] It is easy to see how Europeans initially succumbed to the lure of easy wealth, given the astonishing success of the Spanish, the Dutch, and the English. But have they learned nothing from the ulterior history of Spain or the United Provinces? "Let us not be surprised," Mably concludes, for "commerce is a kind of monster that is destroyed at its own hands."[72]

Mably's condemnation of commercial civilization depended, of course, on his conviction that there existed some plausible alternative to it. This was supplied by his portraits of Sparta and Rome in the two earlier *Observations*. It is here that his differences with a thinker such as Hume emerge most starkly. For the latter had, in fact, admitted that there was at least one great exception to his axiom that "industry and arts and trade increase the power of the sovereign as well as the happiness of the subjects."[73] The ancient Greeks and Romans, Hume asserts, took the energies that the Europeans devoted to manufacture and trade, and instead diverted them into the collectivist institutions that made their republics free and powerful, so that "no probable reason can be assigned for the great power of the more ancient states above the modern, but their want of commerce and luxury."[74] But would it be possible, Hume asks, to repeat this performance? His response is revealing:

> I answer, that it appears to me, almost impossible, and that because ancient policy was violent, and contrary to the more natural and usual course of things. It is well known with what peculiar laws SPARTA was governed, and what a prodigy that republic is justly esteemed by every one. . . . And though the ROMAN and other ancient republics were supported on principles somewhat more natural, yet was there an extraordinary concurrence of circumstances to make them submit to such grievous burthens . . . though the want of trade and manufactures, among a free and very martial people, may *sometimes* have no other effect than to render the public more powerful, it is certain, that, in the common course of human affairs, it will have a quite contrary tendency.[75]

Hume's defense of commercial modernity here depends on figuring classical civilization as a "violent," "exceptional," and "peculiar" experience, contrary to the "natural," "usual," and "common" course of things. In this way, he could simply dismiss the evidence of classical history as beside the point, where modern statecraft was concerned. The world of ancient Greece and Rome was, for Hume, strictly *irrelevant* to modern experience.

Roughly speaking, this was the same position adopted by Mably himself in his first book. But his political thought after *Parallèle des romains et des français* was founded on precisely the opposite assumption. For Mably, who had now completed his move from the *parti des modernes* to the *parti des anciens*, no such chasm separated antiquity from modernity. The same historical principles that governed the rise and decline of the ancient republics also determined the fates of the various European nations. Was it possible then, in his eyes, to reestablish a modern Sparta or Rome? The digression on commerce in the *Droit public* that we have been examining ends with these melancholy reflections:

> I conclude these remarks, which are perhaps as useless as they are long. It would be appropriate to reflect on a state that possesses no more gold and silver than it needs, and to consider the means by which it can and must reduce a fortune which dooms it—but who would listen? I would experience the fate of Horace, when he advised the Romans to gather up their riches and cast them into the Adriatic.[76]

This tended to be Mably's judgment about the general condition of Europe, through the rest of his intellectual career. For the foreseeable future, there seemed to be no prospect whatever for societies that would pursue ends other than the accumulation of commercial wealth. In this sense, the "corruption" of the age was ineradicable. At the same time, much like the situation that obtained in another great age of corruption, Hellenistic Greece, contemporary Europe presented a variety of opportunities for reform and restoration. The palliatives Mably had in mind were mainly political ones, designed to combat or mitigate, above all, the *inequality* that was the necessary effect of an untrammeled accumulation of material wealth:

> There are a few forms of government that discourage the corruption fostered by wealth, which so many others seem to favor and encourage. If a country possesses laws that prevent citizens from being either too poor or too rich, and if the resulting spirit of economy and modesty extends to the public as a whole, then it can possess with impunity riches that would ravage a state in which the natural equality of men was less respected.[77]

The problem was to discover "forms of government" that would neutralize the effects of the division of societies into grossly unequal classes—an aspiration that in fact set the agenda for Mably's subsequent political thought.

The phrase "natural equality of men," however, reminds us that by 1764 Mably had already furnished his thought with philosophical foundations, drawn from the tradition of natural jurisprudence as well as from forms of Enlightenment psychology, that were largely lacking in his earlier writing. These will form the subject of the following chapter. In the meantime, we can briefly summarize the course of his intellectual evolution, as it has emerged thus far. The crucial event in that development was of course Mably's complete reversal of political conviction, as he moved from the enthusiastic monarchism of *Parallèle des romains et des français* to the celebration of republican city-states in his *Observations* on Greece and Rome, and then to the critique of commercial civilization introduced in *Principes des Négociations*. As we noted, however, the precise reasons for this striking change of heart are difficult to establish with any certainty.

That it had a profound personal dimension is hardly to be doubted, since it coincided with Mably's severing of relations with Tencin and his consequent abandonment of a Court career. But there exist no biographical sources to permit an accurate assessment of the relations between his life and thought in this period—or any other, for that matter. Nor do we know much more about the intellectual influences that may have affected the evolution of his early thought. In the preface to *Observations sur les Romains*, Mably writes that shortly after the appearance of the *Parallèle*, "A few persons, for whose intelligence I have a profound respect, honored me with their criticisms; and when, with their help, I was able to consider my work with some objectivity, I discovered that a plan that I had once thought very judicious, was in fact wholly lacking in reason."[78] Unfortunately, the identity of these "persons," as well as the substance of their criticisms, remains a tantalizing mystery.

In any case, it is important not to overlook the considerable degree of intellectual continuity that linked *Parallèle des romains et des français* with Mably's subsequent writings. For what was perhaps most striking about his youthful royalism was the fact that Mably wholly dispensed with the idea of a primordial or "ancient" monarchical constitution, of the sort sponsored by Dubos. Instead, he made his case for the French monarchy using two analytic tools that belonged to the republican tradition of philosophical history, the immediate model for which lay in Montesquieu's *Considérations* on the Romans. These were, first, a comparative framework that drew a sharp contrast between classical antiquity and modern Europe, and second, the standard Aristotelian-Polybian typology of governments, used to produce causal explanations of the evolution of political forms. These two instruments were immediately reapplied in the *Observations* on ancient history, and, as we shall see, formed the basis for all of Mably's subsequent intellectual labors. In this sense, then, the distance between the *Parallèle* and the works that succeeded it is not quite so great as his violent repudiation of that book might suggest.

CHAPTER 4

Dialogues: Conversations with Stanhope and Phocion

In a brief dialogue written in 1776, *De l'étude de la politique*, Mably recorded a conversation with a young acquaintance, for whom he prescribes a comprehensive course of study in politics—thereby providing us with a rare general statement of the basic principles governing his mature thought. It is not surprising that philosophical history figures prominently in the reading list he proposes, which includes, in addition to the expected ancient historians, Montesquieu's *Considérations* ("Far more likely to be of use to you than *De l'Esprit des lois*," Mably comments), as well as his own *Observations* on the Greeks and the Romans. Mably never abandoned the conviction that this form of historical writing should form the central pillar of any political education. But in *De l'étude de la politique* he goes on to warn his young friend that the study of history may be useless or worse, if undertaken without the guidance of two further bodies of knowledge—the "laws of nature" and the "origin, development, and progress of the passions." Indeed, Mably attributes his own youthful "mistakes" to his ignorance of these two domains: "How many errors and prejudices was I subject to at first, and how difficult they were to discard! It was only after having studied natural law and the play of our passions that I began to scorn a large number of things that I had once regarded with a profound respect!"[1] What this seems to suggest, of course, is that the political metamorphosis described in the previous two chapters—Mably's move from royalism to republicanism—was prompted by a mid-life conversion to the *école du droit naturel* and the adoption of a new outlook on the "passions." As we noted, however, the lack of detailed evidence concerning his intellectual evolution in these critical years makes it extremely difficult to establish even the *chronology* of these shifts in Mably's thought, much less to determine their exact role in his change of political conviction. All that can be dated with any precision is the moment when these two new intellectual "languages" make their first appearance in his writings, and this seems to have postdated his conversion to political republicanism proper. In 1758, or shortly thereafter, Mably wrote *Des droits et des devoirs du citoyen*, the first of his works to make any use of the conceptual vocabulary of natural jurisprudence; and in 1763 he published *Entretiens de Phocion*, in which a version of his social and moral psychology makes its earliest appearance. Not coincidentally, these were also his first two exercises in the literary genre that eventually came to dominate his writing, the philosophical dialogue.

The Political Conjuncture of the 1750s

With these two works Mably's thought thus assumed something like its mature shape, approximating the tripartite compound suggested in *De l'étude de la politique*. Before taking up either dialogue, however, it is necessary to turn our attention outward, to their wider political context. For both works were in fact responses to a specific political conjuncture, one which proved, in retrospect, to be a crucial turning-point in the fate of the Old Regime, and which was undoubtedly decisive in fixing Mably's own political convictions. He had begun his intellectual career—appropriately enough, given his initial political views—at the climax of a long period of uncharacteristic political stability and cultural harmony in France, which had begun with the advent of the Regency in 1715, and which culminated in the long and tranquil stewardship of Fleury in the 1730s and early 1740s. But this peaceable season came to a sudden and unexpected end around mid-century. The four decades after 1750 witnessed a spiral of increasingly acrimonious contention among the ruling elites of France, which eventually culminated in the revolution that overthrew the monarchy in 1789. Almost all recent research on the origins of the French Revolution has pointed to the 1750s as the critical juncture in the fate of the Old Regime. What upset the social equilibrium of the first half of the century? A full explanation would naturally have to begin with what was the bottom-line reality for any absolutist government, its martial performance in competition with the other states in Europe—briefly touched on in the last chapter. Yet the effects of French failure in the international arena are ultimately intelligible only in terms of developments within domestic politics. By 1763, when bankruptcy was still a remote prospect, a political and ideological juncture had already been passed: "In terms of ideas and rhetoric, France seems to have been ready for a revolution around 1760."[2] Here, too, however, the major cause of the change that occurred within French public life has traditionally been seen as an "external" one—the advent of the Enlightenment. It was in these same years that its diffuse component parts, mostly English or Dutch in inspiration, were synthesized into a powerful cultural *movement* for the first time. By then the majority of the intellectual leaders of the European Enlightenment were French, and their headquarters was Paris. The measure of the Enlightenment's impact in this period is to be seen above all in the great public controversies that erupted around the publication of the *Encyclopédie* in 1752 and 1757–59, and in the scandal that greeted Helvétius's *De l'esprit* in 1758–59. Yet for all the "publicity" that attended the *mouvement philosophique* in the 1750s, it was hardly sufficient in and of itself to pose any immediate threat to the political stability of the Old Regime. Even at their moment of greatest solidarity, the French *philosophes* never presented a united front in their political outlook. Nothing is more striking, in fact, than the overall lability of Enlightenment political thought, which could combine daring and radical speculative flight with opportunistic resignation to the unalterable monarchical order of Europe—often within the works of a single thinker. This is not to deny that the Enlightenment played its role in the eventual demise of the Old Regime. But like the distress caused by failure in the international arena, the "effect" of Enlightened criticism depended, in the first instance, on certain prior shifts within the French polity itself.

For it now appears that the shocks administered after mid-century to the delicate political equilibrium that sustained the monarchy—the earliest real premonitions of the storm to come—had their origins in the knot of problems that Montesquieu had correctly grasped as being at the heart of the social compact of absolutism: the institutional relations between nobility and monarchy. It is well known how an "Estates" system had developed by the later Middle Ages in France, as elsewhere in Europe, providing revenue to the monarchy as well as serving as a representative forum for the local elites; and how the Estates General, impeded by the immense geography of France, and by the power of the autonomous regional assemblies beneath it, failed to acquire the authority and fixity of, for example, its English counterpart.[3] After its final prerevolutionary convocation in 1614–15, the Bourbon monarchy was able to dispense with the Estates General altogether, with little resistance from the nobility. French absolutism thus reached the furthest extent of its development, in the dictatorship of Louis XIV, at the same moment that the English Parliament assumed sovereign command of the English state. But the question of political representation in France did not thereby disappear. In effect, the long desuetude of the Estates General merely deflected the demand for royal accountability into other channels, the chief of which became the elaborate network of high courts of appeal, the *parlements*, themselves late-medieval creations of royal convenience. The *parlements* gradually acquired constitutional prerogatives that amounted to a system of judicial review: the right to issue *arrêts de règlement*, obstructing the local administration of the monarchy; the right to delay activation of royal legislation until it was properly "registered" with the *parlements*; and the right to present *remontrances* to the king, of an advisory or expostulatory nature. Not even Louis XIV, scarred by the *parlement*-led Fronde of his youth, was able to mount a successful challenge to these privileges.[4] In any case, the long and disastrous dénouement of his reign cast grave doubts on the ability of one-man rule to protect aristocratic interests. With his death, the *parlements* entered their period of greatest efficacy and prestige. After 1715 the parlementary magistrates presented themselves convincingly as the guardians of French constitutionalism and natural representatives of the nobility—the most important of the "intermediate powers" that Montesquieu saw as essential components of European monarchy. It must be emphasized that throughout the first half of the eighteenth century, despite a number of flare-ups between court and *parlements*, the system did indeed form one of the stable institutional pillars of French absolutism, of critical importance to royal legitimacy.[5] This is why the sudden disequilibrium of the parlementary system after mid-century, never again to be restored, proved to be so crucial for the fate of the monarchy.

The parlementary crisis of the 1750s has not always received the attention it deserves, partly because it was unleashed by a religious dispute that seems strangely anachronistic in the century of Enlightenment. But this anachronism is of course a retrospective illusion. The religious legitimacy afforded to monarchy by Catholicism was nearly everywhere a central component of absolutist ideology. Down to the eighteenth century the social groups that had successfully defeated or overthrown absolutism in Europe—in the Netherlands and England—had marched under the banners of a militant Protestantism. The Religious Wars had apparently rescued France for Catholicism. But a fainter version of a Reformation-style opposition promptly appeared *within* the Gallic Church, in the epoch of Richelieu and Mazarin.[6] French Jansenism of the seventeenth century was born of Dutch inspiration, and blended Augustinian theology, Richerist Presbyterianism, and echoes of conciliarist political theory in a potent hybrid; its main adherents were naturally drawn from the ranks of the *noblesse de robe.* The problem was easily contained in the latter half of the century, but Louis XIV's dogged efforts to impose conformity on the French Church culminated in a fateful maneuver: as a parting gesture in 1713, he induced the pope to issue the Bull *Unigenitus,* condemning Jansenism. A long tug-of-war followed, with the Parlement of Paris leading the opposition, from which Fleury apparently emerged victorious in 1732, when *Unigenitus* became the official law of Church and State. However, in 1749 the archbishop of Paris, in an attempt to flush out Jansenist clergy, initiated a campaign of persecution with royal approval, refusing sacraments to those who declined to sign an orthodox *billet de confession.* At the same time, this move coincided with Controller General Machault's unsuccessful efforts to levy new taxes on the privileged orders, the clergy in particular, in an effort to retire the debt from the War of the Austrian Succession. This fatal combination of fiscal and religious imposition detonated an explosion of protest and obstructionism on the part of the magistracy, led by the Parlement of Paris. The ensuing struggle, with alternating judicial strikes by the magistrates and exiles of the Parlement in 1753 and 1757, became a bitter contest of will between the monarchy and the leading stratum of the *noblesse de robe.*[7] Moreover, this dispute among ruling elites quickly spilled into the "public space" being created by the Enlightenment itself in this epoch. The Parlement began to publish its remonstrances for the first time, and a pamphlet war raged throughout the decade, as both sides made strenuous efforts to enlist popular support. In the short term, the privileged orders seemed to prevail. Machault's initiatives were swiftly defeated by clerical resistance; and by 1758 the Parlement had triumphantly returned to Paris from its exile, leaving *Unigenitus* largely a dead letter thereafter. Indeed, the Jansenist party relentlessly pursued its perceived enemies, securing the expulsion of the Jesuit Order from France in 1763—what is often called the greatest defeat suffered by Catholicism in the eighteenth century.

In the meantime, the decade had closed with the attempted assassination of Louis XV and the demoralizing setbacks of the initial phases of the Seven Years' War. The cumulative impact of this series of events lay not so much in any institutional changes, as in the irreversible perceptual switch of "delegitimization"—a rapid and largely permanent loss of confidence in the monarchy among wide sections of the population.[8] In fact, what was probably the most portentous development of the decade was simply the surprising radicalization of parliamentary ideology itself. For resistance to "despotism" had suddenly acquired an institutional shape and contemporary reality that had been unthinkable in the earlier part of the century. The order of the day was no longer merely the nostalgic evocation of a "lost liberty" among a handful of disgruntled nobles, but the active defense of parliamentary privileges and "rights," stirring the political sympathies of large numbers of supporters, both aristocratic and bourgeois. The specific results of this radicalization were to be seen in two claims that now became increasingly prominent in official remonstrances and in supporting propaganda, both of which went well beyond anything to be found in the writings of earlier defenders of the "intermediate powers" such as Montesquieu: the assertion that the various *parlements* together formed a single corporate entity, and the claim that this assemblage functioned as the "representative" of the French nation and protector of its "liberties" in its dealings with the court.[9] The basis for both notions was a historical argument, according to which the *parlements* were not only the guardians of the traditional constitution of the monarchy, but were also the legitimate successors to the various representative institutions of the French past, including the moribund Estates General. Though the first serious calls for the restoration of the Estates were not heard until 1771, its shadow already impended ominously over the failing Bourbon monarchy.

'Des droits et des devoirs du citoyen'

It was against this turbulent background, as French absolutism entered the period of its final senescence, that Mably completed the journey toward his mature political thought. The pivotal work that first introduced most of the major themes and vocabulary of his later writing was also a specific response to the political upheavals of the 1750s: *Des droits et des devoirs du citoyen*. For all of its importance in Mably's intellectual evolution, however, this dialogue has continued to guard certain secrets about itself. One of these is the exact date of its composition. The eight "letters" that make up *Des droits et des devoirs du citoyen* are dated 12–21 August 1758. There is no internal evidence for any date later than this, and most scholars have concluded that the dialogue was written at this time or shortly thereafter. Yet some uncertainty persists, for not only was the work never published in its author's lifetime—for reasons that will be clear in a moment—but there is no extant reference to its existence, on Mably's or anyone else's part, prior to a passage in one of his own later dialogues, itself published only posthumously, but apparently written around 1776.[10] Another enigma concerns the identity of Mably's chief interlocutor in the dialogue, an Englishman named "Stanhope." The autograph manuscript of *Des droits et des devoirs du citoyen* originally used a different name, "Milord Halifax," which Mably then replaced throughout with "Stanope" (the "h" was added in the posthumous printed versions of the work). When the dialogue was first published in 1789, the *Correspondance littéraire* informed its readers that the intended reference was to the famous Lord Chesterfield—that is, Philip Dormer Stanhope (1694–1773), fourth Earl of Chesterfield, whose grandfather had been the Marquis of Halifax.[11] This may well have been the case, since Mably had undoubtedly met Chesterfield during the 1740s, when the latter made frequent appearances at the salons of Madame de Tencin, Madame de Bocage, and Madame Dupin. Yet an even more likely model for the character was Philip, the second earl Stanhope (1717–86), a relative of Chesterfield and the son of James Stanhope, the first earl and leading English commander during the War of the Spanish Succession. Although he remains a somewhat shadowy figure, Philip Stanhope was celebrated not only for his skill in mathematics and his command of Greek, but also for his radically democratic political convictions, which he carefully cultivated in his son Charles Stanhope, the third Earl and Lord Mahon after 1763, who later became a leading radical politician and fervent supporter of the French Revolution.[12] The only other reference to a "Stanhope" in Mably's writings, which occurs in the late dialogue *l'Oracle d'Apollon*, is plainly to this Philip Stanhope: "I will tell you what Milord Stanhope told me during his visit on the way back to Geneva, where he has devoted himself wholly to the education of his son, Milord Mahon."[13] We lack any other sources for reconstructing whatever biographical experience might lie behind *Des droits et des devoirs du citoyen*. Nevertheless, it will be seen that the political views expressed in the dialogue are far closer to the radical opinions attributed to Philip Stanhope and his son than to any that might plausibly be ascribed to Chesterfield.

Mably's general purposes for the character of "Stanhope" are, in any case, clear enough. He serves as a representative and spokesman for the radical Commonwealth tradition, who undertakes the political reeducation of an anonymous and initially rather reluctant French proselyte, as the two wander through the gardens of the royal chateau at Marly (which was in fact Mably's own preferred place of refuge from Paris, particularly during the decade of the 1750s); the Frenchman in turn recounts their conversations to a third party, in a set of eight letters.[14] *Des droits et des devoirs du citoyen* opens with an *avertissement* that consists of the famous fragment from Cicero's *De republica*, preserved in Lactantius, beginning: "*Est quidem vera lex recta ratio naturae congruens, diffusa in omnes, constans, sempiterna* . . . "[15] ("True law is right reason in agreement with nature, universal, unchanging, and eternal . . . "), to which Mably adds: "The work you are about to read is nothing more than a commentary on this admirable passage from Cicero, which ought never to have been lost sight of by those who have written on natural law and the principles of government." The initial topic of discussion—that of political obligation and resistance—is suggested to Stanhope and his French friend by the stark contrast between the splendor of the gardens and the misery of the surrounding countryside. At the outset, the Frenchman advises a melancholy resignation to these realities, based on his own account of the "rights and duties" of citizens. In the state of nature, he begins, mankind enjoyed perfect equality and freedom; the only duty of the first men was to secure their own happiness. "So long as men remained in this state, their rights were as limitless as their duties were limited. Everything belonged to each one of them, and each man was a kind of king with a right to universal monarchy."[16] However, recognizing at length the limitations of this situation, men contracted with one another to transfer these rights to magistrates, thus exiting from the state of nature into civil society—a "singular revolution." The condition of the efficacy of these compacts was that they be made irrevocable and unbridgeable. The result is that all men are born into distinct civil societies, with distinct sets of laws: "I have gone through Grotius, Hobbes, Wolff, and Pufendorf," the Frenchman concludes, thus identifying the authors alluded to in the *avertissement*, "and they all claim that each citizen finds himself subject to the laws of the society of which he is a member. To suggest that these laws are not the measure of the duties of the citizen amounts to the destruction of society. . . . "[17] This account is, of course, a caricature. No attempt is made to distinguish among these four authors, who are all simply tarred with the brush of a generic Hobbesism. This is sufficient for Mably's purpose, however, which is to permit "Stanhope" to set forth a somewhat rambling critique of the conservative wing of the modern natural rights tradition, ostensibly in the name of a return to Ciceronian rectitude.

To begin with, the Englishman objects to the depiction of the state of nature proposed by his French friend. There is an initial concession to Hobbes. A state in which rights were unlimited and duties did not yet exist was perhaps true "for the first moments of the birth of mankind," when men were still half-animals. Significantly, this was at the same time a gesture in the direction of Rousseau, as the sentences that follow make clear: "Lacking reason, they were still classed among the animals, mechanically obeying feelings of pleasure and pain. There were thus neither rights nor duties—morality did not exist for these automatons, just as it does not exist for savages grazing in forests, or for a child in the arms of his nurse. But what interest can this situation have for us, if it is not our own, and perhaps never even existed?"[18] The last question is almost certainly a reference to the famous passage in the *Discours sur l'origine de l'inégalité parmi les hommes* in which Rousseau insists on the importance of describing "a state that no longer exists, that perhaps never existed, that probably never will exist, and yet about which it is necessary to have very clear ideas, in order to pass judgment on our present state of affairs."[19] But it is precisely the latter claim that Mably's Englishman contests. Having initially accepted something like the picture of the state of nature of the second *Discours*, Stanhope then rejects it as irrelevant, reverting to a far more traditional conception. For "once repeated feelings of pleasure and pain had engraved a certain number of ideas in the memory; once men, with the aid of experience, began to grasp the relations between the objects which surround them; once they were able to reflect, compare, and reason—was it true that their rights were still limitless, or that they recognized no duties?" No, for "the idea of good and evil necessarily preceded the establishment of society; without this instrument, how could it have even occurred to men to make laws?"[20] The error of the great natural law writers of the previous century, Stanhope insists—less than accurately in the case of Grotius and Pufendorf—was to conceive of the state of nature as a condition to be ended or canceled rather than secured and perfected. Ultimately, their mistakes all derived from their common desire to defend absolute monarchy, tainting their work with a conformism that ran counter to their own principles.[21] Grotius possessed a "profound genius" and had sensed the truth, only to lack the courage to express it, having published his book under the auspices of Louis XIII. Pufendorf came from a country "in which there was liberty only for the oppressors of the nation," and thus disguised the truths he too had glimpsed. As for Hobbes, he could have rivaled Locke for the glory of having made known "the fundamental principles of society." However, "attached by events or by interest to an unhappy faction," Hobbes "employed all the resources of a powerful mind to establish a system destructive of humanity, and which he himself would have condemned, if, instead of the disorders of anarchy, he had experienced the ravages of despotism."[22] The result is that these modern writers—apparently with the exception of Locke, though he is not mentioned again in the dialogue—totally misconstrued the nature of man and the state of nature. They proposed a "blind and servile obedience which, in defiance of our reason and the nature which has bestowed it upon us, transforms us into automatons."

In order to understand the state of nature accurately, Stanhope continues, one must begin by examining *human* nature, with this rule in mind: "If we find that there are things that belong to mankind so essentially that they cannot be removed without debasing them, then we may conclude that the society and the government erected to ennoble humanity, have no right to deprive citizens of these things." Thus, our "most essential and most noble attribute" is *reason*, "the organ by which God instructs us as to our duties, and our only guide for leading us to happiness." This "reason" is in fact nothing more than the eternal and immutable *recta ratio* spoken of by Cicero in his Republic. And *liberty* is the second essential attribute of humanity, which is in fact inseparable from reason. "For what purpose would nature have given us the faculty of thinking, of reflecting, and of reasoning, if, for lack of liberty, we were unable to use our reason?"[23] Stanhope thus concludes: "The reason that nature has bestowed on us, the liberty in which she has placed us, and that invincible desire for happiness that she has placed in our soul, are three titles that any man can invoke against the unjust government under which he lives. I thus conclude that a citizen is neither a conspirator nor a disturber of the public peace, if he proposes to his compatriots a wiser form of government than that which they have freely adopted, or which events, passions, and circumstances have imperceptibly established."[24] In fact, not only do citizens have a "right of reformation" of this sort, they have a sacred *duty* to exercise it: "I therefore believe that revolutions are still possible; that a good citizen must remain hopeful, and is obligated, according to his position, his powers, and his talents, to work toward rendering these revolutions useful to his country."[25] Prudence, Stanhope concedes, naturally dictates certain limits: "Man never loses his rights, but reason does not always counsel him to insist on them. Reason considers the times and the circumstances, and never counsels us to pursue a chimera." For example, the English attempt to move directly from a monarchy to a republic in the previous century had been far too precipitous, and thus doomed itself to failure. Nevertheless, even the French could hope for a constitutional monarchy, and the path toward one was clear: "In order to make your way securely," Stanhope advises his companion, "you French must first aspire to that sort of liberty we enjoy, that is to say, you must see to the reestablishment of your former Estates General."[26]

Both intrigued and alarmed by the seditious *élan* of these remarks, the Frenchman assures Stanhope that no such outcome is possible in France. Besides, can the Englishman really mean to extend this "right to reform the government" beyond the circle of the "wisest" citizens, to the poor and the ignorant? Isn't this to invite appalling anarchy? Stanhope replies that his companion has forgotten one of the deepest lessons of ancient politics: "What benefits did not result from the eternal quarrels of the patricians and plebeians in the Roman Republic? If the people had preferred repose to everything else, they would have become enslaved to the nobility, and the name of the Romans would be unknown to us today. Instead, their conflicts carried the government to the highest degree of perfection, exciting a spirit of emulation in the whole citizenry."[27] The same lesson was learned all over again in the last century in England, whose citizens would be laboring under Stuart despotism to this day, had they not preferred liberty to repose. But your civil war, the Frenchman protests, was that not a terrible price to have paid for this liberty? "Civil war," Stanhope whispers in his friend's ear, "is sometimes a great good." All war is pernicious. But if foreign war is sometimes useful,

> if natural right even renders it necessary, since it is sometimes the only means a state has for avenging an injury, restoring its possessions legitimately, and preventing its own destruction, I would ask, after you have quieted your imagination, as I have calmed my own, whether a civil war, in the same manner as a foreign war, may not sometimes be authorized by the most exacting morality?[28]

But what if a people has freely entered into a compact with a monarch, the Frenchman objects, as the Danish Estates did in 1660? "We have seen," answers Stanhope, "that there are perhaps some rights that one simply cannot give up; for example, those that so belong to the essence of man and society that it is impossible seriously to contemplate their separation. Even the most ignorant legislators have recognized there such rights exist." A people cannot enslave itself any more than an individual can, Stanhope insists. The natural lawyers have demonstrated a hundred times that the true attribute of sovereignty is absolute independence, and that it is thus incapable of binding itself. He then presses on to the inevitable conclusion: "The people, to whom sovereign power originally belongs, the sole author of political government and bestower of its powers to its magistrates, always has the right to interpret its contract, or rather its gifts, to modify its clauses, to cancel them, and to establish an entirely new order of things."[29] The Frenchman, by now on the verge of conversion to republicanism, makes a final attempt at resistance. If each citizen has the right to disobey an unjust law, then each citizen also has the right to judge the laws of nature for himself—but how could any group of men ever agree on these? The laws of nature, Stanhope answers, are no more than

> the precepts of reason itself. . . . They are so simple, so clear, so luminous, that it is enough to present to men for them to be accepted, so long as they are not in the grip of some passion, or subject to some derangement of the mind. The feeblest mind, the most vulgar peasant, are as aware as the most profound philosopher, that they must not do unto others that which they would not have done to themselves. . . . The more we meditate on these primitive laws of nature, the deeper their impact on all our political laws; and is it not in departing from their rule, that we have spoiled everything?[30]

With these confident declarations, the first half of *Des droits et des devoirs du citoyen* comes to an end. There follows a short interlude, in which Stanhope introduces two topics that would form much of the agenda for Mably's subsequent political writings: first, the question of the "relations between morality and politics"—the topic taken up at length in *Entretiens de Phocion,* to which we will turn in a moment; and second, a brief utopian reverie, starting from Stanhope's claim that private property is the "principal source of all the misfortunes that afflict humanity"—a claim that, in a sense, became the central preoccupation of all of Mably's major writings of the following decade.[31] These concerns are set aside, however, when Stanhope poses what he calls the "great question" of the epoch: "whether the people of Europe who have lost their liberty will be able to recover and preserve it."[32] In other words, given that sovereign authority belongs, by natural right, to the "people," how can the subjects of present-day monarchies—the French monarchy in particular—be expected to exercise this right? What could be done even to begin to overturn the immense weight and power of Bourbon absolutism? It is in response to these questions that Stanhope, in the second half of *Des droits et des devoirs du citoyen*, outlines a three-step recipe for a transition from absolute to constitutional monarchy in France. First, the "intermediate powers" of the monarchy, the *parlements* above all, should reclaim their leading role in the political life of the nation, according to the "ancient constitution" of the realm—a move that Stanhope sees as already accomplished with the political activism of the various *parlements* in the 1750s; second, the *parlements* should use their newly recovered powers in order to force the Court to reconvene an Estates General; and finally, the restored Estates should move to establish its own periodicity and legislative authority within a new constitutional monarchy. As the plan unfolds, the Frenchman poses a series of objections to it, doubting the success of English strategic thinking in a French context. But these are systematically disposed of by Stanhope. *Des droits et des devoirs du citoyen* concludes on a note of cautious optimism about the prospects for the "recovery of liberty" in France—an optimism that was to color much of Mably's political writing of the following decade.

We will return to this "script for a French Revolution," as Keith Baker has aptly termed it, in Chapter Six, where it can be examined in the context of Mably's later writing on French politics and history. Here it is necessary only to indicate something of the place of *Des droits et des devoirs du citoyen* within French political thought as a whole. Some time ago Franco Venturi drew our attention to the remarkable "republican ferment" that gripped France in the decade after 1745, of which *De l'Esprit des lois* and the early political writings of Diderot and Rousseau were only the most visible manifestations.[33] The onset of the parlementary oppositionism described above, as well as major reversals in the international arena, of course help to explain the timing of this new period of ideological turbulence. But Venturi rightly insisted that this change had a specific intellectual leaven as well—the English Commonwealth tradition, which served as the central carrier of radical political thought in Europe between the English and French Revolutions, linking the regicide republicanism of the Commonwealth to the succession of minority Whig and Tory factions whose opposition to the settlement of 1689 extended far into the eighteenth century. For French political thought had gradually begun to claim the Commonwealth inheritance as its own, once the creeping paralysis of French absolutism became evident in the decades following the death of Louis XIV. By mid-century the bulk of the "Whig Canon," from Milton and Harrington to Sidney and Locke, had been translated into French, and progressive thinkers, led by Montesquieu, had undertaken the project of transcribing Commonwealth concepts and categories for usage in the French context.[34]

In light of this background, the significance of Mably's dialogue is evident enough. *Des droits et des devoirs du citoyen* not only provides a striking confirmation of Venturi's claims, but it also points to an entirely new stage in the relationship between English and French political thought. For the first time, a major French thinker had proposed that the English transition from absolute to constitutional monarchy might provide a model for the recovery of "liberty" in France. For what is prescribed in the second part of *Des droits et des devoirs du citoyen* is unmistakably a scenario for a "Whig Revolution"—a repeat of the English revolutions of the seventeenth century, at once more compressed and less violent, directed by a conscious political agency that could profit from the mistakes—as well as the achievements—of the Commonwealth pioneers. At the least, Mably's dialogue marks a major symbolic juncture in the development of the revolutionary tradition in Europe.

But the influence of English political thought on Mably's work was not confined to the domain of revolutionary strategy. It is equally evident in the natural law theory propounded in the first part of *Des droits et des devoirs du citoyen.* We have seen that the dialogue opens with a critique of the conservative *école du droit naturel,* whose target was Hobbes above all, but which was aimed at Grotius, Pufendorf, and Wolff as well. The appeal to the authority of Cicero notwithstanding, "Stanhope's" arguments plainly amount to a declaration of allegiance to the *other* wing of the modern rights tradition, the radical lineage whose inaugural figures were the English Levellers and whose most authoritative voice was that of John Locke.[35] It is probably no accident that Mably's title both echoed and amended the title that Barbeyrac gave to his translation of Pufendorf's *De officio hominis et civis—Les devoirs de l'homme et du citoyen.* For Barbeyrac was the first great popularizer of Locke in France. His translations of Grotius and Pufendorf, the main vehicles for the dissemination of natural law theory in the early eighteenth century, were accompanied by extracts from the Second Treatise, which Barbeyrac used to criticize the political conservatism of the founders of modern natural jurisprudence.[36] As we have seen, Locke is conspicuously exempted from the general condemnation of the other seventeenth-century rights theorists in *Des droits et des devoirs du citoyen.* He is not mentioned again in the dialogue, but elsewhere Mably warmly recommended him as the supreme authority in matters of natural law. In a revealing letter of 1764 to his patron the Duc de la Rochefoucauld, Mably wrote:

> If you took less pleasure than you do in reading the principles of civil government, I would deluge you with tributes to this work; it contains every single truth, or at least the germ of every truth, known to natural and political right. To copy passages from Locke is an effective way to make his principles your own; but truly to succeed at this, you need to make a *extrait raisonné*—that is, to weigh the reasonings of the author, to join new ones to his own, and to draw the proper conclusions. I should apologize, Monsieur le Duc, for recommending so taxing a method of reading; but your initial pains will save you a great deal in the long run. The more you are able to make Locke your own, the easier it will be to read other words on natural right; you will recognize their errors far in advance and avoid them effortlessly.[37]

A decade later, in the work cited at the beginning of this chapter, *De l'étude de la politique*, Mably affirmed that "politics consists solely of the faithful obedience of the laws of nature, and history records so many misfortunes only because we have neglected them." But he goes on to assure his young friend that the study of this subject was not as onerous as was commonly believed: "I do not require that you read all the works written on this subject—God forbid! But I do ask that you read, with great attention, and more than one time, Locke's treatise on civil government. Indeed, it is necessary to make it your own, and to have a firm grasp of his principles, in order to correct the errors that resulted from the bias every Englishman feels toward his own government."[38] Once Locke has been studied, he continues, one can then read a few chapters of Grotius and Pufendorf: "You will find many useful truths in their works, and, if you have read your Locke carefully, you will be able to evade their errors with ease."

Needless to say, *Des droits et des devoirs du citoyen* is very far from being a faithful Lockean text in a strict sense. Even setting aside for the moment the question of property, Mably's doctrine of inalienable rights, his endorsement of full popular sovereignty, and his arguments for the justice of civil war, are all of course far closer to genuine Leveller sentiments than to anything that Locke himself might conceivably have endorsed. But this should not be particularly surprising. For the texts just cited clearly suggest that Locke, corrector of the conservatives, required correction himself, owing to his excessive "respect" for the English constitution, whose monarchical component naturally was too powerful for Mably's tastes.[39] Once again, it is a pity that the evidence to reconstruct Mably's intellectual sources—correspondence, memoirs, manuscripts—is as scarce as it is, for it would be interesting to know, among other things, which edition of the *Two Treatises* he used (Mably evidently did not read

English). The history of Locke's reception in France indeed appears to have been one of a gradual "radicalization," from the initial translation of Mazel in 1691 to the overtly republican edition of Rousset de Missy of 1755.[40] As for other possible sources for the opinions expressed in *Des droits et des devoirs*, one name suggests itself, that of Algernon Sidney. In his remarks on natural law theorists in *De l'étude de la politique*, Mably advises the reading of "a few chapters from Sidney," referring no doubt to the *Discourses concerning government*, which had initially been translated into French in 1702, and which were republished in 1755. As Baker suggests in his essay on *Des droits et des devoirs*, Mably's warm recommendations in favor of civil war—so distant in spirit from Locke's thought—may well have been inspired by Sidney's notorious chapters on the same subject in the *Discourses*.[41] Beyond this, we shall see in fact that the general structure of Mably's mature thought is remarkably similar to the blending of classical republicanism, natural jurisprudence, and neo-Platonic stoicism that characterized Sidney's own political writing.[42] In any case, our knowledge of Mably's sources is obviously hampered by the fact that the complex history of the "reception" of the Commonwealth tradition in eighteenth-century France remains largely unwritten.[43] But whatever the specific results of future research in this area, it seems certain that *Des droits et des devoirs du citoyen* will take its place as a key text in that history—a vivid testimonial to the seminal role being played by English political thought in the France of Louis XV.

'Entretiens de Phocion'

Mably declined to publish *Des droits et des devoirs du citoyen* in his lifetime—perhaps not surprisingly, since the authors of far less incendiary works, Helvétius most notably, had experienced vicious harassment and persecution in the recent past. The dialogue's impact thus had to wait for its appearance during the "pre-Revolution," some thirty years later. The destiny of the second work marking the transition to Mably's mature thought was very different. Probably written in the fall of 1761, *Entretiens de Phocion* was published in 1763 and met with instant success, both in France and abroad. *Phocion* was awarded the prize for the best work of the year by the *Société littéraire suisse*, which bestowed the same award on Beccaria's *Dei delitti e delle pene* the following year. With the possible exception of *Le droit public de l'Europe*, it was by far the most widely known and best received among all the works Mably published in his lifetime, enjoying twelve reprintings in France before the Revolution, as well as editions in Italian, German, Swedish, English, Polish, Spanish, and Greek.[44] Nor does the contrast with *Des droits et des devoirs du citoyen* end there, for *Phocion* appears to be quite distinct from the earlier work in both its setting and its dominant concerns. Equipped with a *trompe l'oeil* preface—one of the few lighter touches to be found in Mably's writing—the dialogue purports to be the translation of a Greek manuscript recently discovered at Monte Cassino, whose author, a certain Nicocles, had been present at a series of didactic conversations between the doomed Athenian commander Phocion and a young fellow-citizen named Aristias.[45] After a long exploration of the "relations between politics and morality," the dialogue ends on a sharply pessimistic note, befitting its somber historical context. With tears in his eyes, Phocion announces that the time for the "healthy violence" of a Lycurgan coup is long since past for Athens. Rather than the defiant defense of Athenian liberty championed by Demosthenes, he counsels a prudent conformity to the vagaries of "fortune"—in other words, submission to Macedonian overlordship. The revolutionary self-confidence of *Des droits et des devoirs du citoyen* seems to have vanished in *Entretiens de Phocion*, written only a few years later.

The differences between the two works should not be exaggerated, however. Despite its classical costume, *Entretiens de Phocion* is certainly no less "contemporary" in its concerns—no less a reaction to the political and intellectual upheavals of the decade of the 1750s—than was the earlier dialogue. The first of its five *entretiens* opens with a melancholy précis of Athenian history from the Peloponnesian War to the eve of Chaeronea, whose parallels with the disasters of the past century of French history will have been transparent to Mably's readers; and the text itself is furnished with a large number of editorial "notes," pointing to contemporary issues and meanings. Moreover, there are some indications that the dialogue had a very specific contemporary reference. In his *discours de réception* in 1789, the Academician Nicolay mentioned that the major work of his predecessor, *De la félicité publique*, had originally been inspired by conversations between Chastellux and Mably. In a response, Claude de Rulhière added that the young Chastellux had even appeared as a character in *Entretiens de Phocion*, information he insisted came from the author himself: "One can hardly tell, and it is a secret that he revealed to few persons, that under the name of the young Aristias, he wished to sketch a portrait of the Marquis de Chastellux, such as he appeared at that age—full of spirit, patriotism, and ardor for virtue, who was then only a philosopher by passion but who wished to enlighten himself through contact with the wise."[46]

Neither Mably nor Chastellux left anything to corroborate this report. But what renders it plausible is the fact that the views attributed to "Aristias" in the first *entretien* quite clearly point to those currents of Enlightenment thought that eventually found expression in works such as *De la félicité publique.* Aristias is introduced as "a young man born to love and respect virtue, but whose mind has already begun to be spoiled by the sophists." His initial move is to praise the enormous wealth and commercial prosperity of the Athenians, which he regards as providing a secure basis for rendering Athens once again the "first republic" of the world.[47] Phocion's reply is that, on the contrary, it was precisely this surrender to the "passions" of avarice and ambition that was responsible for all the miseries to which the Athenians had been subjected; these must be firmly subordinated to the "prudent laws of reason." But Aristias has some confident views of his own on this subject:

> Why suppress the passions, whose salutary fire gives movement and life to society? Nature imperiously commands us to a relentless search for happiness: doesn't she make both her will and our destination perfectly clear to us through the pleasures and pains with which she has armed everything that surrounds us? . . . This "reason," whose uncertain commands we praise and of which we are so proud, is really nothing more than the product of our vanity. It is merely the name that we give to our prejudices, once they have been formed by accident and consecrated by education and habit. . . . Weak, languid, everywhere enslaved—is it really fitting for reason to lay claim to such authority? It is to the passions that nature has granted this authority, in giving them the strength necessary to subjugate us.[48]

There is little doubt as to the specific contemporary reference intended by Mably in these lines. For among the complex series of intellectual adjustments that marked the passage from the early to the later Enlightenment in France, none was more striking than the novel and largely positive emphasis that was placed on the "passions" as the key motor force of individual and collective agency—a move that was one element in the general retreat from the confident rationalism of the early Enlightenment. Few French thinkers were ever tempted to follow Hume to the provocative conclusions advanced in his *Treatise of Human Nature*: "We speak not strictly and philosophically when we talk of a combat of passion and reason. Reason is, and ought to be the slave of the passions, and can never pretend to any other office than to serve and obey them."[49] But readers of *Entretiens de Phocion* might well have been reminded of the famous rehabilitation of the passions which opened Diderot's *Pensées philosophiques*: "People complain endlessly about the passions; they impute all the misfortunes of mankind to them, forgetting that they are also the source of all pleasure. . . . They believe that some injury has been inflicted upon reason, whenever anyone says a word in favor of its rivals. But it is only the passions, the great passions, that can raise the soul to great things. Without them, neither our characters nor our actions could approach sublimity; the arts would return to their infancy, and virtue become trivial."[50] These claims were echoed on a vaster philosophic scale by Helvétius in *De l'esprit*: "The passions are the equivalent, in morality, of movement in physics. They create, destroy, conserve, enliven everything, and without them, all is dead; they are what animates the moral world. . . . It is thus to the strong passions that we owe all invention and marvels in the arts; they must be regarded as productive germ of the mind, the ultimate spring of all great achievements."[51] Of course, neither Diderot nor Helvétius adopted anything like the *anti*rationalism suggested in the passage attributed to "Aristias" above—the idea that "reason" is nothing more than a collection of "prejudices, formed by accident and consecrated by education and habit." But a pointed skepticism toward inherited conceptions of a transcendent rational order was in fact a feature of the writings of both men in this period—visible both in the reductive sensationalism of *De l'esprit*, as well as in Diderot's article on "Droit naturel" in the *Encyclopédie*, in which the traditional conception of natural law as a transcendent and immutable rational order is abandoned in favor of a quasi-historicist notion of a "general will" of the human race.[52]

There is every sign, then, that the "sophistry" to which "Aristias" has fallen victim—celebration of the passions, skepticism about the claims of reason—should be understood as referring to the intellectual innovations of the radical Enlightenment in France: the thought-world, roughly, of the *Encyclopédistes*, of Helvétius, and, later, Holbach. Mably's response comes through the mouthpiece of "Phocion." "If reason is no more than a prejudice," the latter tells Aristias, "you had better tremble, for virtue then becomes a useless and meaningless word." But there are no grounds for such skepticism about the existence of a transcendental rational order. Politics is indeed a rational science, founded on "those luminous, fixed, and immutable principles that nature has given us in order to seek out and secure our own happiness." It was Lycurgus who first established a social order embodying these principles:

> Rather than looking to our prejudices, he consulted nature alone. He descended into the torturous depths of the human heart, and grasped the secrets of providence. His laws, whose goal was the control of our passions, did nothing more than develop and affirm those laws which the Author of nature has made known to us through the ministry of our reason, the sole supreme and infallible magistrate among men.[53]

In a note, Mably cites the same passage on "*recta ratio*" from the third book of *De republica* that served as the epigraph to *Des droits et des devoirs du citoyen*: "This is the 'right reason' described by Cicero with such sublimity and accuracy, and which ought to serve as the standard for all of morality and politics. *Les entretiens de Phocion* have no other purpose than to develop this important truth."[54] As for the passions, Phocion insists that they are indeed responsible for all of the evils traditionally ascribed to them: "Nothing is sacred for the passions: wars, murders, treachery, violence, injustice, cowardice—such are their fruits."[55] Human nature is such that any attempt to eliminate or suppress the passions altogether would be in vain. But to endorse the instinctualist hedonism recommended by the defenders of the passions would be a far more grievous error:

> We have a reason and passions: in smiling at the ill-humor of those severe philosophers whose goal is to detach our souls from the bonds of our senses, let us not fall into the infinitely more dangerous error of those men who invite a total surrender to our passions, only to regret continually their having been misled by the false goods that they present. We go beyond the intentions of nature, if we attempt to destroy the passions; they too are among her immortal creations. But we have been commanded to temper and control the passions by the counsel of reason, since this is the only way for them to lose their venom and to contribute something to our happiness.[56]

This is as much philosophical anthropology as Mably provides in *Entretiens de Phocion*. It is perhaps surprising that there is no explicit reference, not even in his editorial notes, to the sensationalist psychology developed by his brother Condillac, which had already reached its finished form in the latter's *Traité des sensations*, published in 1754. For Condillac's emphasis on the inescapable *limits* imposed on human reason by sensationalism was to play a central role in his discussions of these same themes in his later dialogues. Nevertheless, the core position of Mably's own moral psychology was already established by this point. Against an unrealistic confidence in the autonomous power of reason—the mistake of those "severe philosophers, whose goal is to detach our souls from the bonds of our senses"—Mably always stressed that the passions were ineradicable components of human nature. But he strongly rejected the claims for the benign social role of the passions that were so common in the mid-eighteenth century, insisting on the necessity of their subordination to rational control and guidance. Much like Rousseau, Mably's goal was to restore the classical notion of a profound *conflict* between reason and the passions, which tended to be underestimated or denied altogether by the optimistic naturalism of the later Enlightenment.[57]

At all events, Aristias is soon overwhelmed by the arguments of Phocion. By the start of the second part of *Entretiens de Phocion* he has renounced his earlier views, with apologies. "It is a strange folly," he admits, "to dare to usurp the name of philosopher while at the same time reducing yourself to the condition of an animal, to undertake to reason while maintaining that there is no such thing as reason."[58] This capitulation permits Phocion to turn to the real business of the dialogue, which is to explore the relations between "politics and morality." The topic is introduced via a direct appeal to Plato. Phocion is portrayed as a former pupil of the great philosopher, from whom he acquired the doctrine of "mixed government," described in terms identical to those we have already seen in Mably's *Observations* on Greece and Rome. "This great man," Phocion informs Aristias, after detailing the faults of monarchy, aristocracy, or democracy in their "pure" forms,

> argued that public power, by means of a skillful mixture of all these forms of governments, should be distributed among different parties able to resist, to balance, and to temper one another reciprocally. But he did not stop there, my dear Aristias. The disciple of Socrates knew mankind too well to imagine that even a government whose parts were combined with the greatest wisdom could sustain itself without the aid of *moeurs domestiques*. Read his *Republic*: consider how vigilantly he strives to master the passions and to submit virtue to the most austere standards. Perhaps he surpassed the limits of prudence; but at least his excessive precautions show how necessary he believed *moeurs* were to the conservation of his government.[59]

Thus the "principal object of politics is the regulation of *moeurs*": "It is only by means of the exercise of the domestic virtues that a people learns to practice the political virtues." Now these ideas are of course familiar ones in eighteenth-century political thought. An insistence on the fundamental continuity or even outright identity of "morality" and "politics" was often presented as the deliberate resumption of classical conceptions after the "interruption" of medieval Christianity and the principles of of the early-modern period; as such, it is a common trope in the writing of Montesquieu, Rousseau, and

Helvétius, among many others.[60] What is unusual about Mably's presentation of the theme in *Entretiens de Phocion* is that it leads him to attempt a detailed catalogue of the political "virtues," in full conformity with the classical republican tradition.

The three primary political virtues, Phocion declares at the start of the third *entretien*, are justice, prudence, and courage: "Let us concur with the principles of morality, which show that from these three virtues flow order, peace—in a word, the preservation of every good desired by men."[61] At the same time, precisely because of their preeminence, these virtues cannot be instilled in a body of citizens by mere legislative fiat. Instead, the legislator or political leader must first establish a foundation for them through the cultivation of a set of "auxiliary" virtues, which are more tractable and responsive to political manipulation. The first of these is *tempérance*, "the virtue that reduces the number of our needs and simplifies them, by encouraging us to content ourselves with no more than that which nature demands for our preservation."[62] For examples of institutions that foster temperance, Phocion points to the Spartan common meals, as well as the sumptuary laws and regulations concerning women described in the seventh book of Plato's *Republic*. The second auxiliary virtue is *amour de travail*—but one must not conclude, Phocion hastens to add, that *all* labor is useful to society. The examples of Egypt after Sosostris and of Athens after Pericles demonstrate that industry that is fueled by the passions of avarice and ambition will tend to divide the citizenry into two groups: on the one hand, an over-wealthy elite whose interests diverge from those of the community as a whole, and on the other, a propertyless artisan class, necessarily excluded from political participation. Corresponding to the natural "mediocrity" of human needs, labor should be light, continual, and shared by all. In a remarkable expression of paternalist primitivism, Mably has Phocion declare:

> How I admire the simplicity of *moeurs* that is depicted in Homer, kings who know how many head of cattle, goats, and sheep they possess, and can prepare their own food; a queen who weaves the very garments worn by her husband; a princess who descends to the river in a humble cart in order to wash her family's clothes. Each person sharing in the glory being his own artisan—and, the gods willing, perhaps the wisdom of our *moeurs*, the simplicity of our needs, and the equality of our fortunes can still make this possible![63]

The third virtue is *amour de la gloire*, the "noble and generous sentiment that reminds us of the grandeur of our origins and of our destination—the sentiment that renders us the rivals of spiritual beings, and reminds us that we are the work of a God."[64] Again, this must be tempered by a careful choice of objectives. The fate of Periclean Athens suggests the dangers of an excessive love of glory, twisted into a desire for imperial domination of one's neighbors. The last auxiliary virtue, Phocion concludes, is *respect pour les dieux*, which is explained in the traditional terms of the necessity of a public cult, underwritten by divine sanction, for the maintenance of social order. Lest the contemporary thrust of these remarks be overlooked, Mably has him add that "the Sophists, my dear Aristias, have tried in vain to argue that the most religious men are also the least virtuous; but they are mistaken—they call religion what is mere superstition or hypocrisy."[65]

Needless to say, this picture of the "political virtues" is a thoroughly traditional one. Mably's sole departure from the orthodox Stoic-Christian catalogue is to locate "temperance" among the "auxiliary" rather than the cardinal virtues—an idiosyncrasy that, in fact, he abandoned in his later dialogues. The real contrast here is with Machiavelli, whose texts provided the most commanding, if not the most imitated, presentation of this theme in early-modern European republicanism. For the latter's great and scandalous innovation, of course, was to confine his own list to prudence, courage, and temperance, expelling "justice" from the ranks of the cardinal virtues altogether.[66] If Mably was able to restore the latter to its traditional position, the reason is not hard to see. For his own conception of the virtues rested on intellectual foundations that were unavailable to Machiavelli: the "modern" natural jurisprudence of Grotius and his successors, whose goal had been to found a universalistic ethic free from the "localism" of either Aristotle or Aquinas—the targets, in a sense, of Machiavelli's own critique. As Richard Tuck has recently reminded us, the formation of the seventeenth-century natural lawyers was a thoroughly *humanist* one. The foundation of their theory was a highly refined neo-Stoicism—designed to combat the skepticism of a Montaigne and the authoritarianism of a Hobbes at one and the same time—which placed equal emphasis on self-interested individualism and the natural "sociability" of mankind.[67]

Some further consequences of this fusion of political languages are revealed in the fourth *entretien*, where Aristias expresses surprise that *l'amour de la patrie* has not yet been mentioned by Phocion. Surely this is among the most important of the political virtues? Phocion answers that, on the contrary, it is precisely because the Greeks have always regarded this as the first virtue of the citizen that they have exhausted themselves in a century and a half of civil war and now stand defenseless before the destroyer from the North. A high regard for one's city or nation is an honorable sentiment. But it must always be subordinated to the far greater virtue of *l'amour de l'humanité*, which amounts to an extension to interstate relations of the same principles governing the cooperative coexistence of citizens within the state. Again, the only Greek legislator to have realized this fully was Lycurgus, who institutionalized the virtue of *l'amour de l'humanité* in his ban on offensive warfare and imperial expansion. Here Mably appends a long note recounting the fate of this cosmopolitanism over the centuries. First introduced in philosophy by Socrates and Plato, and passed on by the Hellenistic writers to Cicero and Seneca, the idea of the fundamental unity of humanity was wholly ignored in practice in the classical word, and then forgotten utterly even as a theoretical principle in medieval Europe. It was only the Renaissance rediscovery of ancient political thought and the sobering experience of the Religious Wars that permitted the restatement of the theory by the modern *école du droit naturel*. However, the ceaseless imperialism of modern states, and the endless wars that have ensued, only show how far modern Europeans still are from putting *l'amour de l'humanité* into practice.[68]

We have already considered Mably's critique of modern warfare in the last chapter, and contrasted his anti-imperialism with the expansionist republicanism of Machiavelli. At the same time, it is important to recognize that this does not represent a fundamental break with the republican tradition on Mably's part. Having established the precedence of *l'amour de l'humanité* over *l'amour de la patrie*, and having urged a consequent renunciation of all offensive warfare, Phocion goes on to admit that no state can count on the practice of a similar restraint by its neighbors. A vigilant *defensive* force is an absolute necessity, and it must never be entrusted to any hands other than those of the citizens themselves: "Let our republic thus be a military one, let every citizen devote himself to the defence of his country, let him spend some time each day practising with his weapons, and let the entire city acquire the disciplined character of an armed camp. Not only will this policy provide you with invincible soldiers, but it will give a new force to the civic virtues as well."[69] In the time since Athens permitted the "separation of military and civil functions," Phocion concludes, "we have had neither citizens nor soldiers." In this insistence on the close alliance of military and civic virtue, Mably is at one with the entire republican tradition, from Aristotle and Cicero to Machiavelli and Harrington. In still another editorial note, he points to the conclusions that are to be drawn in the present, with a vigorous attack on the almost universal conviction among his contemporaries that "money is the sinews of war." The futility of this belief, Mably argues, returning to the ideas on commerce that we have already examined in *Principes des Négociations* and the last edition of *Le droit public de l'Europe*, has been exposed by Cantillon, with his depiction of the endless cycle of wealth and poverty to which "commercial" nations subject themselves.[70] The truly invincible nation, Phocion himself declares, is one that is defended by its own citizens; and the latter will only have an interest in doing so where extremes of wealth and poverty have been banished. "Nature, my dear Aristias, did not intend for men to possess great wealth. Why should there be rich and poor? Aren't we all born with the same needs? Nature has distributed her goods in a generous fashion: let us use them with the same wisdom."[71]

The fifth *entretien* takes up a final question, that of the "political mechanisms for reforming a republic whose character has become corrupt." In such a polity, Phocion explains, any direct attempt to instill even the "auxiliary" virtues is bound to fail. However, "there remains a final resource for politics, that is, to make use of the passions themselves to weaken and destroy authority." In other words, "to destroy one vice, it is sometimes necessary to appear to favor another." This is of course only Mably's version of the famous idea of "countervailing passions," which, as Hirschman showed in *The Passions and the Interests*, was an extremely widespread notion in seventeenth- and eighteenth-century moral psychology, from Bacon and Spinoza to Hume and Holbach.[72] The *locus classicus* for the idea in France was Descartes's *Les passions de l'âme*, and Mably's elaboration of the idea is a thoroughly Cartesian one: "It is to the passions of the soul that politics must turn," Phocion explains, "such as envy, jealousy, ambition, pride, and vanity. These passions are dangerous in and of themselves; they urge the soul toward injustice, and left alone, they will carry it to the most vile excesses. However, once brought under political control, they often be turned into emulation, love of glory, prudence, firmness, and heroism."[73] Now this might be seen, of course, as a major concession to Mably's opponents. The case for the social utility of the passions, among their contemporary defenders, tended to rest on precisely the same sort of neo-Aristotelian moral mechanics, in which a guiding rationality carefully measured the strength and effects of opposing drives and impulses, playing one off against the other. Indeed, in his later dialogues Mably drew ever closer to a position that was more or less indistinguishable from that of Holbach, Diderot, or even of Hume himself.

Nevertheless, in *Entretiens de Phocion,* his last word on the passions is spoken with the voice of classic rationalism: "We can be sure that we carry our greatest enemies inside ourselves, in our passions. If you cannot follow their silent, torturous paths, you will be as surprised as a general who neglects to study the movements of his enemy. If you cannot master their artificial language, Aristias, they will speak to you and you will believe you are hearing the voice of reason itself."[74]

At all events, the question of political reform in a "corrupt" republic brings the conversation at last to the condition of Athens itself—to France in the mid-eighteenth century, in other words. To the consternation of his audience, Phocion declares that there is no hope of restoring the republic to its former glory, at least for the present: "It is too late to hope that a Lycurgus will treat us to a healthy violence, freeing us from our vices by force." It is not a question of the possession of a "right" to reform: "I know very well that he is no tyrant who usurps a brief and temporary power in order to reestablish and affirm public liberty. . . . When a society dissolves, every citizen becomes a magistrate, assuming all the power that justice can bestow, and the safety of the republic becomes his supreme law."[75] But any internal agitation in Athens would be disastrous, bringing Philip's armies into Attica and destroying Athenian independence permanently. The only prudent course in these circumstances is a patient biding of time, until "fortune" bestows a more favorable opportunity for reform. Phocion's parting gesture, however, is to return to the Stoic injunction offered in the opening pages of the dialogue: "It is never permitted to despair of the republic. One must meet the greatest misfortunes with the greatest courage; expect miracles from the gods, and perhaps you will perform them yourselves. The republic may well perish, but the consolation of the good citizen, in burying himself within its ruins, is to have done everything possible to save it."[76]

The Shape of Mably's Mature Thought

With *Des droits et des devoirs du citoyen* and *Entretiens de Phocion,* all the elements of Mably's mature political thought were now in place for the first time. As we have seen, he had begun his intellectual career as a philosophical historian, after the model of Montesquieu. The royalism of *Parallèle des romains et des français* was abandoned not long after its publication, but Mably's republicanism initially found expression within the same intellectual framework; his two *Observations* on ancient history, in particular, were still the writings of a "bastard son of Montesquieu," in Voltaire's phrase. Mably's first two dialogues did not, of course, signal a rejection of this basic approach to political theory. It will be seen that "Stanhope" founds his blueprint for revolution on specific interpretations of British and French history; and "Phocion" himself, in his closing speech, expresses a similar confidence in the political uses of philosophical history: "It is in studying the causes of both happy and unhappy events in history that you will acquire a sure body of knowledge. The past is an image, indeed a prediction, of the future."[77] What *Des droits et des devoirs du citoyen* and *Entretiens de Phocion* did bring to Mably's thought was *foundations* it had hitherto lacked: on the one hand, the "laws of nature," which provided a quasi-metaphysical basis for his political theory; and on the other, a grasp of "the play of our passions," which supplied, as it were, the psychological microfoundations for understanding the march of history. At the same time, Mably's adoption of the dialogue as a formal device permitted him, among other things, to pay explicit tribute in *Des droits et des devoirs* and *Entretiens de Phocion* to what he considered to be the sources of his political thought—the Platonic–Stoic republicans of classical antiquity, for whom "Phocion" serves as mouthpiece, and the English Commonwealth tradition which, in Mably's eyes, was the most vital modern incarnation of that republicanism, represented by the figure of "Stanhope."

How should we assess the character of the resulting blend of philosophical history, natural jursiprudence, and moral psychology? Taken together, *Des droit et des devoirs du citoyen* and *Entretiens de Phocion* reveal what were to be two abiding characteristics of Mably's later writing, whose combination, at first glance, might seem paradoxical. These are a relative *philosophical conservatism* and an unswerving *political radicalism*. As we saw in the first chapter, certain recent commentators have found it possible to portray Mably as a philosophical reactionary and "anti-Enlightenment" thinker *tout court*. Giuliano Procacci, in particular, argued that he was essentially a "conservative Catholic" moralist, whose thought was dominated by a "Thomist" conception of political rationalism; while Thomas Schleich has insisted that the sole unifying theme of Mably's mature thought was a deliberate and comprehensive rejection of the French Enlightenment as a whole. The letter of the texts of *Des droits et des devoirs du citoyen* and *Entretiens de Phocion*, however, suggests a rather more nuanced judgment in this regard. On the one hand, there is not the slightest trace in either dialogue—nor in any other of

Mably's works, for that matter—of a *Christian* reaction against the Enlightenment. Everything suggests that Mably adhered to a highly conventional form of Deism, and in no way dissented from the fundamental eudaimonism that was common to all forms of Enlightened thought. As for the theory of natural law adopted in *Des droits et des devoirs du citoyen* and resumed in *Entretiens de Phocion*, there is nothing "medieval" or "reactionary" about it. It is a perfectly recognizable version of the neo-Stoic conception of universal and immutable natural law developed by Grotius and his successors, which served as one of the essential foundation-stones of the early Enlightenment in Europe. Mably's rendering is wholly compatible, for example, with the orthodox summary, itself derived largely from Burlamaqui, that Boucher d'Argis provided in the article "*Droit de la nature ou droit naturel*," published in the same volume of the *Encyclopédie* as the article of Diderot referred to above.[78]

Yet this example also reveals the extent to which Mably's conception of natural law can be seen, in its intellectual context, as a *relatively* conservative or even retrograde one. It was precisely at this point that such a conception was being made obsolete by the work not only of thinkers, such as Hume, who were politically distant from Mably, but also by such figures as Diderot and Rousseau, whose sympathies were far closer to his own.[79] The latter three writers each rejected, albeit for different reasons, the conception of the "natural sociability" of mankind that had formed the core of the theories of Grotius and Pufendorf—signaling, of course, the breakup of the "modern" natural law tradition as a unitary intellectual program. Mably's unquestioning appeal to the idea of an immutable providential order in *Des droits et des devoirs du citoyen* and *Entretien de Phocion* left him, for the moment at least, quite outside this movement of thought. If Mably's intellectual commitments make it implausible to set him outside the Enlightenment altogether—Thomas Schleich's criteria, for example, would plainly entail the exclusion of Montesquieu and Voltaire as well—then it is also clear that when the precarious unity of the early Enlightenment broke up after mid-century, Mably gravitated quite naturally to the conservative camp. Indeed, in his later writings on moral theory, he tended increasingly to bypass the seventeenth-century natural lawyers altogether, referring his readers directly to the classical texts of Cicero and Seneca. Long passages in his late dialogues are little more than paraphrases of the arguments of *De officiis, De finibus*, and the *Tusculan Disputations*. The tincture of a deliberate philosophic archaism colored all of Mably's writing after *Entretiens de Phocion*.

Yet this should not allow us to lose sight of the fact that *Des droits et des devoirs du citoyen* and *Entretiens de Phocion* are at the same time intransigently radical works, in political terms. As we suggested in the first chapter, the notion of Mably as a wholly "conservative" or "anti-Enlightenment" thinker is made plausible only by a consistent disregard for his own political intentions. These are clear and unmistakable in the two works at hand. The 1750s had been a time of unprecedented political upheaval in France, as the nation's political elites initiated the cycle of protest and obstructionism that ultimately culminated in the Revolution. Mably's response to these events in *Des droits et des devoirs du citoyen* was first to rehearse the classic justifications of political resistance according to the radical natural rights tradition—not shrinking from the prospect of a recourse to arms—and then to set forth a strategic scenario for the overthrow of French absolutism, based on the model of the Great Rebellion and the Glorious Revolution of the previous century. The setting and subject of *Entretiens de Phocion* give it a rather less optimistic appearance. But, as we have seen, Phocion himself does not deny the Athenians the *right* to stage a Lycurgan coup; he merely counsels a prudent patience, until a more favorable opportunity for the recovery of Athenian "liberty" presents itself. The combination of a stubborn philosophical conservatism and an intransigent political radicalism should not be particularly surprising. In a sense, Mably reproduces something of the same revolutionary temper that characterizes the writing of the political thinker whom he claimed most to respect, John Locke—the difference being that Locke's own sober Calvinist theocentrism has been replaced by Mably's equally sober neo-Stoic logocentricism. The radical egalitarianism of Mably's mature thought, the subject of the following chapter, was probably inseparable from the studied archaism of his philosophical outlook.

CHAPTER 5

Contemporaries: Communists, Physiocrats, Rousseau

The decade following the writing of *Des droits et des devoirs du citoyen* and *Entretiens de Phocion* was the most fertile and productive of Mably's intellectual career. Above all, it was in these years that he completed the revision of *Parallèle des romains et des français* he had begun two decades earlier. The first two volumes of *Observations sur l'histoire de France*, the masterpiece of Mably's later thought, were published in 1765. Before taking up this work, however, we need to consider three other major pieces of writing from the same period, which together present us with an opportunity to compare and contrast Mably's mature outlook with that of important contemporaries. These works vary considerably in genre and occasion. The first, *De l'étude de l'histoire*, was a byproduct of Mably's brother's tenure as tutor to the young Prince of Parma after 1758: a princely advice-book written in the early years of the 1760s, Mably's contribution to Condillac's *Cours d'études* was first published with the set as a whole in 1777. *De la législation ou principes des lois*, on the other hand, marked a return to the dialogue form of *Des droits et des devoirs du citoyen* and *Entretiens de Phocion*: the record of a series of conversations between two parlementarians, a Swede and an Englishman, it too was first published over a decade after its writing, in 1776. In the third work at hand, Mably adopted yet another format, that of the polemic: *Doutes proposées aux philosophes économistes, sur l'ordre naturel et essentiel des sociétés politiques*, published in 1768, was his long and passionate rejoinder to Le Mercier de la Rivière's presentation of physiocratic philosophy of the year before.

Despite their differences, however, these three works share enough in terms of theme and outlook to mark them unmistakably as a single bloc within Mably's writing as a whole. The central preoccupation of each is an ambitious program of political reform, designed to redress the ills and injustices caused by excessive social inequality; each work moves from general statements of principle to consideration of the specific contexts and prospects for reform in the different European states; and their general outlook, in line with that of *Des droits et des devoirs du citoyen,* is one of cautious optimism. Moreover, these are the books that won Mably his reputation as a "communist" writer, both in his lifetime and beyond. *De la législation,* in particular, has long been seen as one of the most coherent presentations of an early socialist viewpoint to have emerged from the French Enlightenment. It is with these texts, in other words, that we must finally confront the question of Mably's "utopianism."

Mably and the "Communauté des Biens"

A preoccupation with social inequality was, of course, already well established in Mably's work. Both the historical analyses of Greek and Roman history in his *Observations* and the account of modern warfare and diplomacy in *Principes des Négociations* point to the balance of economic forces—within and between states—as the key to explaining the fate of nations. It is not surprising, then, that Mably's turn toward prescriptive political theory at the end of the 1750s should have led to critical reflections on the institution of private property itself. The most striking instance here is the brief intermezzo that divides the two main parts of *Des droits et des devoirs du citoyen.* There Stanhope concludes his long defense of rights of political resistance by suggesting, in a whisper, that the "principle source of all the misfortunes that afflict humanity" is private property. It is perhaps not surprising, he continues, that primitive men should have experimented with forms of exclusive property rights:

> But now that we have seen the numberless evils that have issued from this fatal Pandora's box, if even the slightest ray of hope were to spark our reason, should we not aspire to that happy community of goods so praised and so mourned by our poets, the one which Lycurgus established in Lacadaemonia, and which Plato wished to revive in his *Republic*?[1]

From here Stanhope goes on to describe a secret "folly" of his, a dream of retiring with a group of like-minded individuals to a remote island, in order to found "a Republic in which, all equal, all rich, all poor, all brothers, our first law would be to possess nothing ourselves."[2] Lycurgus and Plato aside, the evocation of an egalitarian society that follows is patently an homage to More's *Utopia*. But the reverie soon ends. Dismissing these musings as nothing more than "agreeable daydreams," Stanhope turns his attention to the very practical concerns that take up the rest of *Des droits et des devoirs du citoyen*—in effect, the making of a "managed revolution" in France, securing a transition from absolute to constitutional monarchy.

This is the inaugural gesture toward communist utopianism in Mably's writing, and for all of its brevity, it appears to mark a divergence from the outlook of his avowed masters within the natural rights tradition. Needless to say, no comparable sentiment or reverie may be found in Locke, the centerpiece of whose *Two Treatises of Government*, after all, is the naturalist theory of private property presented in the fifth chapter of the Second Treatise; Locke later describes the "chief end" of political communities as the "preservation of property."[3] At the same time, Mably is also apparently flouting the authority of Cicero himself, who was of course an even more adamant proponent of private property than was Locke.[4] This is not to say that the natural rights tradition spoke with one voice regarding the nature, origins, and justification of property. By the end of the seventeenth century it offered, roughly speaking, two distinct conceptions. The older, which comprised in their different ways Aquinas, Suarez, and Locke, started from the biblical (Genesis 1:28) and classical assumption that the earth was originally the common property of all men; its subsequent parceling into private possessions was nevertheless in accordance with natural law, as men exercised their rights in fulfillment of their duties. The seventeenth century, however, saw the emergence of an alternate viewpoint, in the tradition that Pufendorf later saw as descending from Grotius. For the "modern" school of rights theorists, the tendency was to deny the existence of any prior state of communal, inclusive ownership of the world by a collective subject; the notion of "property" was by and large restricted to private, exclusive rights of possession and use. If this tradition did not consistently deny that property was "natural," it did share an emphasis on the necessity of a strong sovereign power for its existence and protection. Whatever their specific views on these matters, however, thinkers from either camp agreed that private, exclusive property rights were the very cornerstone of civil society. None would deny that property had often been the occasion for contention and civil strife; but the universal solution was held to be, not its abolition, but the establishment of its absolute *security*—both through the protection of a strong sovereign and by means of rational and just rules governing rights and entitlement to it.

A widespread consensus about the justice and utility of private property did not, of course, preclude the adoption of a range of critical attitudes toward it. Examples of a flirtation—sentimental, nostalgic, or ironic—with utopian communism are to be found in the works of most of the commanding figures of the French Enlightenment, from Montesquieu's Troglodytes to Diderot's Tahitians. Stanhope's island reverie in *Des droits et des devoirs du citoyen* could be regarded as one more of these, had Mably gone no further in this direction. But this is precisely what he did in his major works of the following decade. The principal focus of *De l'étude de l'histoire, De la législation,* and *Doutes proposées aux philosophes économistes* is a sustained critique of social inequality, accompanied by a serious and approving reflection on the notion of a *communauté des biens.* The grounds of the critique are twofold, involving an appeal both to natural principle and to historical evidence. On the one hand, Mably argues, the relative physical equality of human beings places strict limits on the—necessarily very modest—degree of material inequality that may be justified by an appeal to natural principles of justice and reason. "Nature imposed one law on our earliest ancestors," he writes in *De la législation,*

> and made known her intentions in a manner so clear that it was impossible to mistake them. In fact, who can deny that we emerge from her hands in a state of perfect equality? Did she not give all men the same organs, the same needs, the same reason? Did not the goods she spread about the earth belong to them in common? Did she establish an individual patrimony for each one? Did she place boundaries in the fields? Nature did not create rich and poor. Did she single out certain races with specific gifts, in the way that she raised men as a whole above the animals by bestowing superior qualities upon us? The fact is that nature did not create great and small: she did not intend the first to be masters over the second.[5]

Men may well differ in their capacities either to produce or to consume wealth, but these differences could not possibly warrant the immense disparities in wealth and power that characterize historical societies: "I do not deny that nature has distributed her gifts unequally among us, but surely not with a disproportion equal to the monstrous differences we see in the fortunes of men"[6]—an assertion that echoes the conclusion of Rousseau's *Discourse on Inequality.*

At the same time, Mably also argues that the record of history provides a massive empirical demonstration *a contrario* of the truth of this naturalism. The bulk of the miseries and disasters that have afflicted humanity through the ages have had their source in these inequities. First, there is simply the toll of privation itself. Mably's model of economic production was, like that of Rousseau, a precapitalist, zero-sum one, in which the luxury of the few necessarily entails the indigence of the many: the crushing poverty under which the majority of mankind have toiled through the millennia is the direct result of the surfeit enjoyed by the classes that exploit them. But equally important is the fact that these disparities in wealth and power inevitably give rise to struggles between antagonistic classes. "Open all the books of history," he writes in *Doutes proposées aux philosophes économistes,*

> and you will see that all peoples have been tormented by this inequality of fortune. Some citizens, proud of their wealth, refuse to regard those who are condemned to work for a living as their equals; the results are unjust and tyrannical governments, partial and oppressive laws, and, in a word, that crowd of calamities from which all peoples have suffered. Such is the picture presented by the history of every nation: I defy you to return to the original source of this disorder, without finding private property in land.[7]

And in *De la législation*: "Make no mistake: property divides us into two classes, rich and poor. The first prefer their private fortune to that of the state; and the second will never serve a government and laws that have rendered them unhappy."[8] In Mably's eyes, history is thus the record of unceasing struggles between unequal classes, and on these foundations it has proven impossible to erect stable and secure political orders.[9] Mably's conception of "class" is very crude, focused largely on the classical dualisms of rich and poor, the few and the many. Though he often had occasion to recognize the complexity of the European social scene, with its complex distinctions between multiple "orders" and "estates," Mably advanced no terminology capable of differentiating between types of exploitation and property regime; his condemnation of inequality did not distinguish between chattel slave, glebe peasant, and urban artisan, nor between Roman senator, medieval lord, and merchant capitalist. At the same time, it is worth noting that Mably consistently regards asymmetries of political power to be secondary to those of class: where classes exist, he assumes, the state will naturally tend to be the instrument of the wealthy and the powerful.[10]

Social inequality is in any case subject to a double indictment in the writings at hand: condemned for its *injustice*, since the "laws of nature" demand a rough equality of material condition among men; and for its *irrationality*, demonstrated by the disasters that have attended it in human history. For all the passion and conviction of its presentation, however, this critique of social inequality will have been familiar to Mably's readers. Warnings about the political dangers of excessive disparities in material condition among citizens formed a key theme in the republican tradition, central to the thought of Harrington, Machiavelli, Polybius, and Aristotle alike. Nor were contemporary readers likely to overlook the affinities between Mably's attitude toward social inequality and that of Rousseau, especially as set forth in the *Discourse on Inequality*. Yet there was another side to Mably's critique, which was largely missing in Rousseau, as well as ancestors in the mainstream republican tradition. This was the warm welcome that Mably gave to the idea of communal ownership of property. We have already seen the fleeting reference in *Des droits et des devoirs du citoyen* to "that happy community of goods so praised and so mourned by our poets, the one Lycurgus established in Lacadaemonia, and that Plato wished to revive in his *Republic*." In his major works of the 1760s, particularly in *Doutes proposées aux philosophes économistes* and *De la législation*, Mably moved to what was apparently an explicit embrace of communism. The "community of goods," he now insisted, is the only property regime sanctioned by nature and thus the only certain means of escaping the poverty and disorder created by inequality.[11] Not surprisingly, much of the resonance of this claim in Mably's writing depends on the example of Sparta, which serves as a kind of historical test-case for the feasibility of a communitarian regime.[12] But his assertions went beyond a mere admiration for the egalitarian ethos of the classical city-state. Not only did Mably clearly subscribe to the older current of natural rights theory, for which communal ownership of the world was the original condition of human society, but he had now apparently come to see the transition to private property as a tragic fall from a prior state of grace, rendering history a long record of degradation and corruption.

Now it is well known that a specifically *communist* utopianism has little resonance in the works of Rousseau, despite his own admiration for Sparta and gestural doubts about the justice of private property. The local inspiration for this theme in Mably's thought nevertheless seems instantly identifiable. One of the most striking aspects of the French Enlightenment was the emergence, on its radical flank, of a fringe of utopian communists, successors to More and Campanella, but far more strident in their denunciation of inequality and far more revolutionary in intent.[13] The key figures whose writings might have been available to Mably, in one form or another, were Jean Meslier (1664–1729), the obscure curé whose *Mémoire des pensées et des sentiments*, which featured a violent attack on Christian dogma, circulated widely in various manuscript forms by mid-century, especially through the sponsorship of Voltaire; the mysterious Morelly (1713?/1718?–?), whose notorious *Code de la nature*, long attributed to Diderot, was published anonymously in 1755; and Léger-Marie Deschamps, the Benedictine monk who doggedly promoted his egalitarian schemes among a number of the leading *philosophes* in the 1760s, Rousseau and Diderot most notably. These writers formed nothing like an organized or coherent movement, and each had distinctive themes and accents. But Meslier, Morelly, and Deschamps were united by their absolute condemnation of private property as a violation of the laws of nature, by their detailed blueprints for societies from which private property would be banished, and by their earnest explorations of possible means—sometimes quite violent ones, in the case of Meslier—of arriving at these destinations. If Babeuf's testimony is correct, they were among the sources for his own ideas; a century later, Marx and Engels paid tribute to them as the pioneers of socialism. And, as we saw in the first chapter, it is in their company that the opinion of posterity has tended to place Mably.

What in fact did he owe to the *philosophes utopistes*? There are neither citations of their writings nor mention of their names to be found anywhere in his works. Mably does not often invoke authorities or ancestors for his views on the *communauté des biens*, but when he does, they are invariably Plato and Thomas More, two traditional and respectable sources.[14] The lack of any explicit alignment with Meslier, Morelly, and Deschamps means very little, however, in a writer as cautious and taciturn as to his sources as Mably. For it is difficult to imagine that he did not read portions of their works. These were widely available, and were the focus of considerable attention, not to mention scandal, in the 1750s and 1760s—the very period when Mably can be expected to have been most interested in their views.[15] Indeed, it seems clear that he could have owed his critique of inequality as much to these writers as to Rousseau (although the problem of "influence" is all the more difficult to judge here, in that the works of Morelly and Deschamps themselves owed something to Rousseau's early works). The fact is that there is nothing in Mably's own denunciations of the injustice and the irrationality of inequality for which innumerable precedents cannot be found in the *Mémoire* of Meslier or in the *Code de la nature*.[16] It may well be the case that the fundamental inspiration for the *commu-*

nauté des biens was derived from Plato or More—certainly Stanhope's brief reverie in *Des droits et des devoirs* is intended to be a remembrance of More's *Utopia*. But when Mably claims that "nature has established equality in the fortune and condition of citizens as a necessary condition of the prosperity of states,"[17] or when he concedes that he cannot bring himself to "abandon that agreeable idea of the community of goods,"[18] no contemporary reader of his works could have failed to think of the *Code de la nature* or of the various communist schemes of Dom Deschamps. Mably's characteristic reserve and the scarcity of biographical evidence unfortunately prevent us from calculating his exact debt to these writers. But it is safe to conclude that his works in this period contain a deliberate appeal to this contemporary utopian discourse.

Whether they fully belong to this utopian tradition is, however, another question. At least two serious doubts can be raised in this regard. The first concerns the question of private property itself, and whether Mably consistently adheres to the idea that it is the "principle source of all the misfortunes that afflict humanity." For even as Stanhope affirms this in *Des droits et des devoirs*, he adds this qualification: "I know that the earliest societies established it [private property] with justice; and that one even finds it already established in the state of nature. For no one can deny that man even then had the right to regard the hut he had built, or the fruit of the tree he had planted, as his own."[19] What this suggests, of course, is a standard Lockean account of private property, in which it is essentially *labor*, the mixing of what is one's own with portions of the external world, that creates a title to private possession. That Mably was indeed inclined in this direction is confirmed if we turn briefly to the most extended discussion of property rights to be found in the works under consideration. This comes in the first two letters of *Doutes proposées aux philosophes économistes*, where Mably has to contend with the physiocratic claim that the social inequalities of contemporary Europe were part of a *natural* hierarchy, and therefore unalterable. In particular, Mably sets out to deny Le Mercier's argument that "personal property, movable property, and landed property . . . are linked together in such a way that we must regard them as forming one single whole, of which no part can be detached without leading to the destruction of the others."[20] What is notable, first, in Mably's response is that he makes no attempt to disavow the founding premise of Le Mercier's case, indeed the cornerstone of all modern natural rights thought, the notion of "personal property"—the idea, that is, that the fundamental relation of human beings to the world, to their bodies and to external objects, is one of *ownership*. On the contrary, he willingly agrees that "personal property" is a "natural right" in each human individual.[21] Having conceded this crucial point, however, it is virtually impossible for Mably to go on to establish the opposite of the physiocratic case, that "the true order of nature . . . consists in the community of goods and the equality of conditions."[22] Indeed, the last clause reveals the vacillation in his thought on this point, for a "community of goods" and an "equality of conditions" are of course not equivalent at all. Logically, a complete equality of material condition is perfectly compatible with the existence of private property, while the communal ownership of property is also compatible with inequalities of material condition.

Thus when Mably goes on to affirm that "movable property, the right to provide for one's substance," follows necessarily from personal property, he tacitly concedes that some amount of "landed property" can equally be sanctioned by natural law. He makes strenuous attempts to avoid this conclusion, arguing—lamely—that common property in land was nevertheless the only arrangement that would have *occurred* to primitive peoples. But he ends with a frank admission that the justice of communal or private property is undecidable on "natural" grounds: "One of the principal advantages to living in society is that I have the right to demand that it provide for my subsistence, since I consent to work on its behalf; but whether society sees to this by leaving goods in common, or by dividing the public domain into landed property for each citizen, is the most immaterial thing in the world."[23] This, of course, disables any claim that private property in and of itself can be the explanation of the miseries and suffering he denounced, which in turn undermines the case to be made for the *communauté des biens*. These vacillations are striking enough in themselves. But what is equally surprising is that this is the *only* discussion of this sort to be found in Mably's writings. He was evidently driven to it in this case by the claims of his physiocratic opponent, for nowhere else does he attempt a philosophical analysis of property rights in any detail at all. It plainly would have been possible, from within the Lockean tradition itself, to construct a convincing justification for a massive redistribution of property, at the very least, had Mably genuinely been interested in doing so. What all of this suggests, curiously enough, is an underlying *indifference* toward the entire question of the justification of property, communal or private—something that cannot be said of Meslier, Morelly, or Deschamps, or of their opposite numbers within the conventional natural rights tradition.

But the really decisive consideration in judging the relation of Mably to the utopians lies elsewhere—not so much in their respective criticisms of private property and social inequality as in the remedies they propose for them. Here the position of Meslier, Morelly, Deschamps, and others was unequivocal. The *raison d'être* for their work was precisely to propose communist societies as feasible alternatives to present-day property regimes; the centerpieces of their writings are their depictions of these societies and their discussions of how to achieve them. Where did Mably stand on this issue? Plainly, much of the impact of his own critique of inequality depends not merely on the belief that a communal regime had been the original—the "natural"—state of mankind, but also on the claim that such a system actually had functioned successfully within historical memory, in classical antiquity. But the crucial question remains: could a Sparta-style regime be established in contemporary Europe? Given the persistence of Mably's reputation as a "utopian" and "early socialist," a great deal depends upon this question. Fortunately, his texts provide a very clear answer to it. Mably explicitly raises the possibility of establishing a communist regime at a critical point in each of the three books we are examining in this chapter, and in each case he dismisses it as impossible—an "agreeable dream," a "chimera."[24] The reason is that it is simply too late, for our "corruption"—the "degradation of our customs and manners"—has advanced to such an extent that an abolition of private property has been rendered impossible:

> We have arrived at such a state of corruption that extreme wisdom must appear as extreme folly, and in fact would be. Lacking wholly new men to make citizens out of at will, how can we change their very ideas? How can we reach into their hearts to extract the roots of those innumerable and always resurgent passions, whose empire has been rendered so unshakeable by education and habit?[25]

In other words, our attachment to property and inequality has, after so many millennia, put down roots that are simply too deep to be extracted. In *De la législation*, Mably argues that not merely would the possessing classes violently resist any threat to their property, but that even the poor in Europe would feel no attraction for a Spartan regime: "The people are often motivated by insolence, but never by equality."[26] These claims are clearly based on a psychological model whose basic filiation with Rousseau's early work again seems unmistakable: the psychic constitution of mankind—the shape of the "passions"—has evolved in such a way as to eliminate the possibility of certain social arrangements. Mably can be seen to have returned here—with regret rather than satisfaction, of course—to the same basic judgment he had already adopted in *Parallèle des romains et des français*. The decisive juncture in human history, when a whole range of political and social possibilities was closed off for good, was the end of Graeco-Roman antiquity. As we shall see, the transition from the classical to the modern world, never quite explicable from within Mably's categories of thought, would continue to haunt his writings to the very end.

Whatever the precise reason for the impossibility of a communal regime, Mably never betrays the slightest hesitation in ruling out any chance of a major redistribution of property in Europe, much less the abolition of private possessions altogether. Indeed, his exclusion of communism from the horizon of the possible is so complete that his final position turns out to be equivalent, for all intents and purposes, to a conventional natural rights outlook. Having ruled out a communist solution to the problems created by inequality, Mably actually declares that "in every state in which property has once been established, it is necessary to regard it as the foundation of order, peace, and public security"—an axiom that would have been endorsed by Grotius, Hobbes, and Locke alike. When he writes: "At the start, any law that departed from the community of goods, by favoring the establishment of property even in the most indirect manner, was a mistake; today, however, all sound laws will aim at depriving our passions of any means or pretext to make even the slightest injury against the rights of property"[27]—the bulk of modern natural law writers might well reject the claim of the first clause, but all would approve of the conservative sentiment expressed in the second.

What is the meaning of this surprising about-face? It seems to mark a profound impasse within Mably's thought. On the one hand, he echoes the utopian denunciation of social inequality as the source of all the "misfortunes that afflict humanity"; on the other, he joins the mainstream natural-rights thinkers in regarding the private property that preserves and protects this inequality as the fundament of "order," "peace," and "public security." It is at this point, naturally enough, that many commentators have located a fundamental indecision in Mably's thought, or at least an unbearable and perhaps incoherent pessimism. This judgment would indeed be justified had this been Mably's last word on the subject. But it was not. For the weighing and rejection of the possibility of communism turns out to be merely a necessary prelude to the real purpose of the works at hand, which is to lay out a feasible program of *political* reform in Europe, one of a resigned accommodation to the "second best."[28] If the "first best" solution of the *communauté des biens* is out of the question, we are not thereby invited to believe that the evils created by inequality have lessened—that "our errors, by reason of their age and the credit they have taken on, have now become truths, and that after having created our misfortune, will now secure our happiness." In the present circumstances, our guiding principle must thus be: "If it is no longer possible to obey the simple laws of nature, we must at least learn by what resources human industry can still remedy part of the evil caused by the inequality of conditions."[29] It was merely because a direct assault on property is impracticable that Mably advises its protection. But this leaves the field clear for an indirect attack: "Rather than entering into open combat, the legislator must thus make use of ruse and artifice."[30]

What sorts of "ruses" and "artifices"? Having ruled out a wholesale remodeling of society, the key to an indirect strategy against inequality lies in the adoption of a republican form of government ("a state can have good laws only so long as it is itself its own legislator"[31]), but—it will come as no surprise—of a particular kind:

> The passions of the prince are too free in despotism, those of the people in pure democracy, and those of the great in aristocracy; the consequence is that spirit of injustice that forms their character, and those biased laws that, nearly everywhere, sacrifice one part of the state for another. . . . The only legislators to have succeeded in creating a flourishing society are those who have grasped how to make a kind of mixture of the diverse governments, and to establish, by means of a careful balance of temperaments, a moderate administration that prevents the abuses or excesses of both power and liberty. . . . The Romans, and a good many modern peoples, will tell you that it is necessary for powers to balance one another reciprocally, and that it is only by means of this balance that the citizens, despite their inequality of fortune, can draw closer to natural equality, and enjoy the security for which they first entered into society.[32]

The model of "mixed government" presented in *De l'étude de l'histoire*, *Doutes proposées aux philosophes économistes*, and *De la législation* is a very consistent one: legislative power is to be placed in the hands of the entire body of the people or in an assembly of their elected representatives; there is to be a strict separation between legislative and executive power; and the latter, finally, is to be divided into multiple branches, their offices made elective, of limited tenure, and open to all ranks of society.[33] How would such a constitutional arrangement be expected to remedy the effects of inequality? The general idea is an appeal to a notion of "countervailing powers." The participation of every social order in the exercise of political power can be expected to prevent its being turned against any one of them; since "mixed government" cannot be made the tool of any single social class, it instead becomes the instrument of their reconciliation. In addition, as we shall see in a moment, in *Doutes proposées aux philosophes économistes* Mably advances very striking claims for the role of democratic *deliberation* in producing rational consensus.

"Mixed government" is thus the key to Mably's political remedialism. But his proposals do not end with it. Precisely because the root cause of the "misfortunes" of humanity cannot be eliminated, even the most carefully constructed balance between social orders has a built-in tendency to degenerate. In the long run, the state will tend to pass from the hands of the people into those of the wealthy, and from there into the control of a despot, the final terminus of the process of "corruption." It is to combat these tendencies that Mably suggests that "mixed government" should be buttressed with two further sets of measures. The first is roughly economic in character. His strictures about the sanctity of property notwithstanding, Mably advises a stringent regulation of commercial activity and of the disposal of property. His proposals include various kinds of sumptuary and agrarian (anti-"vinculist") laws and the regulation of testaments; basing himself on Swedish precedents, he even recommends the establishment of a separate patrimony for each class.[34] The minimum goal for every state must be to "prohibit poverty." Second, as we have already seen, Mably shared the extraordinarily widespread conviction among his contemporaries that *moeurs* were the key to understanding and mastering social life among men. He writes in *Doutes proposées aux philosophes économistes*: "*Moeurs* should be the principle object of politics . . . good or ill, they decide the fate of states."[35] A second set of supports for maintaining mixed government are thus "ideological" in character, designed to mold and regulate the opinions and morals of citizens. The most schematic presentation of such measures comes in Book Four of *De la législation*, in which Mably advises the well-ordered republic to establish a system of free public education for all citizens, a "public and tangible" religious cult, and, finally, censorship for the protection of both.[36] The purpose of these measures, of course, is cultivation of the political "virtues" according to the recipe set forth in *Entretiens de Phocion*.

Such then is the basic shape of the reform program Mably outlines in the three texts we are examining: a mixed government is established, for the purpose of restoring as much of "natural equality" as is possible without compromising basic rights of private property; the stability and durability of this system is then reinforced by economic measures that try to impede the accumulation of private wealth, and ideological measures whose function is to instill egalitarian morals and manners. It cannot be emphasized enough that Mably's program is intended to be very practical, which could feasibly be made a reality in contemporary Europe. "Theory is nothing, if it is not followed by practice"—such is the general motto of these works.[37] In particular, Mably was perfectly aware of the obstacles facing such a set of reforms and of the need to tailor it to differing circumstances: "But it is necessary to advance toward liberty by different routes, according to the difference in one's forces, means, resources, and the distance of one's starting-point."[38] One of the most striking features of the works at hand is the way in which Mably adapts his general program to the widely differing circumstances of Europe: Book Three of *De la législation* consists of a long meditation on the various reformist strategies one must adopt in either monarchies or republics; and *De l'étude de l'histoire* includes brief assessments of the prospects for reform in every major state of Europe.[39] Finally, it should be noted that each of these works is quite confident about the prospects for republican advancement in Europe. Recalling the successful overthrow of absolutism in England and Holland, Mably has Stanhope declare in *Des droits et des devoirs du citoyen*: "I believe that revolutions are still possible, that a good citizen must keep up hope, that he is obligated, according to his condition, his power, and his talents, to work to make these revolutions useful to his country."[40] States do not have a life span alloted by nature, Mably assures the young Prince of Parma; they can and should aspire to immortality: "Why should politics be unable to bring about what fortune can do? By studying revolutions, and controlling events accordingly, why should not the reformers of a state enjoy the same success?"[41] With these confident expressions, Mably had arrived at the peak of his political optimism.

It can now be seen why a straightforward identification of Mably with the contemporary utopian communists would be mistaken, despite his evident debt to this tradition.[42] It is not quite accurate to say that the problem is one of a conflict between "utopian" and "realist" tendencies in Mably, even though his own proposed reforms were obviously meant to be feasible in a way that those of Morelly and Deschamps were not. On the contrary, the evidence suggests that it was precisely Mably's commitment to *another* utopian discourse that blocked a full embrace of the schemes of the *philosophes utopistes*. This is of course the tradition of classical republicanism, in which the model of the best society is not the anarchist communitarianism of the *Code de la nature*, but "mixed governments" of ancient Sparta and Rome. It is this tradition that furnished all the elements found in Mably's ultimate program for reform, whose continuity with his two *Observations* on Greece and Rome and *Principes des Négociations* scarcely needs to be underlined. The republican and the communitarian traditions need not necessarily be counterposed, of course. There is certainly a general field of compatibility between these two visions of the *optimus status reipublicae*—perhaps indicating a fundamental affinity among all Western utopias—which often makes it difficult to distinguish the two. Quentin Skinner has in fact argued that Thomas More's work, the founding charter of the modern utopian tradition, can itself be read as a classical republican document—an internal, Platonist critique of Renaissance humanism.[43] As we have seen, Mably goes a very long way toward accepting this critique. When one of his interlocutors in a later dialogue complains about being forced to read the "follies" of Plato and More, Mably responds that not only must he read them, he must accept them as "incontestable truths."[44] Yet in the end he regretfully surrenders the unattainable "perfection" of More's *Utopia*, settling for the far more modest—more brittle and pessimistic—utopianism of the Machiavellian tradition.

For all the basic similarity of their critique of inequality, there is thus a huge gulf between the respective plans for the alteration of society in the works of the *philosophes utopistes* and those of Mably. For not only was he immune to the attractions of erotic liberation or millennial deliverance that tempted so many of his contemporaries; but—and this is the most important point—his vision of an alternate society was ultimately a far more *political* one, in the deepest sense of the term. The political stance of Meslier, Morelly, and Deschamps was essentially anarchist: their goal was not merely the abolition of private property, but also the elimination of the state itself. Political institutions and activities, in their vision, would simply dissolve into the associated life of the community of equals. For Mably, far closer to the mainstream of classical republicanism, the situation is nearly the opposite. For his deepest preoccupation was precisely *political* community, in the classic sense of a self-governing, participatory citizenry; his paramount interest was in describing institutions that would maintain communities of this kind where they existed, and in discussing strategies for their restoration where they did not. The deepest charge he levels against social inequality, in the end, is its tendency to cripple or destroy political community of this kind. Even as Mably resigns himself to the permanent division of human society into unequal classes, it is precisely to the renascence of a classical politics that he looks for means of restoring some of the losses incurred in this choice.

The Critique of Physiocracy

Having explored Mably's relation to the *philosophes utopistes*—their common ground as well as their divergences—we can now take advantage of the very different perspective afforded us by his critique of physiocracy. *Doutes proposées aux philosophes économistes* and a brief dialogue he later contributed to the debates over the grain trade, *Du commerce des grains*, are unique among his works. They provide the only opportunity we have of seeing Mably, who normally avoided polemics, arguing at length *against* an opposing system of thought. At first glance, the sources of his antipathy for physiocracy may not seem particularly obvious. Mably might be expected to have sympathized with the general agricultural ethos of the thought of Quesnay and Mirabeau, to have shared both their hostility toward luxury manufacture and mercantilist protectionism and their desire to restore vitality to the backward and underdeveloped French countryside. In fact, his criticisms give us no reason to believe that he rejected what might be called the scientific kernel of physiocracy, the doctrine of the exclusive productivity of agriculture; nor do they suggest that he was fundamentally opposed to the specific policy demands of Quesnay and Mirabeau in the areas of public revenue and commercial regulation. Indeed, Mably opens his *Doutes* by declaring that he has long been an admirer of the *philosophes économistes*, whom he had considered his "masters" on matters of taxation and commerce.[45]

The mid-1760s, however, were the critical turning-point in the fortunes of the physiocratic school, the moment when it reached its maturity, after years of intellectual isolation and official persecution. Between 1764 and 1767, the movement won its most famous converts, Le Trosne, Saint-Péravy, Le Mercier de la Rivière, and Baudeau; it acquired its own propaganda organ, in Baudeau's journal *Ephémérides du Citoyen*; and it sponsored the publication of a host of works designed to popularize the doctrine and extend it into new territory—Mirabeau's abridgment of *La philosophie rurale*, Du Pont's edition of Quesnay's writings, which first launched the name of "physiocracy," and Quesnay's own *Le despotisme en Chine*, which introduced the notion of "legal despotism." Above all, 1767 saw the publication of Le Mercier's hugely successful *L'ordre naturel et essentiel des sociétés politiques,* which for the first time provided physiocracy with a comprehensive social and political philosophy, beyond its core economic doctrines.

Le Mercier's starting point was a ruthless materialism, in which the "social order" was seen to be merely a department of a "natural order" that was itself only a branch of an overarching "physical order." The transparent function of this reductionism, of course, was to claim an ironclad scientific certainty for the social philosophy being expounded. The epistemological linchpin of the system was thus the notorious notion of "evidence":

> One can say in all truth that nothing is simpler nor more evident than the fundamental and invariable principles of the natural and essential order of societies; in order to grasp them at their natural source, in their essence, and even in the practical consequences that result from them, it is necessary to understand the physical order; once this order has become evident, these same principles and their consequences will become equally evident. No human power would dream of establishing laws to order sowing in the season proper to harvesting, or harvesting in the season proper to sowing. It is the same for all other parts of the social order: once they become evident, their evidence will determine *necessarily* and invariably the social order that positive laws must adopt.[46]

In other words, the correct shape of society could be determined with the same certainty as the "the truths of geometry." What, then, does "evidence" teach us? The results, of course, are fairly predictable. The "fundamental base" of social order turns out to be private property, in its present distribution. Le Mercier, as we saw above, considers "personal," "moveable," and "landed" property to be bound into an indivisible whole: "The order essential to any society is to conserve all three in their entirety; nothing can be permitted to injure any of the three forms of property."[47] The form of government best suited for the protection of property, in turn, is that of "legal despotism," in which a hereditary monarch not only possesses absolute sovereignty, but serves as the "coproprietor" of the nation as well.[48] Following Quesnay, Le Mercier professed to find a blueprint for this scheme in imperial China, with its forms of private landownership, its professional bureaucracy, and its dazzlingly productive agriculture. But behind this exotic model, it is not hard to glimpse an idealization of the social order of European absolutism itself, modernized and rationalized under the guidance of a physiocratic mandarinate, free to implement the fiscal and commercial measures demanded by "evidence." It will come as no surprise that the central preoccupation, or rather obsession, of Le Mercier is that of *order*—already announced in the epigraph from Malebranche's *Traité de morale* which appears beneath his title: "Order is the inviolable law of minds; nothing works, except in conformity with it." For all of the abstruse scienticism of its presentation, Le Mercier's solution to the problem of political order reproduces all of the commonplaces of absolutist apology:

> Tutelary authority is essential *one*; it cannot be divided without destroying it; it can be exercised effectively only by a single person. Sovereignty must therefore be hereditary; this is essential for ensuring that the government of a single person is *necessarily* the best form of government. Where there reigns an evident and public knowledge of natural and essential order, this form of government is the most advantageous, because it establishes a true *legal* despotism.[49]

The one novelty in Le Mercier's argument was the notion of "evidence" itself, a characteristic token of Enlightenment epistemology. But the political function of this idea was a familiar one: just as "reason" was the distinguishing characteristic of Bossuet's "royal authority," it was the possession and implementation of "evidence" that separated "legal" from "arbitrary despotism" on Le Mercier's account.

It was this book, with its perverse mixture of economic progressivism, political conservatism, and studied scandalousness of expression, that impelled Mably to produce the only real polemic of his career, *Doutes proposées aux philosophes économistes sur l'ordre naturel et essentiel des sociétés politiques*, published in 1768. He did not reject Le Mercier's work in its entirety. Near the end, he remarks that its final sections—containing expositions of the familiar economic doctrines of physiocracy—are full of "important truths" on taxation, agriculture, and commerce. The main focus of Mably's criticisms is political. The bulk of the *Doutes* is devoted to an extended attack, from every conceivable angle, on the model of "legal despotism"; and it was against this physiocratic reproduction of Hobbesism that Mably made his most detailed and deeply felt defense of "mixed government." First, to no one's surprise, he rejects the distinction between "legal" and "arbitrary" despotism as a spurious one. For Mably, men could consent to a dictatorship of "evidence" *only* where a genuine *communauté des biens* created an objective unity of interests, tangible and visible to all. In the real world, it was precisely because men's interests were divided and opposed by property that a mixed government, enjoining the participation of all classes in self-rule *as* classes, was necessary: "It is precisely because the different classes that compose the notion have opposing interests, that it is necessary to draw them together, and, by giving them a common interest, to place them in a position to compromise with one another. The country or the public good is a first bond uniting the citizens of a republic; permit them to debate their claims, and you will perhaps find that they learn to make reciprocal sacrifices, and that, little by little, each will grow accustomed to being content with the place they occupy in society."[50] Interestingly, Le Mercier had anticipated that a political model of this kind would be seen as the main alternative to his own. His presentation of "legal despotism" thus included a preemptive attack on what he called the "chimerical system of counter-forces."[51] Le Mercier does not identify this enemy by name, but it is plainly Montesquieu and his notion of "moderate government." ("In order to form a moderate government, it is necessary to combine the powers, regulate them, temper them, make them act; that is to say, give each one a ballast so as to put it in a position to resist the others."[52]) This is embodied above all in the English "constitution" of Book XI of *De l'Esprit des lois*:

> Here then is the fundamental constitution of the government of which we are speaking. Its legislative body being composed of two parts, each will be connected to the other by their mutual possession of a veto. Both will be tied to the executive power. These three powers ought to form an equilibrium or inaction. But since they are constrained to act by the necessary movement of things, they will be forced to act in concert.[53]

For Le Mercier, this was of course a recipe for impasse and anarchy in government, the diametrical opposite of "legal despotism."

Now it is a sign of the fundamental affinity between his thought and that of Montesquieu that Mably was perfectly willing to accept the label of "counterforces" to describe his own conception of "mixed government." In fact, as a closer look at his depictions of the latter reveals, the similarities with Montesquieu's "moderate government" can be quite striking:

> Why not establish within the state rival powers that can only act by compromising with one another? This method seems to me to be especially useful for a people that has not yet arrived at a knowledge of all the truths of politics, since it would force them to think and to instruct themselves. . . . The division of authority, which results from counterforces or mixed government, prevents those who govern from surrendering to their own indolence, indifference, avarice, and ambition; it forces them to think before acting, and never to favor brazenly their personal interests over that of the public good.[54]

Such competing interests

> will compel mutual recognition, since the passions of the prince or of a favorite will never suffice to regulate and order everything, and since each person will bring the strongest reasons to bear on behalf of his opinions. It is impossible wholly to suppress particular interest; but it can be constrained to disguise itself under the mask of the public good.[55]

The reason this language is so reminiscent of Montesquieu's is that the political mechanism appealed to by both is essentially the same: countervailing or rival "powers" "moderate," "temper," and "balance" one another, thereby establishing a certain "equilibrium," "conciliation," or "concert" among them. At the same time, these texts also suggest important differences within this common field. For Montesquieu, the achievement of a "moderate government" is primarily the liberal one of preventing the abuse of power: "To prevent the abuse of power, it is necessary, by the disposition of things, for power to block power."[56] His guiding conception is what Judith Shklar has suggestively named a "liberalism of fear."[57] This theme is not without resonance in Mably's writings, but his own main emphasis lies elsewhere. For the distinctive motif of Mably's depiction of "mixed government," especially in the *Doutes proposées aux philosophes économistes*, lies in the unique role it ascribes to public deliberation. Mably does not spell out his theory here systematically, but its general thrust seems to be that the *public* nature of democratic deliberation will ensure the emergence of rational solutions out of the clash of private interests. Even to be heard, public enunciations are forced to assume the "mask of the public good"—some minimum of attention to the interests of others—which in the long run tends to produce exactly this. The debates of the assembly thus take on something like a pedagogic function, as they transform private interests in the direction of "the public advantage." For Mably, of course, has a purpose beyond the Montesquieu's "liberalism of fear":

> It is thanks only to a tempered administration that all classes of citizens, brought together in a single place, can arrive at the truth by means of discussion, and grasp how important it is to them to strengthen the rule of law. I emphasize, monsieur, that in this way all of the orders of society balance each another, compel recognition, and hold each other in equilibrium; neither the people, the grandees, nor the prince possess enough authority to impose partial laws; and thus the nation, which has moved as close to the natural equality of men as is possible today, is truly the depository and protector of the laws.[58]

In other words, where Montesquieu proposes what is essentially a *protective* or liberal conception of republicanism, Mably instead offers what might be called a *restorative* one. A "mixed government" is intended not merely to protect one social class from domination by another, but also actively to transform the "private" interests that keep them divided, to arrive at "truth by means of discussion." The forum thus becomes the instrument of reconciliation between classes, the consensus it creates—the "common interest" discovered by citizens in the course of debate—serving as compensation for the unequal division of the spoils of labor.

The *gouvernement mixte* of *Doutes proposées aux philosophes économistes* is thus no mere copy of the *gouvernement modéré* or that of the "counterforces" of *De l'Esprit des lois*. What this indicates, in turn, is that Mably's criticisms of Le Mercier go some distance beyond those that might have been shared by Montesquieu, despite the revulsion the latter surely would have felt for the idea of "legal despotism." For although the main thrust of Mably's attack was political, it was by no means confined to this level. It would have been difficult indeed to ignore the provocation of the social philosophy of Le Mercier, who did not shrink from offering a very specific conception of the ends of human society, summed up in this revealing formula: "Humanly speaking, the greatest happiness consists for us *in the greatest possible abundance of objects that serve for our enjoyment, and the greatest possible liberty to profit from them.*"[59] Mably, indignant at this transposition of priorities, angrily responds:

> Alas, monsieur, where are we? I would never have thought it possible to carry rural mania to such a point. As if we were animals, concerned with nothing other than our fodder. . . . Let us at least try to consider ourselves as intelligent and sensible beings, in whom intelligence and sensibility have been conjoined, and we will discover many other needs besides those of agriculture. We will see that justice, prudence, courage, and so forth, are every bit as necessary as the fruits of the earth. For the fact is that without the social virtues, your countrysides will lie fallow or will be devastated. No, monsieur, in the condition to which property in land has reduced men, it is not at all certain that politics consists solely in maximizing one's *disposable revenue*, in establishing only indirect taxes on land, and in religiously seeing to the capital necessary for the reproduction of the harvest. No doubt it is important to produce good harvests; but one must start with the creation of excellent citizens. A flourishing agriculture is ordinarily the result of good government—it cannot be its cause. Let us not confound things: it is the cultivation of men, that is to say, it is the social virtues that serve as the basis for the happiness of society. That is the first object of politics; our fields will come later.[60]

It is worth pausing over this exchange. For with it, we seem to have arrived at the confrontation that is so central to modern liberal thought, between "two concepts of liberty," one "ancient" and the other "modern." In the mid-seventeenth century, we already find Hobbes drawing this distinction:

> The Libertie whereof there is so frequent, and honorable mention, in the Histories and Philosophy, of the Ancient Greeks, and Romans, and in the writings, and discourse of those that from them have received all their learning in Politiques, is not the Libertie of Particular men, but the Libertie of the Common-wealth.[61]

A century later, Benjamin Constant returned to the same contrast, in the wake of another revolution:

> The goal of the ancients was the sharing of social power among citizens of the same country: this is what they called liberty. The goal of the moderns is the enjoyment of security in private pleasures; and they call liberty the guarantees accorded by institutions to these pleasures.[62]

More clearly than Hobbes, Constant insisted that these two conceptions of liberty were not only distinct, but even mutually exclusive:

> In order that a people enjoy the greatest extent of political rights, that is, in order that each citizen may participate in sovereignty, it is necessary to have institutions which maintain equality, which prevent the growth of fortunes, which prohibit distinctions, oppose the influence of wealth, talent, even the virtues. Now all these institutions limit liberty and compromise individual security.[63]

In other words, there was a deep tension between individual and collective liberty, such that they could not be possessed simultaneously: the exercise of either necessitated the reduction or extinction of the other. The political lesson of this zero-sum model of freedom, naturally, was that one was forced to make a choice, for behind these two different ideas of "liberty" were two opposed and incommensurate modes of social life. Needless to say, this notion has proved enormously attractive to the more conservative successors to Hobbes and Constant within the modern liberal tradition.[64]

Now at first glance, the collision between Mably and his physiocratic opponent just cited appears to provide us with a textbook case of a clash between "ancient" and "modern" liberty. This is certainly the case from the point of view of Le Mercier, whose conception of liberty is both "negative" and strictly individualist. He is in fact far more candid than most liberal thinkers in disclosing the umbilical cord that joins "negative" liberty and private property in his system:

> Even in chains, a man preserves the metaphysical liberty of desiring and willing; but he does not then possess the *physical* liberty of action. . . . Now it is evident that the latter is the only kind of interest to society, for in society everything is physical. . . . This is the way to think about social liberty, that liberty which is so inseparable from the right of property that the two merge into one, such that one cannot exist without the other.[65]

At the same time, Le Mercier's rejection of "positive," collective freedom could not be more complete. The core of his political philosophy consists of an attack on the very notion of self-government by a community or nation: the "physical liberty" to enjoy one's property can be secured only were men to have surrendered all collective power to an absolute and hereditary sovereign. Moreover, the other essential element of "happiness" cited by Le Mercier—a flourishing abundance of commodities, with its promise of a veritable *société de consommation*—could hardly seem more "modern."

If we turn from here to Mably's response, however, it is immediately clear that the binary contrasts of Hobbes or Constant, not to mention later liberal writers, are wholly inadequate for grasping the sense of his objections to Le Mercier. It is true enough that he objects to the crude behaviorism of the conception of human nature sponsored in *L'Ordre naturel et essentiel des sociétés politiques*. But what is striking is that this leads Mably neither to substitute some alternate vision of human "happiness" to that of Le Mercier nor to express a preference for "collective" or "positive" as opposed to "individual" or "negative" liberty. Mably plainly accepts the goals of agricultural development and the liberty to enjoy this "abundance" as valid in themselves; the main thrust of his argument is simply that Le Mercier's means for achieving these goals are incapable of bringing them about. In *Doutes proposées aux philosophes économistes* and elsewhere in his writings, he consistently rejects the equation between "ancient liberty" and poverty that was so essential to eighteenth-century apologists of commercial civilization. Mably always credits the Greek city-states and the Roman Republic with flourishing and productive countrysides, precisely because their citizens were free to govern themselves. The cultivation of the "social virtues" is never portrayed as an alternative to rural prosperity, but rather as a condition of it. As for the question of "liberty," Mably neither repudiates nor neglects "negative" or individual freedom as values. The very passage from *Des droits et des devoirs du citoyen* that designates "liberty" as an "essential attribute" of humanity makes it clear that Mably considers this to be the inalienable possession, first and foremost, of individuals;[66] while we have already seen that he is no less willing than Le Mercier to regard the exercise of rights to private property as the "foundation of order, peace, and public security." Far from attempting to force a choice between individual and collective liberty, Mably's purpose is rather to argue for their *interdependence*: the condition for the secure enjoyment of the property rights cherished by Le Mercier, and for the "abundance" that flowed from their exercise, is the freedom of the community from domination by the will of another, whether despotic or oligarchical. In other words, he clearly reproduces here a Machiavellian conception of republican liberty, according to which individual liberty, in the "negative" sense of a "free area of action," could be secured only in a community that was the master of its own fate.[67] It was their grasp of this richer, more profound understanding of "liberty" that led to Mably's admiration for classical political thinkers:

> Recall what is said by Plato, Aristotle, Xenophon, Thucydides, Cicero, Tacitus, Plutarch, and the rest. The essence of their doctrine is that a nation must make its own laws, because it is composed of intelligent beings, to whom God has given reason to judge what is suitable for them. They say that it is only children and madmen who are destined to be guided by the reason of another. They say that nature has imposed on all men the same duties, and given to each the same rights. They add that she would not have made them free, had she wished politics to render them slaves. They argue that a society can flourish only when its citizens are devoted to the public good, and that they show such devotion only when they obey laws of which they are themselves the authors.[68]

Of course, the political philosophy of Le Mercier, like that of Hobbes, with its insistence that "liberty" could be purchased only at the price of submission to "legal despotism," was a fairly easy target for these criticisms. But Mably's properly republican conception of freedom is equally distant from the caricature of "ancient liberty" found in the thought of more moderate liberals such as Constant. The latter, despite his far greater appreciation for the attractions of "ancient liberty," still believed that the full possession of "political rights"—understood as participation in democratic self-government—was incompatible with "individual security" as well as material prosperity. Mably, on the other hand, did not see individual and collective liberty as antithetical in this fashion, but rather as *complementary*: the security of the individual and the prosperity of the state as a whole—as opposed to the wealth of the few—could be maximized only within a particular form of self-governing political community.

In the eighteenth-century context, of course, the terms "liberty" and "abundance" were far more than merely the objects of abstract speculation by political theorists. For the physiocrats and their supporters, consideration of this topic was crystallized around one concrete objective above all—the liberalization of the grain trade. Together with the establishment of a single tax on land rent, it was freedom in the buying and selling of grain that was supposed to rescue the French economy from its epochal backwardness.[69] The first great experiment in liberalization, conducted largely under physiocratic inspiration, had already formed one of the turning points in the history of Enlightenment political thought: the debates that attended it shattered the fragile unity of the *parti philosophique.* Mably scarcely refers to these exchanges in *Doutes proposées aux philosophes économistes,* where, as we have seen, his attention was largely trained on the politics of "legal despotism." But the second experiment in liberalization a few years later under Turgot provided him with an opportunity to address the subject himself. At the height of the *guerre des farines* that brought Turgot's reforms to an end in 1775, Mably wrote one of his finest shorter dialogues, *Du commerce des grains.* Set in the Luxembourg gardens, it records a conversation with a physiocratic sympathizer who is nearly frantic with anxiety that the riots of the capital will spread to the countryside, and that this new *jacquerie* will spell the end of Turgot's experiment. Mably tries to assure him that food, not rebellion, was the object of the Parisian mob: "I saw them [the rioters] in the middle of their exploits; they acted gaily rather than with anger; a trifle sufficed to calm everything."[70] But when Mably adds that it would perhaps be a good idea to restore controls to the grain trade, the physiocrat responds in dismay: "It is the liberty to sell, to buy, and to transport grain at will, that will animate everything. The countryside no longer lies fallow. Little by little, abundance will spread from the landowning classes to all the other orders of citizens." These are not vain hopes, he insists, but "evident truths."[71]

It is not necessary to linger over the arguments Mably uses to reject this primitive "trickle-down" theory, since they largely reprise those of Galiani or Diderot from the earlier round of debates. Essentially, his claim is that subsistence is simply too critical an area to be left open to experimentation; in the present situation, this "liberty" is only a "new tax" on the poor.[72] But when his opponent complains that a return to a regulation of the grain trade would be to violate the deepest natural rights of property owners, Mably reverts to the themes of *Doutes proposées*:

> Once the community of goods is gone, and men have consented to a division, I concede that there is no law more sacred than that of property.

> No doubt I must enjoy my fortune, and the whole public force must be the guarantee of my enjoyment, so long as one wishes to affirm public tranquillity. But it seems very strange to imagine that my right to property is somehow threatened, if I am asked to submit to the laws of reason, and to restrain my avarice and prodigality. Far from permitting the wealthy, out of a false respect for property, to abuse their fortune in order to swell it still further at the expense of the public good, the legislator must oppose this with all his strength. If the poor are citizens as well as the rich, if too great a concentration of wealth on the one hand, and excessive poverty on the other, multiply the vices of society and plunge it into the greatest misfortunes, what man is so irrational as to claim that politics cannot stipulate for the rich the conditions according to which they will enjoy their fortune, and prevent them from oppressing the poor?[73]

Here again we find the same endorsement of the rights of "negative" liberty, coupled with the claim that the condition of the secure possession of these rights is some minimum of attention to the interests of one's fellow citizens—"the public good." Moreover, this text makes it clear how central Mably's critique of inequality is to his case for "republican liberty." The need to impose these conditions on the exercise of "negative" liberty arises only because property is concentrated in the hands of a minority of citizens. If every citizen possessed enough property to ensure his own independence—if all members of society enjoyed the "negative" liberty secured by the ownership of property—then there would be no need for a form of government whose function was to restore a semblance of "natural equality." But:

> Since the laws of our fathers lacked the prudence to establish some kind of equality and to prevent all property from falling into the hands of a small number of men; since the rich have left no heritage whatsoever to the poor, which is a very great mistake; is it necessary, to make them still more powerful, to permit them to oppress the people, to extract even more than they are able to produce from the sweat of their brows?

A heedless drive to accumulate still more wealth, Mably insists, could only result in the rebellion of those who produce it without sharing in it. The rioters of Paris had been easily subdued in this instance: "But you may be sure that a second time they will be less timid and thus more enterprising. If they see no other recourse, if they are driven by desperation, they will burn the farms and the castles, and the government, which has failed to foresee these disorders, may well be helpless before them."[74] So long as such a grossly unequal division of wealth and power persists, the only means of establishing a stable and durable social order is to establish a "mixed government," thus bringing all classes of citizens into active self-government.

Naturally these arguments fail to persuade Mably's opponent, who soon quits the field, declaring that "people are right to say that you are a very difficult person to please." The dialogue is then concluded with a postscript, in which Mably expresses his own exasperation to the friend to whom he has described the conversation:

> Could you please tell me what they mean by this great principle of liberty which is supposed to procure so many blessings for us? A grand word, I believe, which its enthusiasts have made fashionable, echoed a thousand times over, and which is completely empty, indeed disguising a great deal of ignorance. Do they mean to say that each person must be free to engage in commerce just as he wishes, without the constraint of any rules other than those dictated by his own interest and his own industry? If that is the sort of liberty they demand, then no one has ever proposed anything more foolish.[75]

It is important to keep in mind that Mably's bafflement over what he regarded as an absurdly constricted and impoverished notion of "modern liberty" was not merely the reflex of an indignant moralism. He was certainly repelled by the injustice of the distribution of property that the physiocrats, and eighteenth-century political economy as a whole, worked so hard to legitimate: "Consult your own conscience and swear in good faith that you would not be so jealous of this liberty of which you speak with such enthusiasm, if you did not intend to abuse it. If you are convinced that everything belongs to you, that society is nothing more than this, then you are hardly worth listening to further, and you should be treated as public enemies."[76] But he also believed that the physiocratic program was *irrational* as well, in the specific sense that it was self-defeating—incapable of bringing about the very ends its proponents desired. The possessing classes of France, in Mably's eyes, seemed to be suffering from precisely the same myopia that had visited destruction on the possessing classes of the fourth-century Greek city-states and the first-century Roman Republic. The Greek aristocracies had come to regard the pursuit of private wealth and power as far more important than the maintenance of the democratic institutions of the previous century; the result was to render their communities, now deprived of the "social virtues" that had protected their freedom, easy prey for Macedonian and Roman imperialism. The Roman senatorial class then repeated the same errors on a vaster and far more destructive scale, plundering the entire Mediterranean basin in a frenzy of accumulation, plunging themselves headlong into the long night of imperial despotism and the ultimate collapse of their civilization. As we have seen, Mably had reason to believe that the political conjuncture of the 1750s and 1760s had presented the French with an unprecedented opportunity to reclaim their "liberty" (in the republican sense) and move toward the establishment of a democratic republic. In this context, the physiocratic drive for an accumulation of wealth at all costs seemed an invitation to the kind of collective suicide committed by the landowning classes of classical antiquity. It was no otherworldly moral imperative that suggested that the possessing classes of France would do better to adopt the reform program advocated by Mably in his mature works: it was dictated by "the laws of reason"—that is, by a prudent regard for their own self-interest. "Mixed government," in other words, was the only effective means of durably achieving both the abundance and the liberty aimed at by physiocracy.

Mably and Rousseau

We began this chapter by attempting to calculate Mably's debt to the communist utopians of his own epoch, among whose ranks he is so often placed. It might be useful to conclude by considering his relationship to the contemporary thinker to whom he was undoubtedly closest, politically and philosophically—Jean-Jacques Rousseau. Their relationship was in fact more than an intellectual one. The two men first met at Lyon in 1742, where Rousseau was engaged as a tutor to Mably's nephew and niece. They maintained fairly close relations in the years that followed. Mably provided Rousseau with letters of recommendation on the latter's move to Paris in 1744; later it was Mably who suggested the work that led to Rousseau's commentaries on the abbé de Saint-Pierre.[77] Their friendship was not strong enough to weather Rousseau's time of troubles, however. By the end of 1764, the attack on Rousseau, inaugurated by the Parlement of Paris's condemnation in 1762, had reached its crescendo. A month after receiving the heavy blow of Voltaire's cruel pamphlet, *Sentiments des citoyens*, Rousseau was shown a letter then circulating in Geneva, purportedly sent by Mably to a Genevan friend, harshly criticizing his *Lettres de la montagne*.[78] Mably's letter was plainly a private and sincere one, quite distinct from the commination of *Sentiments des citoyens*. Rousseau nevertheless felt deeply betrayed, and immediately wrote to Mably, demanding a confirmation or denial of his authorship.[79] In the *Confessions*, written some years later, Rousseau reports that Mably, embarrassed by the letter and jealous of his greater celebrity, did not respond; from that time,

Rousseau realized that "I would have no worse enemy."[80] The truth was slightly different. Mably had in fact responded immediately, with a letter of notable frankness and delicacy:

> It is quite true, Monsieur, that, one of my friends having spoken of the troubles in Geneva caused by your latest work, I made the response from which you have sent an extract. I cannot guarantee that my expressions have not been altered; but if they have been copied faithfully, it is certain that I would like to correct many of them. . . . You are outraged, but, in sacrificing your resentment, one will not merely admire your talents, one will love your philosophy. No one wishes to merit your friendship more than myself, Monsieur, and I will always be very attached to you.[81]

Despite Mably's efforts, this was the end of their relations. He was, of course, not the only acquaintance of Rousseau to break with him in these difficult years, but Mably seems to have withstood the trial with relative dignity. He certainly maintained a profound respect for Rousseau as a thinker, and seems genuinely to have regretted the breach.[82]

What in fact did Mably owe to Rousseau intellectually? As usual, his own reticence and the lack of other evidence would seem to rule out an exact calculation of his debt. But the traditional assumption that Rousseau's thought played at least a catalytic role in Mably's intellectual development remains plausible enough, considering their friendship in this period and the fact that Rousseau plainly anticipated by some years many of the themes of Mably's mature thought. The basic similarity of their outlook is perfectly clear. If Mably went further than Rousseau in the direction of communist utopianism, his reluctant conclusion that a radical redistribution of property was wholly impossible in eighteenth-century Europe meant that the central problematic of his mature thought would, in the end, be the same as that of Rousseau—how to find means of remedying the evils of social inequality without the abolition of private property altogether. In Rousseau's own words, "My intention is not the total destruction of private property, since that is impossible, but to confine it to the strictest limits, my giving it a measure, a rule, a bridle to restrain it, which will direct it, dominate it, and subordinate it always to the public good."[83] In fact, if we compare the political program set forth in Rousseau's later works—the *Discours sur l'économie politique*, *Du contrat social*, the *Projet* on Corsica, and the *Considérations* on Poland—with the one offered in Mably's writings, their overall consonance is very striking indeed. Both conceive of political life as a kind of compensation for the loss of "natural equality," and both see the principal means of achieving this goal in the adoption of a particular form of political government. The basic identity of the models for a democratic republic described in *Du contrat social* and in the three works we have examined in this chapter needs no demonstration. Moreover, Rousseau recommends precisely the same sort of ancillary supports for his political scheme as does Mably: the agrarian and sumptuary laws of the *Discours sur l'économie politique* and the *Projet* on Corsica, and the proposals for "ideological" regulation that close out *Du contrat social*. The fundamental affinity of the political thought of Mably and Rousseau has not, of course, gone unnoticed.[84] What has not been sufficiently recognized, however, is that the source of this affinity is their common racination in the tradition of classical republicanism, of which their writings together represent the creation of a distinctive French variant.

At the same time, the political thought of Mably and Rousseau was obviously not identical, by any reckoning. A detailed comparison reveals a number of important divergences, including both omission in the work of one writer of themes or concepts central to the work of the other, and certain instances of explicit disagreement. On the one hand, the centerpiece of the *Discours sur l'économie politique* and *Du contrat social*—the notion of a "general will" that expresses the common interests of the sovereign community—is virtually ignored in the writings of Mably, who hardly so much as mentions the term.[85] Conversely, the idea of "mixed government," which is in many ways the central token of Mably's thought and which reaches back directly to Polybius and Machiavelli, is effectively missing in Rousseau.[86] On the other hand, there seem to be some cases of outright discord. We have seen the enormous importance that Mably places on public deliberation and debate: not only does this find far less resonance in Rousseau's writings, but it seems directly incompatible with the latter's notorious prohibition of "communication" between citizens.[87] Even more striking is the fact that while Mably displays a complacent and unconcerned acceptance of political representation, Rousseau of course launched a famous critique and denunciation of it as wholly incompatible with his political system.[88]

What is the meaning of these differences? What they seem to point to essentially is the contrast between the quality and depth of Rousseau's engagement with the modern natural-rights tradition, and the relatively limited role that natural jurisprudence played in Mably's thought. The question of Rousseau's relation with the *école du droit naturel* is of course one of the most vexed issues in the study of his thought. But on any account he must be seen a pivotal figure in the history of that tradition. In part this was due to his reworking of a specifically Gallic inheritance: the conceptual set based on the binary antithesis of *particularité—généralité,* whose history has recently been meticulously traced by Patrick Riley. Originating in seventeenth-century theological thought, the notion of a divine *volonté générale* underwent a striking process of secularization, which Riley traces in a lineage running from Pascal through Malebranche, Montesquieu, and Diderot, until it emerged as the republican General Will of *Du contrat social.* In any case, the fact is that Rousseau's masterpiece marks a turning-point in the histories of *both* of the great political "languages" of the age: indeed it seems likely that the reason for his preeminence and originality within eighteenth-century political thought lay precisely in his unprecedented efforts to synthesize these two traditions—to deploy the language of the "state of nature" and the "social contract" for what were essentially republican purposes.

As for Mably, it would be wrong to deny the importance of natural law in his development altogether. His "conversion" to the *école du droit naturel* provided his thought with metaphysical foundations it had hitherto lacked, making possible both the radical populism of *Des droits et des devoirs du citoyen* and the radical egalitarianism of his works of the 1760s. But his interest seems to have stopped at this point. Not only was his conception of natural law a philosophically backward—or at least unexamined—one, but he seems to have avoided the concept of a *volonté générale* altogether. Above all, Mably never went on to make any extensive use of the conceptual instrumentarium of modern rights theories: the "state of nature," the notion of a passage to "civil society" through the exchange of rights in a "social compact," the idea of "sovereignty" itself—all of the central concerns of *Du contrat social.* Despite the admiration he professed to have for Locke, Mably evidently lacked the sort of sympathy for and grasp of natural jurisprudence possessed by Rousseau. In one sense, of course, this refusal to follow the latter into the intricacies and paradoxes of the *volonté générale* and the social contract is a sign of the limits of Mably's vision—a failure to see as far as Rousseau into the fundamental political dilemmas of the age. Yet it also serves to establish the autonomy of his thought as a distinctive variant within French republicanism. For if Mably wrote no work to compare with *Du contrat social,* Rousseau, for his part, never ventured onto the terrain of philosophical history, of which Mably was to demonstrate such mastery in *Observations sur l'histoire de France,* the subject of the following chapter.

CHAPTER 6

History: The Politics of the French Past

The central, abiding concerns of Mably's thought, from beginning to end, were the politics and history of his native land. We have seen that his first book, *Parallèle des romains et des français,* was conceived as a historical apology for the French monarchy; and that the whole course of his early thought consisted of a long process of revision of the *Parallèle,* once he had abandoned the political standpoint it defended.[1] It remains for us to consider the last step in this process, which was completed with the publication of the first two volumes of *Observations sur l'histoire de France* in 1765 (a third volume was written shortly thereafter, but was published only in 1788). This was without any doubt the greatest—at once the most eloquent, the most deeply felt, and politically the most important—of Mably's works. In order to grasp its full import, however, we need to begin by taking a closer look at the long historical debate over the "fundamental laws" of the French monarchy, which furnishes the intellectual and polemical context for all of Mably's later writing on France. Earlier we noted that this debate has been strangely neglected in recent scholarship. There exists no contemporary treatment of it of the same scale and seriousness as Pocock's classic study of seventeenth-century English historical thought, *The Ancient Constitution and the Feudal Law.*[2] In fact, a comparable survey of French historiography in the eighteenth century would form a very revealing contrast to Pocock's book, for the debate over the history of the French monarchy was both near to and far from its English counterpart.

The Debate Over the French "Constitution"

The doctrine of the "ancient constitution" in England was initially developed for the defense of common law prerogatives and parliamentary legislative authority—two institutional expressions of the unique strength of the English landowning class—in the face of Tudor and Stuart attempts to move in the direction of continental-style absolutism. Pocock's study demonstrates the immense power of the belief in a traditional parliamentary constitution, chronicling the ways in which its supporters repeatedly overcame all serious intellectual challenges. Both sides in the Civil War raised their standards in its defense; the sole important change effected in the doctrine in the interregnum was its fusion with the quasi-republican theory of "mixed" government, which helped to give it a highly flexible political shape. The ideology of the ancient constitution triumphed in the Restoration of 1660, and even more decisively in the final clearance of the remaining vestiges of absolutism in 1688. Thus the entire settlement of 1688–1715, sealing the transition to parliamentary sovereignty—a novel political order in Europe—was legitimated as the "confirmation" of a customary constitution that was supposed to have existed from the Saxon epoch onwards. The two central leitmotifs of English ancient constitutionalism, from Coke to Burke and beyond, were, first, *immemorialism*, the claim that the various components of the constitution were "traceable to no original act of foundation"—since to discover the origin of any right or prerogative would be "to admit an indelible stain of sovereignty upon the English constitution."[3] The second was a belief in the mystic *continuity* of English history, such that all historical change was seen, in Burke's famous words, as "re-affirmance of the still more antient standing law of the kingdom," and all revolutions as ones according to the "principle of reference to antiquity."[4] The political advantages of such a deliberate repression of the consciousness of historical change were enormous. Forged to combat the encroachments of royal authority, the notion later proved to be an equally formidable weapon against the claims of popular sovereignty. Its service, in effect, was to render the political order of Hanoverian England immune to rationalist political criticism of any sort. This accomplished, ancient constitutionalism naturally lost some of its potency in the eighteenth century. Indeed, the greatest historical work on England in the Enlightenment, Hume's *History*, can be read as a critique of the very idea of an "ancient constitution."[5] But the doctrine was never far from reach when necessary. The threat of the

French Revolution itself was of course enough to call forth an impassioned recapitulation of the whole tradition—its most eloquent statement—by Burke.[6]

As for France, the example of English ancient constitutionalism was naturally tantalizing, both for the aristocratic opponents of the regime of Versailles, who launched their own vindications of "ancient liberty" after the turn of the eighteenth century, and for the royalist historians who undertook to defend the monarchy from these attacks. The long debate between supporters of the *thèse nobiliaire* and the *thèse royale*, which started in the last years of Louis XIV and was ended only by the Revolution, seems in many ways to be a reprise of the English exchanges of the previous century. We find precisely the same sort of effort to use historical arguments for the legitimation of political programs, all based on the assumption that historical study revealed an immemorial and thus legitimate "constitution." Yet the political context of the French debates was wholly different. Their *object*, instead of the immature and enfeebled absolutism of the Stuarts, was the powerful, historically accomplished, absolutist state of Louis XIV. This meant that any attempt to match the central feat of English ancient constitutionalism, the creation of the illusion of continuity through the ages, was crippled from the start. For the French past fell massively and inescapably into two distinct periods—pre-absolutist and absolutist. The result was that the proponents of the *thèse nobiliaire* and the *thèse royale* were forced to divide the assets of an English-style ancient constitutionalism—vindication of "ancient liberty" and defense of a standing political order—between themselves, creating a fatal polarization that neither side was able fully to overcome.

Paradoxically, it was the royalist version of French history that presents us with perhaps the closest intellectual equivalent of English prescriptivism. It is true, of course, that history was not the chosen terrain for absolutist legitimation in either England or France. The examples of James VI and I and Bossuet suggest that the natural impulse of royalism was to retreat to some mixture of religious and rationalist arguments, precisely because these were immune to historical criticism. Once faced with a mounting challenge, however, from the last years of Louis XIV onward, royalist writers and propagandists in France proved more than capable of sketching a portrait of an absolutist ancient constitution, stretching unvaryingly from the time of Clovis to the present. We thus find in royalist historians something like the same effort to efface all traces of historical change—to effect a total identification between past and present—

that characterized the Whig defenders of the English ancient constitution. Of course, the great difficulty with this—the neuralgic zone of royalist historiography—was how to account for the medieval period, with its images of monarchical weakness and aristocratic independence. In other words, the success of royal prescriptivism depended on disproving the apparent priority of "feudal liberty" in the French past. As we have seen, Dubos found the most ingenious solution to the problem. He portrayed the monarchy as purely absolutist at the outset, since Clovis and his successors merely inherited the quasi-immemorial mantle of Roman imperial sovereignty. The entire medieval period could then be figured as an "interruption" of French history, as the feudal nobility "usurped" royal authority and plunged the nation into centuries of barbarism and anarchy. The rise of absolutism, finally, was depicted as merely the "restoration" of the original monarchical constitution, thus freeing the nation from the aristocratic usurpation of the Middle Ages.[7] Such was the basic royalist case. Presented modestly and defensively by Dubos, it was repeated endlessly through the century, on an ever vaster scale. This process reached its climax, decades later, in the work of the propagandist and royal historiographer Jacob-Nicolas Moreau, who devoted an entire career and an enormous archival "arsenal" to the description and defense of a royalist ancient constitution.[8] Both the theoretical justification and the political lesson of this use of history were summed up in the lapidary formula of Moreau's fellow royalist, Goudar: "Nothing should be changed in a state that has survived twelve centuries in the same order."[9]

As for the sponsors of the *thèse nobiliaire*, their initial thrust was precisely the opposite: to restore a sense of historical difference, to demonstrate that absolutism—"despotism"—was not immemorial in France. At the same time, precisely because its aim was not to defend the existing privileges of common law or Parliament, but instead to celebrate the lost liberty of a distant past, the anti-absolutist appeal to history could not base its claims on prescription or custom alone. In France, such prescriptivism, at least at the outset of these debates, was really only at the disposal of royalist historians. The *thèse nobiliaire* was thus "partially rationalized"—a phrase we can borrow from Pocock[10]—in its first incarnation: that is, it had to supply some *reasons* for its vindication of "liberty," beyond its mere historical precedence. This can be seen nowhere better than in Boulainvilliers, the most acute and influential of the proponents of the *thèse nobiliaire*. For his doctrine of the conquest was quite distinct from any immemorialist account of an "ancient constitution." However illiberal, or even reactionary, it later seemed, its purpose was still to establish the "liberties"—the rights—of a body of citizens, in a determinate historical *event*. For Boulainvilliers, liberty and property were bound together in classic liberal fashion. More than this, his account of French history is presented in what is unmistakably the language of civic humanism or classical republicanism.[11] Boulainvilliers's *gouvernement féodal* is plainly an idealized model of a Greek *polis*, in which an egalitarian (if exclusive) citizenry exercises participatory self-government. At the same time, his account also reveals a trait that would become central to almost all later versions of "opposition" history, the appeal to the English model of ancient constitutionalism itself: "We must conclude that the safety of a people can be secured only by those states that are governed on the model supplied by the ancient destroyers of the Roman Empire, of which there remains more than a trace only in England."[12] The role played by the English example in *De l'Esprit des lois* needs little comment; we shall soon see that Mably too came to conceive of the divergence between England and France as the central drama of European history.

Symptomatically, while the shape of the *thèse royale* changed very little through the century, the *thèse nobiliaire* was soon succeeded by a variety of opposition *thèses*, which built on the case established by Boulainvilliers, but which also transformed it in certain fundamental respects. Denis Richet once aptly described this evolution in terms of an "enlargement of an ideal elite."[13] In effect, the precedence and privileges that Boulainvilliers believed to be the possessions of the feudal nobility alone were gradually extended to an ever-wider portion of the population until, by the eve of the Revolution, they were widely seen as the patrimony of the French "nation" itself. As we shall see, Mably's *Observations sur l'histoire de France* played a decisive role in this evolution. But two earlier moments in the debate, prior to Mably's intervention, need some comment. First, Montesquieu has traditionally been seen as the pivotal figure in French historiography of the eighteenth century. There is no doubt that this centrality is overstated in Carcassone's study, whose major fault is its attempt to view the entire debate over the French constitution through the selective lens of *De l'Esprit des lois*. Carcassone's book does, however, have the merit of demonstrating the extraordinary political heterogeneity of Montesquieu's thought, which could literally provide arguments for all sides in the ideological contest being described. On the one hand, the historical books that conclude *De l'Esprit des lois* certainly provided a more authoritative and attractive version of the *thèse nobiliaire*, establishing it on far securer historical grounds than did the quasi-racial, voluntarist account of Boulainvilliers.[14] Yet Carcassone probably exaggerated the contemporary impact of these parts of Montesquieu's treatise. Far more important was the portrait of the English constitution in Book XI, which was perhaps the single most influential piece of political writing of the entire century, a source to be mined on both sides of the Channel and both sides of the Atlantic. At the same time, however, *De l'Esprit des lois* as a whole offered anything but an unequivocal endorsement of the English constitution or even of the *thèse nobiliaire* itself. Over and against both is the portrait of monarchy in the first eight books of Montesquieu's treatise: the government in which the prince is "the source of all political and civil power"; whose "fundamental maxim" is "no monarch, no nobility; no nobility, no monarchy"; and which is a moderate, and therefore "free" government. These formulae were not merely prudent concessions to monarchical sensibilities. It was Montesquieu, far more profoundly than any of his contemporaries, who recognized that the fortunes of the "regrouped" French nobility of the eighteenth century now depended more than ever on the fate of the absolute monarchy whose highest offices in the state, church, and military it occupied. *De l'Esprit des lois* is the greatest literary exploration of this complex symbiosis. If it bears witness to the ineradicable friction that persisted between aristocracy and absolutism in France, it nevertheless faithfully reflects the broad self-confidence of the eighteenth-century nobility, now free to enjoy the fruits of its final rapprochement with the monarchy. Montesquieu's measured yet satisfied depiction of modern European monarchy reminds us, in other words, that *De l'Esprit des lois* really belongs, in tone and message, to the relative political calm of the first half of the century.

For the real watershed in the development of the *thèse nobiliaire* away from the quasi-racial exclusivism of its origins came only after 1751, with the advent of the parliamentary opposition discussed in Chapter Four. The predictable result of the startling new claims that appeared in the remonstrances and pamphlet literature of the period was the transformation of the *thèse nobiliaire* into a *thèse parlementaire*, in which the defense of the rights of the nobility gave way to those of the more nebulous "nation," while the horizon of this defense shifted dramatically from the past to the present. By far the most influential version of the *thèse parlementaire* was the Jansenist magistrate Adrien Louis Le Paige's *Lettres historiques, sur les fonctions essentielles du parlement, sur le droit des pairs, et sur les loix fondamentales du royaume*, first published in 1753.[15] Like Boulainvilliers and Montesquieu, Le Paige stayed within the bounds of a formal monarchism: "According to the fundamental constitution of the state, it is essential that we have a king; that the king unites in his person all legislative and coactive power; that he is eminently the principle and source of all justice and of all authority in the realm."[16] Yet there are two "fundamental laws" that are coterminous with the monarchy itself, both involving very strict limitations on the power of the king: "One is that the Kings may not put anyone to death. . . . It is not that there is no death penalty in our state . . . but that this can only be pronounced in the Assembly of the Nation, about which I will speak, and which is the first origin of our Parlements." As for the second "fundamental law":

> It does not permit the King to do anything, even in regard to the slightest affairs, without the counsel of his princes elected by the Nation to pass judgment with him; and in regard to affairs of particular importance, without the counsel of the Nation itself. . . . You recognize in this a certain rule of our public law, just as ancient, just as unshakable as the Monarchy itself, and which has always been religiously maintained by our Kings . . . that no edict, ordonnance, or other act, has the force of public law in the realm, before it has been deliberated in the Parlement, which today represents these princes and these assemblies.[17]

The final sentence hints at one of the chief polemical purposes of the *Lettres historiques*: to argue that it was the *parlements*—that of Paris in particular—and not the failed Estates General, that have inherited the role of the earlier assemblies of the nation. But the most memorable feature of Le Paige's work is its insistence, repeated with what eventually becomes a near-pathological monotony, that the fundamental laws of the French monarchy have never undergone the slightest alteration in their thirteen centuries of existence: "Thus when you ask me what the extent of the authority of Parlement once was, when it passed edicts or laws, and what is its extent today, the answer is simple. Its authority today is the same as it was in the time of Clovis."[18] The contrast with all earlier versions of aristocratic ancient constitutionalism is remarkable. In the parliamentary literature of the 1750s and 1760s, the "ancient liberty" of the French, whose *loss* was so vividly felt and described by Boulainvilliers, was now fully *restored*—defended, that is, as a living inheritance. In other words, the *Lettres historiques*, in what can only be described as a classic case of wish-fulfillment, simply denies that the historical rupture represented by the advent of absolutism had ever occurred—the mirror inverse of the censorship of the memory of "feudal liberty" in royalist historiography. At the same stroke, the aristocratic account of French history now largely ceased to be "partially rationalized" in the sense described above. The case Le Paige makes for allegiance to the *lois fondamentales* is as pure an example of prescriptivism as any to be found in English historical thought.

The harvest of a half-century of debate over the history of the monarchy thus seems to have been a remarkable ideological impasse, one that accurately reflected the fatal political stalemate that had now developed between court and nobility in France. The contest had begun with the nostalgic celebration of a lost "feudal liberty" among disgruntled nobles; royalist historians responded with depictions of an autocratic "ancient constitution" (i.e., the retrojection of the image of absolutism into the distant past); and an increasingly self-confident magistrature then countered with the creation of an aristocratic "constitution" (i.e., the projection of the shape of a late-medieval Estates monarchy into the present). What is striking, however, is that no participant in the debate had yet sought to disown or even seriously to question its founding premise, the idea that there was a single set of "fundamental laws" to be found in the records of French history. On the contrary, the effect of the political agitation of the fifties had been to propel both parties into a far greater commitment to the notion of an immemorial and prescriptivist "constitution" than had ever been the case before.

How to Make a French Revolution

How did Mably view the evolution of the debate over the history of the monarchy in these years? It will already be clear that prescriptivism as such can have had no attraction for him, for one very simple reason. As we have seen, by the end of the 1750s Mably had adopted a radical conception of popular sovereignty: "The people, to whom sovereign power originally belongs, the sole author of political government and bestower of its powers to its magistrates, always has the right to interpret its contract, or rather its gifts, to modify its clauses, to cancel them, and to establish an entirely new order of things"—in Stanhope's words in *Des droits et des devoirs du citoyen.*[19] Naturally, such a conception wholly precludes any idea of a prescriptivist "ancient constitution." Thus when Stanhope first expounds this doctrine, his French companion initially recoils from the apparent prospect of perpetual change entailed by it. If the "people" can alter the shape of the constitution at will, he asks, what will become of the "fundamental laws"? "What they may," is Stanhope's reply: "New fundamental laws will take the place of fundamental laws that have been destroyed."[20] In *De l'étude de l'histoire*, written not long afterwards, we find a more extended rejection of the notion of "fundamental law" as used by Mably's contemporaries:

> This is a beautiful phrase, on the lips of the whole world, but which no one understands. If you mean that the legislator must himself conform to the laws as long as he permits them to subsist, then nothing is more true. But if you are claiming that he is not capable of abrogating them in order to replace them with others, then that is an absurdity: I ask you tell me by what name you call the power that can oppose him? I would like someone to explain to me why these laws that are called fundamental should have the privilege of being impossible to annul. They are the work of a legislator; why should they not always be under his control? Isn't it in the nature of legislative power to be incapable of prescribing boundaries for itself? It would be ridiculous to think that new laws must never be contrary to old ones; for different circumstances demand laws whose spirit is entirely different. Besides, old laws can be faulty: they may have been imposed by an ignorant or unjust legislator; why should an enlightened and just legislator be forbidden to correct them?[21]

And in the preface to *Observations sur l'histoire de France* itself the notion is dismissed with a similar impatience:

> No one is so ignorant as to confuse the first laws that a nation has with its fundamental laws. The fundamental law of a state is not a mass of proscribed, forgotten, or neglected laws, but the law that regulates, prescribes, and constitutes the form of government.[22]

From this vantage point, then, the whole project of attempting to found political legitimacy on the historical priority of a set of "fundamental laws" was utterly chimerical: "fundamental law" was merely the expression of sovereign authority, any coherent notion of which wholly precluded prescriptivism as such. Yet this was unlikely to have been Mably's last word on the subject of the "ancient constitution." As a closer look at the second half of *Des droits et des devoirs du citoyen* reveals, he was profoundly impressed by the power of a belief in "ancient liberty" for the mobilization of political energies. As was mentioned above, the last part of the dialogue is devoted to what is essentially a *strategic* question: assuming that sovereign authority belongs, by natural right, to the "people," how can the subjects of present-day monarchies—the French monarchy in particular—be expected to exercise this right? It is in fact the Frenchman who specifies the initial problem most precisely. Resistance to "despotism," he argues, is one thing where some form of representative institution, sharing in legislative power, already exists. The prerogative powers of the English king, for example, are far too great, yet Parliament nevertheless was able to refuse Walpole's excise scheme in 1733. "But things are different," the Frenchman continues, "in nations that have a legislative monarch armed with all the powers of the state, whose presence and activity is felt everywhere, by means of officials who are instruments of his will and who believe they can extend their own power by removing any limit to that of their master."[23] What practical route was open to the subjects of the French monarchy? What could be done even to begin to overturn the immense weight and power of Bourbon absolutism?

It is in response to these questions that Stanhope, asserting that "politics prescribes a certain order of conduct to peoples who wish to make themselves free," offers to his French audience what Keith Baker has accurately termed a "script for a French Revolution": that is, an impressively detailed and realistic recipe—in three major steps—for the overthrow of absolutism in France and its replacement with a constitutional monarchy.[24] Stanhope begins by conceding that the voyage toward liberty will be long and difficult, since the prejudices of absolutism have long since become part of the political common sense of the French.[25] Nevertheless, the French monarchy possesses certain resources that are wholly lacking, for example, in the "purer" despotisms of the East. "In the midst of this ocean of arbitrary power," Stanhope asks, "do you not glimpse floating here and there some of the debris of your former independence?" These "planks" should be regarded as the fortunate means for escape from the impending shipwreck:

> You must cling to them forcefully, for with their help you can keep your heads above water. Swim on, have courage and do not despair, perhaps an unexpected wind will bring you safely to port. Keep a close watch, for despotism is extreme in Turkey only because they possess no corporate bodies, no privileged order of citizens. Provinces, cites, towns—everything there is governed by a minister of the tyrannical seraglio, whom, for all the power he wields in his own sphere, the sultan can have strangled as easily as one kills a rabbit in the forest. You, on the other hand, have assemblies and corporate bodies; your clergy still forms one such body; your nobility still preserves the memory of its past grandeur and its particular privileges, and must be treated with discretion and respect. You have parlements everywhere, and several of your provinces are still governed by their Estates assemblies. One does not strangle all of that, the way one strangles a vizier or a pasha whom one has raised up from the dust.[26]

We are, of course, in the world of Montesquieu, for these "planks"—i.e., "companies," "bodies," "privileged orders," "parlements," "Estates"—are none other than the "intermediate, subordinate, and dependent powers" of Book II of *De l'Esprit des lois*, which constitute the "nature" of European monarchy and mark its distance from Asiatic "despotism." Not accidentally, Mably here offers one of his rare accolades of Montesquieu's book. *De l'Esprit des lois*, Stanhope declares, "has many faults: the fundamental ideas of its system are false, everything is rambling, incoherent, and unconnected." What offended Mably most, naturally, was Montesquieu's defense of hereditary nobility.[27] Nevertheless: "The work still merits a great deal of attention: it renders arbitrary power detestable by the multitude who read it and believe they understand it, and in reading it they gradually become accustomed to liberal ideas."[28] In fact, it indicates precisely what the *first* duty of any group of citizens who hope to see their nation recover its "liberty" must be:

> It is necessary to try to return, little by little, to the abandoned and nearly forgotten principles of the former government. This method, confirmed by constant and uniform experiences, will prevent people from being shocked by the novelty and difficulty of the undertaking; it will reveal hearts already prepared for a revolution, since we are naturally led to respect the wisdom of our fathers. . . . You see then that this debris of rights, privileges, and prerogatives that some bodies and some provinces have retained from the ancient constitution, are, in a sense, so many milestones marking the route that you must follow. . . . So long as the parlements defend their policy, their forms, and their dignity with vigor, the people will know that the king is not, like the great Turk, the master of all he surveys.[29]

Thus the initial step in Stanhope's scenario for a French Revolution is simply an endorsement of parlementary ideology itself—an effort to secure the existence of the "intermediate powers" of the monarchy and to restore their privileges where they have lapsed.

However, any political strategy that called on the French to "return little by little" to their "former government" was bound to confront one crucial question: what of the Estates General? A century earlier, with the memory of 1614 still relatively fresh in mind, the convocation of such an assembly had formed one of the central demands of the leaders of the Fronde. But with the maturity of absolutism, the possibility of restoring the Estates seemed to grow ever more remote and ever more unnecessary.[30] A few muted calls for one were heard with the advent of the Regency, but after this the "space" that had belonged to the Estates in the French political imagination was decisively occupied by the *parlements*. No index of the eclipse of the Estates General is so eloquent as Montesquieu's silence on it: not merely is it excluded from the ranks of his "intermediary powers," it is not even so much as mentioned in the text of *De l'Esprit des lois*. As for the parlementary literature of the 1750s and 1760s, we have already noted that it was common to see the Estates General and the *parlements* depicted in it as two rival, mutually exclusive institutions. Nothing could seem less likely in 1758 than to imagine any link between the crisis of the *refus des sacrements* and the calling of an Estates. Yet this is precisely what Mably's "Commonwealthman" does. He insists that a magistracy in full possession of its constitutional prerogatives, backed by the support of the populace, has the power to take the decisive *second* step toward the recovery of sovereignty by the nation—to call for the convocation of the moribund Estates General. In fact, Stanhope claims, a great opportunity had just passed for doing so, with the imposition of the second *vingtième* in 1756. Had it wished, the Parlement of Paris could have rallied the people against this act of "despotism": "I am assuming that it would have established, as an incontestable truth, the easily proven principle that the nation alone has the right to tax itself, that it would have sketched a portrait of royal usurpation over the years, and that in consequence it would have demanded a meeting of the Estates General."[31] To imagine such a possibility was the crucial innovation of the strategy recommended in *Des droits et des devoirs du citoyen*: it was not until 1771, when the long episode of parliamentary oppositionism came to an end in the Maupeou "coup," that the momentum for the calling of an Estates began to build in France.

By this point, it is clear that Stanhope's plan has passed beyond anything imagined in the parlementary ideology of the 1750s, which was limited to calls for the restoration of a prescriptive "ancient constitution." This is confirmed when he sketches in the third and final step in his revolutionary program. Once the Estates General is restored, its most important task, the "fixed and determined object" of the revolutionaries, must be to give it a form and periodicity that it never possessed in the past, amounting to nothing less than a transfer of sovereignty: "Thus before dispersing, the Estates must necessarily have announced a fundamental law, a PRAGMATIC SANCTION, by which it is ordered that the representatives of the nation, armed with all of its powers, will assemble every three years, without meeting any impediment, and without the need of some particular act for their convocation."[32] All other goals are secondary to this one: "everything must be sacrificed to this end." Nor, once this has been secured, does Stanhope hesitate to offer a variety of practical recommendations for the restored Estates. Above all, as a true spokesman for the Commonwealth tradition, he advises the establishment of a rigorous separation of legislative and executive power. Since in all likelihood the French king will continue to exercise some legislative authority, it is the encroachment of ministerial power that will pose the greatest threat to the autonomy of the new assembly.[33]

At the same time, Stanhope's program of deliberate political reconstruction has certain limits. He issues numerous warnings about the dangers involved in making too sharp a rupture with the past, taking pains to emphasize that this whole process must be very deliberate and peaceful. The lessons of the English Civil War are never very far from Stanhope's mind in these passages—the primary example of how easily the revolutionary process can escape the control of its leaders through too sharp a breach with the past and too easy a recourse to force: "A *révolution ménagée*, on the other hand, of the kind I have recommended to you, will be all the more advantageous in that a love of order and of law, and not of a licentious liberty, will be its guiding principle. I mistrust a liberty that needs soldiers to establish itself: if they suppress the tyrant, it is rare indeed that they do not usurp the tyranny—Cromwell will always have his imitators. The wisdom of your magistrates would instead spread to all orders of the state and would dispose people to act in favor of the laws with courage, but also with prudence and with method."[34] In particular, "prudence" and "method" suggest that no attempt to reduce the privileges of the nobility should be made. If anything, these should be enhanced: "Far from requiring the nobility to surrender privileges that may well belong to the nation, it is necessary, on the contrary, to give them hope for still more flattering privileges and for a more real grandeur."[35] Nor should monarchy itself be abolished, even though its prerogatives are greatly to be reduced: "Royalty is no doubt a vice in a government, but all the same, it is a necessary one once a nation has lost those primitive ideas of simplicity and equality that men once possessed, but that can never be regained."[36]

Such is the scenario for a "French Revolution" outlined in *Des droits et des devoirs du citoyen.* The defense of the "ancient constitution" is essentially used as a *lever* to overturn absolutism, permitting a reconstructed national assembly to assume control of a modern constitutional monarchy—in essence, a moderate "Whig Revolution," applying the cumulative wisdom of the English experience of the seventeenth century to the monarchy of eighteenth-century France. This recipe for a "*révolution ménagée*" was, of course, an astonishing prognostication. Thirty years before the fact, Mably had accurately forecast what were to be the basic mechanisms of the Revolution of 1789—a parliamentary revolt against ministerial "despotism" (the protests over the reform program of Calonne and Loménie de Brienne in 1787) leads to a call for an Estates General (first issued by the Parlement of Paris in July 1787; conceded by the monarchy in August 1788), which, once convened, assumes full legislative power and proceeds to the construction of a constitutional monarchy (the passage from the Estates General to the National and then the Constituent Assembly in the summer of 1789).

At the same time, the intellectual and literary achievement of *Des droits et des devoirs* is all the more impressive, in that the work is a genuine *dialogue*, with a serious exchange of views. Once Stanhope's plan is sketched in, the Frenchman, who has hitherto offered only token resistance to the ideas of his "English Socrates," begins to register serious doubts about its prospects for success in the French context. His initial target is the second step in Stanhope's plan, the suggestion that parlementary protest could ever lead to a convocation of the Estates General. The Englishman, he argues, has completely misjudged the character and motives of the French magistracy in its struggle with the court—the *parlementaires* are in fact a selfish oligarchy whose claim to represent the "nation" is part of a cynical and self-serving attempt to extend their own power: "Putting itself in the place of a nation that no longer exists, it has concocted a plan to govern the king by means of the authority it exercises over the people in the king's own name."[37] Stanhope's mistake, the Frenchman suggests, is essentially historical. The record of history shows that, far from ever having resisted the encroachments of "despotism," the *parlements* have always been its willing accomplices. They were and have remained creatures of the monarchy, whose objective function was not to limit but to *extend* royal power. If the recovery of liberty in France depended solely on the willingness of the magistrates to surrender their authority and prestige to an Estates General, then its prospects were remote indeed.

But Stanhope is unmoved by these arguments. The recovery of the nation's "liberty" may well form no part of the magistrates' intentions, he responds; nevertheless, they will be driven in precisely this direction in spite of themselves:

> I can safely predict that if they attempt to do violence to public wishes, by establishing a parlementary aristocracy dividing authority with the king, they will necessarily fail. If the parlement examines the progress of royal power since the time of Philip the Fair, it will have to confess to having betrayed the state, or, to make amends, to agree that the burden that it has taken on is too heavy for it, that it is incapable of representing the nation and sustaining its rights.[38]

The magistrates, in other words, will sooner or later discover that it is in their own interests, and those of the nobility they represent, to issue a call for an Estates General: "for it is clear that this order can never be free and powerful in a country in which the people remain under the yoke."[39]

Yielding reluctantly to these arguments, the Frenchman then turns his attention to the third major step in Stanhope's scenario, which seems hardly more plausible to him—the assumption that a reconvened Estates assembly would be able to challenge the authority of an absolute monarch and transform France into a durable constitutional monarchy. Here again, it is the record of history that clearly suggests otherwise, since the whole early modern experience with the Estates General had produced nothing in the way of permanent accomplishment:

> We have had them, but what good did they do, and what good could they still do? We lack the tenacity, the constancy, the strength—in a word, the character to render them useful; and once they no longer do any good they do great harm. The deputies of the three orders will be corrupt, lazy, and foolish, and these personages will form a mob impermeable to common sense.[40]

For the Frenchman, his compatriots seem to be the victims of their own history, trapped by an inescapable syllogism:

> It is necessary to have a good moral character to recover one's liberty, since one cannot even preserve it without its help. But ours is bad, very bad indeed; and thus this liberty that you have described so pleasingly, can never be anything but a beautiful chimera for us.[41]

But Stanhope, undaunted, insists that the *moeurs* of the French are not irretrievable at all. The agitation of the past decade in fact suggests precisely the contrary:

> Agree at least that for the past several years you have been inflamed against despotism; that you desire to see an end to the abuses, and that in the ongoing ferment of today you are speaking, in public, words a good deal bolder than your most secret thoughts of a dozen years ago.[42]

If the crisis over the *refus des sacrements* was able to engender this sort of "ferment," how much more could be expected from the call for an Estates General?

> You will see that the mere proposal by the parlement to convoke the Estates General would instantly increase your courage, your understanding, and your love for order and the good. . . . If your Estates, proceed-

ing in the manner I suggested to you yesterday, were to deal tactfully with both public prejudices and private interests, and give to the laws the authority they took away from the prince, you would see your nation's still uncertain taste for liberty evolve into a very active passion. Don't you see that your character would start to correct itself in spite of you, once you understand the necessity of a reform?[43]

Indeed, Stanhope assures his partner that the very first steps of his "*révolution ménagée*" will initiate a kind of "cultural revolution," which will soon take on a life of its own, sweeping all resistance before it:

Take my word for it, or rather base your opinion on the always constant operation of the human passions: once your nation is wise enough to demand a convocation of the Estates General, and is strong enough to obtain it, it will never be stupid enough to content itself with an empty representation—extremes do not meet. Today, now that you are no longer wallowing in monstrous ignorance, now that you possess the discipline for study and for reasoning and know the sources from which you can draw the truths of history and politics—a thousand brochures will appear to instruct the public about its interests. They will seek out the faults of the former Estates, examine their form and their policy, study the general and particular causes of their decline and the oblivion into which they finally fell. Seafarers rely on charts for their navigation; you will make for yourselves, if I can put it this way, political charts that clearly mark the reefs and shoals, currents, safe or unsafe coasts, ports, and so forth.[44]

We recognize here precisely the same claims for the thaumaturgic powers of public discussion and deliberation that Mably was to make a few years later in *Doutes proposées aux philosophes économistes*. Mably's Englishman conceives of his "*révolution ménagée*" as something like a vast project of civic education for French society as a whole, in which the mere practice of free political speech and action provides the guarantee of its own success. And in an apparent simulacrum of precisely the same sort of learning process, the Frenchman himself finally yields to the force of the better argument. By the end of their discussions, Stanhope judges that his friend has become as "proud and zealous a Republican as any I know in England."[45]

The final word of *Des droits et des devoirs du citoyen*, however, is far less triumphant or optimistic than the apparent unanimity of the two conversants might suggest. For at the same moment that Mably's Frenchman is won over to an enthusiastic confidence about the likelihood of a recovery of "liberty" in France, the Englishman himself attempts to lower these expectations. In the final conversation before his departure from Marly for Italy, Stanhope characterizes his revolutionary plans as no more than "agreeable dreams" with no real prospect for success. He concludes in a posture of melancholy stoicism: "Why should we hope to see something that the world has never yet seen? No matter, these dreams are perhaps the most real of our goods, and I sometimes allow my imagination to lose itself in them, in order to console myself for all the human miseries that offend reason."[46]

Mably's initial reaction to the political watershed of the 1750s, and the new claims on behalf of the "fundamental laws" that accompanied it, was thus one of considerable complexity. No doubt he was already convinced of the fundamental *illegitimacy* of the Bourbon monarchy, indeed of any government not founded on popular sovereignty, no matter what the precise shape of its "ancient constitution." Nevertheless, Mably had correctly grasped, far in advance of most of his contemporaries, that conflict between the court and the corporate bodies of the monarchy, of the type represented by the crisis over the *refus des sacrements*, offered a real hope of practical escape from absolutism. The model of the English revolutions of the seventeenth century, whose lessons were summed up and preserved in the radical Commonwealth tradition, suggested that agitation on behalf of the "ancient constitution" and the "fundamental laws" of the monarchy could be used as a lever for toppling the monarchy, leading to the establishment of the sovereign authority of a proper legislative assembly. Mably's prescience here was no accident. It was the perfectly intelligible result of an accurate reading of the revolutionary potential contained within the events of the crisis over the *refus des sacrements*.[47] Yet Mably also perceived that the use of the lever of the "fundamental laws" was fraught with difficulty. The successful prosecution of Stanhope's plan depended on a number of conditions that were anything but obvious in the French context. Above all, it assumed that the French nobility would somehow recognize that it was in their own interests, not only to submit to, but even to lead the way in a passage from absolute to constitutional monarchy. Stanhope's "prolegomena to liberty" show that Mably believed that such an outcome was at least within the realm of the possible. But his Frenchman's hesitations also suggest that he knew that to require the *ancien régime* to submit to self-liquidation in so pacific a fashion was perhaps to expect too much—at the least, he anticipated that such a revolution might be a good deal less "*ménagée*" than his Commonwealthman imagines.

The Nightmare of History: Mably's Observations

Plainly it was only on the terrain of history—through an exhaustive reconstruction of the national past—that Mably could arrive at a final judgment of the prospects for a "*révolution ménagée*" in France. It is with this background in mind that we can now turn to *Observations sur l'histoire de France*, the first part of which was published in two volumes at Geneva in 1765.[48] Mably's preface opens with this memorable declaration of purpose:

> My goal in this work is to describe the different forms of government that the French have obeyed since their establishment in Gaul; and to explain the causes for the lack of stability that has condemned them, through the centuries, to continual revolutions. This side of our history is entirely unknown to readers who confine themselves to studying either our ancient annalists or our modern historians. I have experienced this myself; for once I discovered the true sources of our history, that is, our laws, capitularies, ancient formulas, charters, diplomas, treaties of peace and alliance, etc., I recognized the crude and numberless errors to which I was subject in my *Parallèle des romains et des français*. There arose before my eyes a nation completely different from the one I thought I knew.[49]

What were the "true sources" of French history, in which Mably discovered a wholly "different nation"? He is referring to those monuments of antiquarian erudition that assembled the primary sources for the early history of the monarchy: above all, the *Capitularia regum Francorum* edited by Baluze (1677), and the *Receuil des historiens des Gaules et de la France* of Dom Bouquet, eight volumes of which appeared between 1738 and 1754.[50] Much of the power of *Observations sur l'histoire de France* derives from Mably's remarkable grasp of these and other standard sources, which he often employs with devastating effect in settling accounts with earlier participants in the debate over the history of the monarchy. Fully *half* the book's pages are given over to an enormous apparatus of critical notes, under the label of "Remarks and Proofs."

At the same time, the scholarly achievement of *Observations sur l'histoire de France* is inseparable from the profound alteration of perspective implied in the characterization of French history as one of "continual revolutions." The term *révolution* itself was not, of course, unusual or unfamiliar in eighteenth-century historiography. Aided by the English designation of the "Glorious Revolution," the notion had already made its migration from the astronomical to the political and historical spheres. But as scholars have often noted, the concept had not yet crystallized in its modern form.[51] Conventionally used in the plural, "revolutions" were still largely associated with a realm of epochal change and vicissitude that operated beyond the limits of conscious human control—as in the abbé Vertot's *Histoire des révolutions de la république romaine*, referred to above.[52] It was only with the French Revolution itself that the term took on its modern sense, as a punctual political event directed by deliberate human agency. Now as Keith Baker suggests, in *Des droits et des devoirs du citoyen* Mably did come close to using the term in the latter sense—but *only* by modifying it with the adjective "*ménagée*," in a significant alteration of its meaning. Elsewhere, in *Observations sur l'histoire de France* above all, he uses "revolution" in the conventional eighteenth-century sense of the term. Mably's polemical purpose in doing so is perfectly clear. *Observations sur l'histoire de France* was an intervention in a debate whose common purpose had become the search for continuity and order in the historical record. In effect, what Mably promises here is to turn the present debate on its head, restoring the sense of historical discontinuity and disorder in the French past that had been forgotten or repressed by his predecessors. *Observations sur l'histoire de France* must be read, in other words, as a long critical meditation on ancient constitutionalism, from a classical republican standpoint, in which Mably offers, not another version of *the* "fundamental laws" of the monarchy, but a history of the "forms of government"—the *many* "fundamental laws"—that the French have obeyed through the centuries.

The narrative recounted in *Observations sur l'histoire de France* can be divided into three main parts, dealing, respectively, with the earliest foundation of the monarchy in the Dark Ages, the watershed period of Estates activity in the Middle Ages, and the "modern" era down to Louis XIV. The first, covering the period from the entry of the Franks into Gaul to the accession of Hughes Capet, can be rapidly summarized. For Mably, the "original" form of government of the Franks was the rude democracy described in Tacitus's *Germania*: "Tacitus informs us that the government of the Germans was a democracy, tempered by the power of the prince and the aristocracy."[53] This was the government first established in Gaul:

> The nation remained free and formed a true republic, in which the prince was only the first magistrate; it ruled as a body over the various peoples who lived in the lands it had conquered. The assembly of the Champ de Mars still met; the nobility continued to act as counsel to the prince; and the cities of Gaul were governed as had been the villages of Germany.[54]

However, the "democratic government of the French" did not long survive. The occupation of Gaul brought about a social situation that was in "contradiction" with their previous way of life. A rough democracy was a suitable form of government for migrant warrior bands:

> But hardly had they settled in Gaul, than a love of liberty ceased to be their guiding passion. The conquests relaxed the springs of their government; new needs and new circumstances gave them ideas completely different from those they had brought from Germany, and gradually detached them from their original political principles.

The public good was sacrificed to private interests, Mably continues, "and this change in character announced an impending change in government."[55] What had occurred was essentially a process of social stratification, as Frankish warriors moved to strengthen their grip on lands "granted" them by their leaders: the original democracy of the Franks began to give way to a "nascent aristocracy."

An unexpected change of dynasty led, however, to a memorable interruption of this process. This was, of course, the work of Charlemagne, whose reign forms "the most curious, interesting, and most instructive episode of modern history." Charlemagne's solution to the problem of increasingly sharp divisions between social orders, which had brought the realm to the brink of collapse, was to "restore the French to the ancient principles of government that their fathers had brought from Germany."[56] That is, he not only returned full legislative authority to the biannual Champ de Mars meeting, but he also induced the nobility to permit the reentry of the "people" in the assembly, such that the government became a true "democracy" once again—or perhaps more accurately, a "mixed government":

> By dividing authority and involving all the citizens in the government, he wished to divert their attention from their private interests alone. He hoped that the rivalry of the clergy, the nobility, and the people would force them to a mutual recognition, that they would balance one another, in a kind of equilibrium; that each order would learn to fear and respect the others; and that by lowering their ambitions, each order would take up some common ideas of the public good, and so learn to work together.[57]

History soon showed, however, that there were limits to the powers of even a French Lycurgus: "It is not enough to order a people to be free, for it to happen; it was not enough merely to pass laws: you must change the manner of seeing, sensing and thinking in citizens, or their old prejudices will triumph over the wisdom of the magistrates."[58] A certain collective "character" had long since begun to coalesce among the French, which even Charlemagne's reforms were incapable of overcoming. With his death, the process of social stratification already under way merely resumed its course. In the epoch immediately following the collapse of the Carolingian empire, the Frankish aristocrats decisively gained hereditary control over the territories that they had originally received as temporary possessions, arrogating rights of "justice"—that is, political authority—in them. The bulk of the native rural population was ground steadily down toward a state of complete servitude, while the Franks gradually constituted themselves as a caste-like nobility. The end-point of this process was the creation of the "feudal government," whose hallmark was the disappearance of public authority altogether, replaced by a tenuous and unstable hierarchy of personal dependency, at whose apex stood a largely powerless king.

This completed the first great "revolution" of French history, which had taken the French from the primitive and unstable democracy of their German forebearers, to the "monstrous anarchy of the feudal government."[59] By this point in the narrative, in fact, it is quite clear that the "revolutions" that form its subject are very far from the "*révolution ménagée*" whose plan is outlined in *Des droits et des devoirs du citoyen.* Mably emphasizes again and again that the process he describes was not directed by any human agency, but was merely the unintended consequence of actions undertaken for other purposes entirely. Even those who seemed most to benefit from the change had not brought it about, but were themselves merely swept along by forces beyond their control: "But it is most likely that fortune, circumstances, and events took the place of deliberate policy among the families and lords in question."[60] This surrender to the compulsion of "circumstance" and "event"—that is, to causal processes "behind the back" of the individual—gradually becomes the dominant preoccupation of *Observations sur l'histoire de France.* The result of this "inattention," in this instance as in all later ones, was to create a situation that was worse for all parties concerned: "All the parts of the state, enemies to one another, tended not only toward a separation from each other, but also to a mutual destruction."[61]

If we turn, meanwhile, to the "Remarks and Proofs" that accompany this narrative, what do we find? The pre-Capetian epoch had been the main focus of the historical debate in the first half of the century, and it is in his critical notes that Mably confronts the claims his predecessors had made in regard to the original "constitution" of the monarchy. We have seen that he showed no sympathy for the *thèse royale* even as a royalist historian. Here, where it is represented for the most part by the much-maligned figure of the abbé Dubos, it receives a curt dismissal. All of Dubos's efforts to establish the existence of a strong centralized monarchy in the time of Clovis—the denial of a Frankish "conquest," the legend of an imperial or Armorican "invitation" to enter Gaul, the claim of continuity in taxation—are summarily dispatched as patent fictions: "It seems to me that one cannot read the work of the abbé du Bos, without being convinced that he first imagined a history of France, and then set about reading our ancient histories only to pick out whatever might favor his opinions."[62] Of far greater interest is Mably's treatment of earlier proponents of the *thèse nobiliaire*, Boulainvilliers and Montesquieu above all, precisely because he shared the general antimonarchism of their outlook, their conviction of the "ancient liberty" of the French prior to the advent of absolutism.[63] Yet in his notes Mably subjects Boulainvilliers's account of the "conquest" of Gaul to a complete demolition. As we have seen, the latter's goal was to locate the source for the social compact of feudalism—free nobility over a subject peasantry—in a punctual historical event, thereby legitimizing it. Mably does not deny the basic fact of the Conquest, in the sense of a gradual resettlement of Frankish warriors in Gaul, largely unsupervised by imperial or monarchical authority, as had Dubos. Nor does he deny that French society eventually took on precisely the polarized shape described by Boulainvilliers. But he marshals as much evidence as he can to demonstrate that social stratification during the entire Merovingian period was extremely fluid and unformed. No unified, hereditary nobility had yet emerged, and, above all, nothing approaching serfdom itself yet existed.[64] For Mably, "feudal government" in that sense did not come into existence until the evolution of fiefs from conditional possession to hereditary property was finished—not, that is, until some three centuries after the initial entry of the Franks into Gaul.

Now these criticisms of Boulainvilliers were not new. Mably was largely anticipated in them by Montesquieu, who, in a famous phrase, had termed the former's account of the origins of serfdom in the conquest a "conspiracy against the third estate."[65] Mably nevertheless finds it necessary to criticize Montesquieu himself in these notes, albeit with far greater circumspection and respect. For the latter was finally no less interested than Boulainvilliers had been in attempting to establish a secure historical ancestry for the French nobility. Discarding the notion of the "conquest," with its unsettling connotations, Montesquieu instead portrayed the "feudal government" as the achievement of a relatively smooth and continuous evolution, which simply reproduced in different contexts the "spirit" of the pristine relationship that had attached the Germanic warrior to his war-leader. The result was a considerably more subtle and attractive version of the *thèse nobiliaire* than that of Boulainvilliers, but one whose basic filiation with the latter is still unmistakable. For Mably, however, all of this amounted to an unwarranted universalization of feudalism, denying its exceptional (and disadvantageous) character as a form of government: "In every nation there are faithful men pledged to one another by their word; and yet no one has ever claimed that the government of fiefs has been the government of all nations."[66] If, as Montesquieu seems to suggest, "benefices" and "fiefs" are essentially expressions of some prior relationship of honor and dependence, then "it is pointless to look for the origins of fiefs in the histories of the barbarians who destroyed the Roman empire; who could fail to see that fiefs would be as old as the world and would be found under all forms of government?"[67] Above all, Mably attempts to deny the most cherished of Montesquieu's claims, the assertion that vassalage involved, from its very inception in the forests of Germany, not only the exchange of military service and protection, but also the transfer of rights of jurisdiction—i.e., political power—to vassals.[68]

It is easy to see what was at stake in Mably's painstaking criticisms of Boulainvilliers and Montesquieu. For all three writers shared a fundamentally similar conception of the basic shape of French history: like Madame de Staël at a later date, all would have agreed that "It is arbitrary power that is new, and liberty that is old." But for Boulainvilliers and Montesquieu, the "ancient liberty" of self-government had been the privilege of the feudal nobility alone, whether acquired through punctual conquest or immemorial inheritance: in their different ways, the deepest goal of each had been to secure the *priority* of the nobility in French history. Mably, on the other hand, plainly thought that it was an anachronism to speak of the existence of a "French nobility" at any moment before the collapse of the Carolingian empire. This may well have seemed an insult to the pride of the present-day nobility:

> But for them to be offended at not being noble before there was even a nobility—that just shows a touch of lunacy. If this is a mortification for them, then I am sorry, but it cannot be otherwise. For I cannot imagine that Montesquieu really believes that nations started out with nobilities. Equality must first have united the citizens of any nation, and the distinction between nobles and commoners can only have been the result of many events and revolutions, from which certain citizens profited by assuming particular prerogatives and forming a separate class. Our great

> families must be very difficult to please indeed, if they are dissatisfied by not having been nobles since the time of Clothaire II.[69]

Dubos had made a similar rejection of the pretentions of the nobility, but Mably is obviously not resurrecting the *thèse royale*. Instead, it is far more accurate, as Durand Echeverria has suggested,[70] to see in *Observations sur l'histoire de France* the earliest statement of a *thèse démocratique*, in which historical priority has been assigned to neither the aristocracy or the monarchy, but to the French "people" or "nation." Mably is, of course, still some distance away from Sieyès's summary expulsion of the nobility from French history in *Qu'est-ce que le Tiers Etat?* His guiding vision here remained one of harmony between Third Estate, nobility, and monarchy, realized in the "mixed government" briefly established by Charlemagne.[71] Nevertheless, the cocoon of aristocratic exclusivism in which "ancient liberty" had been preserved now seems to have been punctured for the first time.

The second part of *Observations sur l'histoire de France* resumes the narrative from the end of the Carolingian period, when the fragmentation and dispersal of political sovereignty among the class of hereditary nobles was at its height. Mably recognized that for all of its faults, the "feudal government" was not pure anarchy. It was necessary to explain such structure and stability as feudalism was able to achieve—why it took so long, in other words, for this system to give way to a more regular authority. He thus sketches four specific "causes" that assured a minimum of political fixity for the *gouvernement féodal*: the harsh servitude imposed on the peasantry, which supplied the nobility with the economic power of a regular and growing income; the judicial authority the feudal lords wielded over their territories, which constituted their "political" power; the ability of the nobility to maintain private armies; and last, the relative equality of fortune among the nobles, which long prevented any one of them from dominating the rest.[72] The subsequent history of France, then, could be told through the very slow destruction or removal of these four constitutive elements of the feudal government, in a "flux and reflux of contrary revolutions." The first, most fundamental step was the gradual dissolution of serfdom, partly through royal sponsorship of towns outside the jurisdiction of the nobility, but mostly owing to the heedless willingness of the lords to "sell" their liberty to the peasantry.[73] The relative equality of the nobles was soon canceled as well, as the monarchy began to encourage a differentiation of rank, separating a higher peerage from the bulk of the aristocracy. The kings also gradually divested the lords of their exclusive exercise of justice, by extending an alternate royal judiciary all over France. Finally, during the ordeal of the great wars of the late medieval period, the nobles lost their right or ability to maintain private armies and surrendered to the growing military power of the crown.

All these developments tended in one direction only, for the economic, military, and political power of the feudal nobility eventually passed, in every instance, into the hands of the Capetian and Valois kings. This was of course precisely the outcome that Mably had praised in *Parallèle des romains et des français*, where he saw it as the deliberate achievement of a series of far-sighted and benevolent rulers, eager to unburden their subjects of the yoke of feudal "despotism." Mably's new account is very different. For now this great "revolution" appears as no more than the transfer of power from the microdespotisms of the feudal nobility to the macrodespotism of absolute monarchy:

> In fact, nothing was more absurd than to have an executive power prior to the establishment of a legislative branch. One needs laws before they can be obeyed: for without a legislator, nothing is fixed, and customs, which by their nature are always equivocal, uncertain, and wavering, will obey without resistance a thousand accidents and a thousand events, changing them without end.[74]

The Valois kings had been able to attain a complete monopoly of political power, but this had not freed them from the constraints imposed by a national "character" whose chief trait was "inattention." Their advent did not mark a rupture in the unhappy history of their country, but merely a repetition of the same problems, at a different level.

The great tragedy of this slide into despotism, in Mably's eyes, was that it was determined by no teleological necessity. Instead, it was the unintended consequence of a series of unforced errors on the part of the French. In order to explain this, Mably turns at this point in his narrative to some remarkable comparative considerations, which form the real centerpiece of the second volume of *Observations sur l'histoire de France.* These are made possible by the striking homogeneity of the "feudal government," whose basic shape, in Mably's view, was the same in every region of western Europe. First, there is the case of Germany, where the *gouvernement féodale* managed to acquire a stability and durability that it never possessed in France, evolving into a relatively benign form of federalism. Public authority never fully disappeared in Germany, since the meeting of Estates assemblies continued uninterrupted; the emperors were never able to mount a successful challenge to the power of the nobility, and the imperial seat remained an elective office. "A government that in France amounted to nothing more than uncertain and wavering customs, acquired a certain solidity in Germany. It was able to see to its needs, make beneficial adjustments according to circumstances, and establish a kind of equilibrium between the emperor and his vassals."[75]

What made the difference? Essentially, the blame lay with the French nobles themselves, who missed every opportunity to follow in the path of their German counterparts:

> The French were blind to the dangers that threatened their government, and took no steps to avoid them and to preserve their independence. Driven by the accident of events, and the fortune that governed them, they were simply unable to bring about the regulation of their customs that would have prevented the unification of seigneurial lands, or at least the greatest of them, under a single head.[76]

In effect, this was a failure of collective rationality—an inability to mount the cooperative effort it would have required to prevent the loss of their independence: "On the contrary, as jealous of each other as of the prince, and continually misled by vain hopes or by some fleeting present advantage, they did not grasp that on the posterity of each individual depended the safety of all."[77]

From Mably's point of view, of course, missing the German road to aristocratic federalism was perhaps not particularly to be regretted. The essential counterpoint to French history was provided by England, where the power of the feudal nobility had been broken, as it had in France, yet where the result was the eventual replacement of absolute monarchy by parliamentary self-government. Here Mably inserted in *Observations sur l'histoire de France* a brief précis of English history, drawn chiefly from Rapin de Thoiras, Hume, and Blackstone. The common stamp of Norman feudalism rendered English and French political development remarkably similar down to the turn of the thirteenth century; if anything, royal centralization went even further in England than in France in the Middle Ages. The decisive point of divergence between the two was reached in the reign of King John, when the English nobility seized the opportunity to impose a "fundamental law" on a momentarily weakened monarchy:

> He [John] wished to restore fear and respect to the authority he had degraded, and the united barons forced him to grant a charter that fixed in the most specific way the still uncertain and changeable freedoms of the nation. . . . These laws, so celebrated by the English, did not stop at

> establishing a temporary and provisional order. This was a fundamental law, intended to prevent abuses rather than to punish those who have committed them; by serving as a basis for the government, it affirmed its most basic principles.[78]

Here, as elsewhere in Mably's writing, "fundamental law" is the expression of sovereign will—or rather, a first attempt to establish sovereign authority, since English history by no means came to an "end" at this point. What the Magna Charta did, in Mably's view, was to provide the foundation for a long secular transition from royal-aristocratic to more democratic rule:

> If one compares the great charter to the political institutions of the ancients, or if one judges it according to the precepts that philosophers have laid down for the happiness of society, then much of it is apt to seem barbaric. Yet if one compares this law to the charters granted by other princes of the same epoch, in response to the complaints and threats of their vassals and subjects, then it is clear that the English were infinitely more advanced than their contemporaries in regard to knowledge of society. The English now began to consider the entire population of the nation, each of the parts of which formed a single whole. Elsewhere, different orders of citizens, still enemies to one another, failed to see the hidden connections that linked individual happiness to the happiness of all, and strove only to offend and to take offense; they gloried in winning separate and opposed privileges for themselves, which, since they tended only to divide the interests of all, could never acquire permanence and solidity.[79]

This process reached its climax, of course, in the seventeenth century, when the mutual contention of opposing religious and political factions threatened to tear the country apart. A permanent oscillation between anarchy and despotism might have been the result, if the English had not possessed the "anchor" of the Magna Charta:

> Citizens who were enlightened, or naturally more moderate, found in it the titles of their liberties, the rights of the crown, and the principles of a government that occupied a middle ground between the two factions and thus served to reconcile them. . . . In fact, the England of our day owes its existence to that same act that four centuries before had established the foundation of its liberty.[80]

Needless to say, Mably was never an uncritical admirer of the English constitution, in the manner, say, of Montesquieu. Indeed, his frequent criticisms of party factionalism and royal prerogative in England—in particular, what he saw as the Whig failure to reduce the power of the Crown once and for all on the occasion of the Hanoverian succession[81]—led Frances Acomb to rank Mably among the "anglophobe liberals" in her classic study of French attitudes toward England in the later part of the eighteenth century.[82] But this judgment is impossible to reconcile with the "Whig interpretation" of English history that Mably provides in *Observations sur l'histoire de France*—not to speak of the general attitude implied in the choice of "Stanhope" as his mouthpiece in *Des droits et des devoirs du citoyen.* For all of the distance that separated it from the standards established by the republican regimes of classical antiquity, the English constitution remained in Mably's eyes the most vital incarnation of "liberty" in the modern world. Above all, it provided Europe with tangible proof of the possibility of stable, post-absolutist self-government.

The English road had in fact been no less open to the French than the German had been, in Mably's view. The disasters of the first decades of the Hundred Years' War—the blows of Crécy, the Black Death, Poitiers, and the Regency that followed the capture of Jean-le-Bon—presented the French with precisely the same opportunity to rein in royal authority that the English had exploited a century and a half earlier. The famous Ordinances of the Estates of 1355 and 1356–57 were in fact a close equivalent to the Magna Charta, as an initial attempt to impose some legal limitations on royal prerogative.[83] Yet unlike the Great Charter, these documents remained a dead letter in French history:

> Among the two peoples, the princes attempted both to seize a limitless power, and the two nations each made their effort to throw off the yoke that was being imposed on them. The English and the French obtained, or rather gave themselves, the same rights and prerogatives. But why then are our two ordinances of 1355 and 1356 nothing more than a vain title for us, while the famous charter of King John, surviving every effort by avarice and ambition to destroy it, remains the basis for the present government of England?[84]

What was the explanation for this divergence? Here Mably turned to the Montesquieuean notion he had already introduced in *Observations sur l'histoire de France*, that of a specific "national character," which was itself the product of the earliest events and circumstances in the life of the nation. From the start, the central problem imposed on the French by geography and history was the "lack of a superior power," while in England, by contrast, it was rather the "weight of too great a power":

> There thus arose in the two nations different fears, desires, hopes—in a word, a different outlook. Since one experienced the misfortunes that arise from anarchy, and the other the abuses of arbitrary power, it was natural that the French hoped to erect an authority capable of restraining the license of feudal customs and favored its advances, while the English on the contrary wished to reduce this kind of unlimited power, which the prince could abuse with impunity. In this way a different political outlook and character formed in the two nations. They set opposite goals for themselves, and royal power, in the court of public opinion, was bound to make as much progress in France as liberty did in England.[85]

It was for this reason that the opportunity presented to the French in 1356–57 was lost. The momentary desire to reduce the authority of the king, embodied in the "Great Ordinance" of 1357, was more than overbalanced by a "national character" whose grain ran in the opposite direction entirely. The consequences of this failure, however, were dire:

> The English owe their present government to the charter of King John; in the most difficult times, after the most violent upheavals, they have had constant recourse to this law, as if it were their oracle. . . . It is because France, on the contrary, had no such fundamental law, consecrated by the esteem and respect of the nation, that it has been condemned to be guided at every step only by the interests of the moment. The French obeyed events without resistance, while the English struggled against their compulsion; thus, among one people the ruin of feudalism gave way to a monarchy, and among the other, a free government.[86]

The lesson of English history, then, is that the precondition to the recovery of liberty in the modern world was the establishment of a "fundamental law" in the medieval epoch—the historical kernel of a later constitutional order, to serve as "oracle" and "compass" in the struggle against absolutism. The weight of the "national character" was such in France that it deprived the nation of any equivalent "fundamental law" to serve as a barrier against royal centralization. Once the revived Valois monarchy emerged from the other side of the Hundred Years' War, it had little difficulty in reducing the Estates General to a docile instrument of monarchical rule, before eliminating it altogether to pave the way for Louis XIV.

After the Maupeou "Coup"

The two volumes of *Observations sur l'histoire de France* that Mably published in 1765 contained Books I–IV, taking the story down to the comparative reflections on Germany just considered.

Books V and VI, ending with the reign of Charles VIII, were apparently written by the mid-1760s as well. The final parts of the *Observations*, Books VII and VIII, were completed shortly thereafter, although Mably was still adding notes to his "Remarks and Proofs" as late as 1771. By this time, of course, the political climate of France had altered considerably, as a result of the constitutional "revolution" engineered by Maupeou and Terray.[87] As we have seen, the monarchy's attempt to impose conformity on the French clergy through persecution of Jansensim inaugurated, after 1751, a long period of parlementary opposition and obstructionism. The climax of the power and prestige of the *parlements* was reached in 1762, when the *parti janseniste* secured the expulsion of the Jesuit Order from France. By then, however, the government had already launched its counterattack on the fiscal front: the Parlement of Paris was powerless to prevent the doubling of the *vingtième* in 1756 and its trebling in 1760. When radical leadership passed from Paris to the provincial magistrates, the government was able successfully to remodel the *parlements* of Pau and Rennes in 1765. The prosecution of the intransigent governor of Brittany, d'Aiguillon, in 1770, which coincided with Maupeou's own power struggle with Choiseul, then provided the new Chancellor with the opportunity he needed. Beginning with the exile of the Parlement of Paris late in 1770, Maupeou was led, through a series of escalating improvisations, to a complete reorganization of the upper judiciary by the end of the following year. Among other things, the size of the magistrature was drastically reduced, a general streamlining and elimination of corruption imposed, and venality abolished. What most astonished contemporary observers was the ease with which Maupeou carried out his "coup," despite the loud and violent protests that attended it. To all appearances, the power of the *parlements*—the most cherished of Montesquieu's "intermediate powers"—had been utterly broken by a French absolutism suddenly restored to a vigor it had not known for decades. As it happened, the truth was otherwise. Despite the apparent success of Maupeou's "revolution," the government proved incapable of building on its success: no serious attempt to resolve the deepening fiscal crisis of the monarchy followed. At the accession of Louis XVI the judicial reforms were abandoned with the same ease that they were imposed, and the old *parlements* restored. By this point, of course, all "victories" in this dispute were pyrrhic ones. The irresolvable deadlock between monarchy and magistrature was soon to prove fatal to French absolutism.

Nevertheless, for most contemporary observers, the Maupeou "coup" remained a watershed in French political life—for none more so than Mably. Indeed, this was in many ways the critical event in his later intellectual career, propelling him into the deep pessimism that colors all the writings of the last decade of his life. The initial record of its impact on his outlook is contained in the concluding sections of *Observations sur l'histoire de France.* The main narrative of Books VII and VIII simply brings the story of the development of the monarchy to a close, traversing the difficult period of the sixteenth century, toward the climax of absolutism in the seventeenth, when the iron dictatorship of Richelieu paved the way for the gilded tyranny of Louis XIV. Two further national convulsions repeated the lesson of the Hundred Years' War at a lower loop down the spiral: the Religious Wars and the Fronde both appeared to present an opportunity for braking the decline into despotism, yet ended by advancing it. Thirty years earlier, in his first book, Mably had described the absolutism of Louis XIV as the masterpiece of modern politics, surpassing the achievements of the Roman imperial order itself, and he had predicted an "eternal duration" for it. Now he described the legacy of Versailles in these bitter terms:

> During a very long reign, Louis XIV presided over the formation of a new generation, which then passed its character on to its descendants. The nobility, the clergy, and the people all took on the same ideas. At the accession of Louis XV, the parlement recovered its right to discuss laws before their registration; but this was on condition of uncomplaining obedience—a right that can be lost and recovered, which one enjoys only precariously. The regency put the final seal on our degradation. We no longer believed in integrity; money and the most corrupt pleasures became our sovereign goods.[88]

As these lines reveal, however, the real object of Mably's attention had shifted in the final parts of the *Observations* from the monarchy itself to the *parlements* and to what he saw as their central contribution to the political abasement of the French nation. As Baker suggests, the parlementary magistrates, and not the monarchy, are the real "villains" of the latter half of *Observations sur l'histoire de France.*[89] From the outset, Mably argues, the *parlements* were creatures of royal convenience. The bureaucratic aristocracy that bought and sold its offices deliberately colluded with the monarchy in the elimination of the Estates General; the whole apparatus of registration and remonstrance was a cruel deception, whose purpose was not to limit or restrain royal authority so much as to safeguard it, by supplying it with the appearance of public approval. Here Mably came close to abandoning his claim that the main collective actors in French history were merely swept along by forces beyond their control. Instead, he conjures up the picture of a deliberate deal struck between the monarchy and a venal magistrature:

> This usurpation of the rights of the nation was not an error that one must attribute to ignorance or to some passing inattention. . . . In order to justify, if that were possible, its injustice, the *parlement* became accustomed to insisting that the right of taxation belongs to the prince alone.[90]

The *parlements,* in other words, were not the last defenders of "ancient liberty," but rather the instruments of its destruction:

> We are grateful for its remonstrances, its feeble and puerile instruments of resistance; we regard it as a plank after a shipwreck, without imagining that the Parlement itself was one of the principle causes of the disaster. Because it offers the endless repetition of a theater of resistance, we go on hoping that it will one day triumph over evil; our eternal inattention prevents us from judging the future by the past.[91]

In his "Remarks and Proofs" Mably thus unsurprisingly trained all of his critical attention on the work that had served as the central historical apology for the *parlements* since the mid-1750s, Le Paige's *Lettres historiques,* attacking it at such length that he finally had to apologize to his readers:

> I am sorry to have devoted so many pages to my refutation of the *Lettres historiques.* But it was necessary, because it presents the whole doctrine concocted by the Parlement since its respect and authority grew with the total elimination of the Estates General. Besides, this work has been so popular, and its author been regarded as such an oracle, that it is important not to let its errors take root.[92]

The main object of his critical wrath, naturally, was Le Paige's attempt to create the illusion of continuity through the centuries, as if the "fundamental laws" of the monarchy had never been altered since the days of the "first race": "One must be thoroughly enchanted," Mably comments with evident impatience, "to see the principles of our present government in the Salic or Riparian laws, the capitularies of Charlemagne, or even in the edicts of Saint Louis."[93] In the end, however, it was the contemporary performance of the *parlements* that gave the lie to the historical picture confected by Le Paige and the other parlementary apologists. Invoking a Tacitean imagery, Mably declared that it was the *coup de main* of Maupeou that finally destroyed the illusion and revealed once and for all the "the imperial secret":

> The veil has been torn away by the revolution that the royal magistrature has experienced in our days. The Chancellor Maupeou has broken the chain linking the doctrine and the ambition of the parlements. He has

> shown that these bodies lacked the strength that we attributed to them. He has demonstrated a great truth for us: that any order of citizens who favor despotism in the hopes of sharing it with the prince, is in fact digging its own grave and bringing a storm down on its head.[94]

For once, Mably found himself in agreement with Voltaire. His own final judgments on the *parlements* were only slightly less caustic than the latter's in his *Histoire du Parlement de Paris*, published in 1769.[95] But their reasons were very different. Voltaire's hostility had been fueled by the Calas and La Barre cases, and he welcomed the constitutional "revolution" as the prelude to long-awaited reforms of the French monarchy "from above." For Mably, on the other hand, the "coup" meant the end of the heroic period of parlementary agitation that had begun at mid-century, and with this vanished any prospects for a genuine revolution "from below."

The brief conclusion to *Observations sur l'histoire de France* thus contains passages that are among the bitterest ever written by Mably. The entire history of the nation, he insisted, was the record of the successive attempts of one social class to found its own wealth and power at the expense of another. But these efforts were all in vain:

> One order simply cannot maintain a constant condition for itself by attempting to oppress another. The result is continually fruitless efforts, an endlessly uncertain conduct, a lack of fixed interests and of steadfast character, and unceasing revolutions—of which our historians, however, never speak. Always governed by accidents, events, and passions, we have at length lost all respect for our laws.[96]

This was French history rewritten as republican nightmare, as a Polybian cycle of unwilled and irresistible change, until coming to rest in the full stop of despotism. The remote example of Charlemagne, and the more proximate one of England, were there to demonstrate at least the *possibility* of another outcome. But the weight of a "national character" built up over so many centuries made change of any sort ever more unlikely:

> Great nations never act with forethought. They are pushed and pulled, restrained and agitated, by a kind of interest that is merely the result of the habits they have contracted. This national character is a weight that drags everything along with it.[97]

Despite the political ferment of the mid-eighteenth century, "we are without any principle of revolution of our own." None of the three orders of the nation, in other words, possessed either the power or the disposition to offer any resistance to absolutism. Both the clergy and the nobility had long since concluded a separate peace with the monarchy, separating their "interests" from those of the "nation" as a whole. "The nobility," in particular, "are persuaded that it is in their interest to have an absolute master."[98] The great fear of the nobility had been that to oppose the monarchy in the name of a free government would lead to a loss of their own social power—a tragic error, Mably insisted, since the example of England and Sweden demonstrated that a landowning aristocracy would benefit rather than suffer from the placing of constitutional constraints on royal power. As for the Third Estate, Mably described its status in terms virtually identical to those that Sieyès was to make famous two decades later: "The third estate is nothing in France, because no one wishes to belong to it. . . . The people is in effect merely that part of the population that is without credit, respect, fortune, and that can do nothing for itself."[99] The *parlements*, lastly, had performed the function of keeping the very *idea* of a constitutional order alive and before the public, even if they added almost nothing to its reality. But now they too had succumbed to the blandishments of absolutism. Barring some unforeseen national catastrophe, Mably could see no way to undo the knot that had been tied in the course of French history. He thus concluded his book with a melancholy prophecy. Unless the grip of royal despotism could be broken, the future of France was to be seen in the misery of its Iberian neighbor. The Spanish Monarchy, once the mightiest power of Europe, had been reduced a century before to a weak and decadent giant, unable even to defend its borders against its freer and more energetic adversaries. Mably already perceived in France the signs of

> that despotism that everywhere brings misery and poverty, which are accompanied in turn by discouragement, corruption, meanness, and a spirit of servitude—the unmistakable symptoms of decadence, and the signs of an inevitable ruin, once a formidable enemy appears at one's door.[100]

The conclusion to *Observations sur l'histoire de France* was not quite Mably's last word on French history and politics. Despite his conviction that the nation no longer contained "any principle of revolution," he monitored the final efforts at ministerial reform in France with a kind of fascinated exasperation, convinced of their uselessness, but unable to ignore them. Mably's valedictory observations on the French political scene came a decade after the Maupeou "coup." Their occasion was the Swiss banker Jacques Necker's innovative tenure as finance minister during the American War, which came to an abrupt end in the spring of 1781. A few months earlier, Necker had galvanized public opinion in France by publishing his famous *Compte rendu au roi*, in which he claimed not only to have financed a major war without recourse to new taxation, but actually to have produced a *surplus* of revenue while doing so. This self-advertisement—not incidentally the first exposure of royal finances to public scrutiny—naturally unleashed a storm of controversy.[101] Mably's own response was a brief dialogue, left unpublished at his death, recording a conversation with an aristocratic acquaintance who is scandalized by the effrontery of this "Genevan petit-bourgeois." Mably first teases his friend by praising Necker's achievement as finance minister, declaring his confidence in the essential accuracy of the calculations of the *Compte rendu*. Then, in a sobering about-face, he expresses his fears that having acquired so large a reputation, Necker will one day become prime minister—a disaster for France, since the Genevan shows every sign of a willingness to devote his considerable skills to the irrational and self-defeating purposes of monarchical "despotism."[102]

Necker had in fact already overreached himself politically. He was dismissed in May 1781, partly as a result of his ongoing experimentation with provincial assemblies. Although he had already issued a promise to say nothing further on the subject, Mably now wrote a follow-up dialogue to *Le compte rendu*, in which he repeated the dire predictions of the conclusions to *Observations sur l'histoire de France*. Necker would indeed return to power one day as prime minister, but not before the debt accumulated from useless warfare—of which the proxy war being fought against the British in America was a prime example—would sink the monarchy in a fatal bankruptcy and abasement before its enemies. "I am in my seventy-third year," Mably writes, "and death will overtake me before I am witness to all the misfortunes that I am afraid posterity is preparing for us." He then announces his resolve to refrain from further comment on political matters, not sparing himself some harsh words. "You are very wise," he tells his interlocutor in *La retraite de M. Necker*,

> never to have dwelt on what makes for the happiness or unhappiness of nations. For you, this world is simply a comedy. In the fall of ministers, you see only them and their fate, and you laugh at the intrigues that drive the comedy forward to its ridiculous end. But for me—cursed Greeks, cursed Romans, how bitter it is to have studied in your successes, your disgraces, and your revolutions, the sure signs by which one can measure the different degrees of decadence that finally bring a people to certain ruin. . . . I have promised, my dear friend,

never to talk politics with you again, and I have broken my promise—but this will be the last time.[103]

There is, of course, a poignant irony in Mably's final writing on France. He died in April 1785. Slightly over a year later, the gathering fiscal crisis he described in *Le compte rendu* and *La retraite de M. Necker* was officially acknowledged by the monarchy, which attempted to rescue itself by means of a series of convulsive and increasingly desperate reforms. Within a year, these had in turn provoked a grave constitutional crisis, as the ministries of Calonne and Loménie de Brienne collided frontally with a newly combative Parlement of Paris, whose calls for a convocation of the Estates General now mobilized public opinion on an unprecedented scale. In August 1788, the monarchy surrendered to its fate. A meeting of the Estates General, the first in nearly two centuries, was scheduled for May 1789; in the meantime, a caretaker government was formed under the leadership of—Jacques Necker. All of this proceeded more or less exactly according to script—Mably's own script for a French Revolution, set down nearly thirty years earlier in *Des droits et des devoirs du citoyen.* Indeed, as we saw in the first chapter, Mably himself made a decisive contribution to the political ferment of the "prerevolution" of 1787–89: the clairvoyant *Droits et devoirs du citoyen* was itself published for the first time, while the full text of *Observations sur l'histoire de France* probably contributed more than any other work to fixing the historical self-understanding of the Revolution of 1789. Yet Mably himself had gone to his grave in a mood of bitter pessimism, having concluded that a revolutionary transformation of the political regime, on the model of the English revolutions a century earlier, was no longer possible in France—Spanish decadence was a more accurate mirror of the future. Despite his own insight into the dire state of French finances, Mably failed to see that a fiscal crisis could issue directly into the sort of constitutional revolution he had predicted and called for years before.

What accounts for the excessive pessimism of Mably's final years, which seems to have blunted his own skills at political prognostication? As we shall see in the next chapter, this somber mood had more than one source. But everything suggests that it was Maupeou's *coup de main* against the magistracy in 1771 that decisively and permanently punctured Mably's earlier optimism. He lived for another decade and a half, but his political judgment seems never fully to have recovered its equilibrium: Mably never altered his belief that the last great opportunity for a "*révolution ménagée*" in France—a last chance to join the thin ranks of "free governments" in Europe—had been passed up at some point between 1751 and 1771. A revolution of this sort depended wholly on the convocation of an Estates General. For two decades, it had been just barely possible to imagine that parlementary resistance might lead to the resurrection of the Estates—Stanhope's basic proposal in *Des droits et des devoirs du citoyen*. But with the Maupeou "coup" any prospect of such an outcome seemed permanently to have vanished. In effect, both his study of French history in *Observations sur l'histoire de France* and the course of events in French political life after 1758 appears to have led Mably to adopt the pessimistic judgment of the Frenchman in *Des droits et des devoirs*—that Stanhope's plan for a "*révolution ménagée*" was a chimera, totally unsuited to the French context. In the event, of course, both characters in the dialogue had their point. Stanhope's optimism was a brilliant premonition of the actual origins of the French Revolution; the Frenchman's pessimism was a no less impressive augury of the convulsions and reversals of the revolutionary process, once it was unleashed—of everything that would separate 1789 and its sequels from 1688 in European history.

CHAPTER 7

Last Works: Constitutions and the Consolation of Philosophy

As it happened, however, the Maupeou "coup" was not the only blow to Mably's political optimism as he entered the final phase of his intellectual career. We noted earlier the high regard Mably had for the parliamentary regime of eighteenth-century Sweden, which he believed to be superior in every respect to the British Monarchy admired by so many of his contemporaries. The curbs on royal prerogative that inaugurated the "Age of Liberty," the separate representation accorded the peasantry in the Swedish Diet, the high level of commercial regulation and conspicuous sumptuary laws—all these prompted Mably to describe Sweden's constitutional settlement of 1720–21 as the "masterpiece of modern legislation."[1] However, in the very years of Maupeou's reconstruction of the French judiciary, events suddenly conspired to deprive Mably's Swedish model of much of its force. By the end of the 1760s, the party equilibrium that sustained the "Age of Liberty" had collapsed, and mounting political chaos then set the stage for the restoration of royal authority by the francophile heir to the throne, who succeeded in February 1771. Gustavus III ended the "Age of Liberty" with a bloodless coup in August 1772 and proceeded to the reconstruction of a modernized Swedish absolutism. Philosophic opinion in France was nearly unanimous in its approval for the Swedish variant of "enlightened despotism." Voltaire and the physiocrats, in particular, launched an enthusiastic propaganda campaign on its behalf. There was, however, one notable holdout among French philosophers—Mably, who in fact threatened to publish a book denouncing the coup d'état. "The King of Sweden can change his country," the abbé grandly declared, "but he will not change my book." The threat was never carried out, but Mably remained stubbornly convinced that the Swedes, dazzled by the mirage of British economic power, had needlessly surrendered their political liberty.

For all of his disappointment over Sweden, however, the real test of Mably's hopes for political reform outside of France lay elsewhere. This chapter begins by looking at two central episodes of the last phase of his intellectual career, as Mably turned his attention to experiments in state construction at opposite ends of the European world. The first of these was Poland, which had itself entered a period of intense political agitation in the late 1760s—the death-throes of the state, as it turned out. Mably was the first French thinker to respond to the invitations for reform proposals issued by the gentry Confederation of Bar, once it had raised the banner of anti-Russian and anti-absolutist revolt at the end of the decade. His *Du gouvernement et des lois de la Pologne* of 1771 in turn helped to inspire Rousseau's famous contribution to the "patriot" cause, *Considérations sur le gouvernement de Pologne.* The First Partition of Poland, which was consummated in 1772 at the exact moment of the restoration of absolutism in Sweden, deprived these texts of their original purpose. But Mably did not lose interest in Poland. He made a long visit there in 1776–77, the only excursion outside French borders of his lifetime, which prompted a further set of writings; and he went on to publish his initial text on Poland in 1781. By this point, of course, another experiment in state-making had been launched on the other side of the globe, which promised a far happier outcome than the Polish. Responding to the polite suggestion of his American friend John Adams, Mably produced a brief commentary on the state constitutions of Pennsylvania, Massachusetts, and Georgia. Published in 1784, *Observations sur le gouvernement et les lois des Etats-Unis d'Amérique* provoked a storm of controversy, as much for the circumstances of its writing as for its content. At all events, these writings on Poland and the United States form a fascinating set, not merely for the poignant contrast between Polish and American circumstances, but also for the retrospective light they cast on Mably's political thought as a whole. Together, they provided in many ways a more lucid and sober estimation of the prospects and difficulties of political reform than Mably had been able to achieve in regard to France itself.

The Polish Tragedy

Among the series of events that shook or destroyed the European Old Regime in the last decades of the eighteenth century, none was more surprising and dramatic than the complete disappearance of an independent Polish state in the three "partitions" of 1772, 1792, and 1795. Poland had long since been marked out for a separate fate in European history.[2] Descending from the union of the medieval Kingdom of Poland and the Grand Duchy of Lithuania in 1378, the Polish Commonwealth reached the peak of its political and cultural fortunes at the end of the sixteenth century, in defiance of all the ordinary rules of early modern statecraft. Its wealth, and the lack of potent enemies on its borders, permitted the Polish nobility, or *szlachta*, to dispense with the centralization of royal authority that tended to be a historical necessity for other agrarian aristocracies of the epoch. The political regime over which it presided was a baroque confederation of heterogeneous territorial units, united under a bicameral national Diet, or Sejm; by 1577, the monarchy had been rendered definitively elective, and was never to regain political potency in Polish history. There was, however, a price to be paid for the aristocratic "liberty" of the *szlachta*. The seventeenth-century crisis arrived in Poland in the form of the Ukrainian Rebellion of 1648, followed by the Swedish invasion of 1655, which together devastated the economy and produced a grave demographic collapse. There was a temporary recovery of international influence and prestige under the famous warrior-king Jan Sobieski toward the end of the century, but no alteration in the basic political structure of the commonwealth followed. The Great Northern War, which turned Poland into a battlefield for Sweden and Russia, thus came as a second great national catastrophe, leaving further economic decline and demographic regression in its wake. The political result was the Treaty of Warsaw of 1717, which in effect made Poland a Russian protectorate. Down to 1764, the foreground of local politics was dominated by the fierce rivalry of two great native "clans," the Potockis, who tended to act as "patriot" defenders of the aristocratic constitution, and the Czartoryskis, who emerged as pro-Russian advocates of an enhanced royal authority. But the realities of Polish politics were henceforth determined elsewhere, in St. Petersburg, Berlin, and Paris.

The era of the partitions arrived with the election of Stanislaus Poniatowski, former lover of Catherine II, as king in 1763. Poniatowski was linked to the Czartoryski faction, and his initial cautious moves toward political reform—administrative and fiscal centralization, rejuvenation of the Polish army—soon provoked local aristocratic resistance, as well as a mobilization of Russian troops in Poland. The immediate occasion for direct foreign intervention was then provided by the nation's diverse religious map: while the *szlachta* as a whole was staunchly Roman Catholic, there were sizable Protestant and Orthodox minorities in the West and the East (as well as the largest Jewish population in Europe). Prussian and Russian intervention on behalf of these groups led to the forcing of a scheme for full religious toleration on the Diet early in 1768. This last move unleashed civil war. A large section of the *szlachta*, including both magnates and petty nobles, proclaimed the General Confederation of Bar (a small fortress-town in Podolia) in late February and raised the banner of "patriotic" revolt—in the name of "Freedom and the Church"—against both the Russians and Poniatowski. The machinery of international diplomacy wasted no time in widening the conflict beyond Polish borders: the French, in particular, secured a Turkish declaration of war against Russia, which prolonged the conflict beyond anything that could have been achieved by Polish resistance alone. It was only after a string of Russian victories two years later—especially the spectacular destruction of a Turkish fleet in the eastern Mediterranean in 1771—that secret negotiations between Russia, Prussia, and Austria could produce the First Partition. Its terms were announced in August 1772: at a stroke, Poland lost 30 percent of its territory and 35 percent of its population, as Russia annexed White Russia, Austria Galicia, and Prussia all of West Prussia and the Baltic coast.

In the meantime, the Polish rebellion itself had naturally become the occasion for intense debate among the intelligentsia of Western Europe.[3] At the outset, the reformist aspirations of Poniatowski aroused a good deal of sympathy among Western *philosophes*, particularly in Great Britain. Poniatowski and the Czartoryskis, in fact, were admirers of British constitutionalism, and their first moves seemed to promise an evolution in the direction of a constitutional monarchy in Poland on the British model: this was in effect the recommendation of the major English contribution to the debate, John Lind's *Letters concerning the present state of Poland*, published in 1773. Commentary in France, on the other hand, was dominated by Voltaire, for whom, unsurprisingly, the central issue was not political but religious liberty. The partnership of Poniatowski and Catherine II promised a new era of toleration in the East, and Voltaire devoted a good deal of energy to its promotion, in a flood of published pamphlets and private correspondence. The outbreak of the war, forcing the Polish king and the Russian empress apart, did little to change Voltaire's sympathies: his support for Catherine II persisted into the 1770s, despite official French sponsorship of the Confederation and the fact of the First Partition itself. This view continued to have a wide resonance among Enlightened opinion in France. These were also the years of Diderot's propagandizing on behalf of Eastern "enlightened despotism," which also had its attractions for a whole range of physiocratic opinion.

Intellectual support abroad for the Confederation of Bar and for the "patriot" camp in general was far slower to mobilize—hardly a surprise, given the thoroughly reactionary cast of traditional Polish "republicanism." That such support was eventually to emerge was owing chiefly to the efforts of Count Michal Wielhorski, who arrived in Paris early in 1770 as the emissary of the Confederation, armed with a library of "patriot" propaganda. A member of the petty Lithuanian nobility, Wielhorski was well placed to build bridges between the Polish conservatives and their potential sympathizers in the West: while his "patriotic" credentials were impeccable, he was also a well-informed admirer of Western political thought, who could cite Grotius, Locke, and Montesquieu with authority.[4] In Paris, Wielhorski was able to call upon the services of Claude Carlomane de Rulhière, who acted as the indispensable intermediary in his contacts with French thinkers. Rulhière's *Anecdotes*, which arose from his military-diplomatic career in the East and which fixed the image of the Russian court for the later eighteenth century, had already made his fame; at the outbreak of the Polish conflict he was back in Paris, working for Choiseul and drafting his own contribution to the debate, which was only published some forty years later—the famous *Histoire de l'anarchie de Pologne*. It was almost certainly Rulhière who put Wielhorski in contact with Jean-Jacques Rousseau: in Jean Fabre's view, the latter was probably persuaded to undertake his own response to the Confederation's invitation for reform proposals by early autumn 1770.[5] As for Mably, Rulhière was in fact a close friend of his, and it seems quite likely that he played a role in bringing the abbé into contact with Wielhorski as well. But we lack any specific knowledge of the date or means of Mably's involvement with the Confederation—except to note that it clearly predated that of Rousseau by some time. The work eventually published as *Du gouvernement et des lois de la Pologne* was written in two distinct parts, each addressed to Wielhorski; the first, and by far the more substantial of the two, was completed by 31 August 1770.

Mably's text was thus the earliest major French comment on the

Polish crisis, written at the moment that the military fortunes of the Confederation of Bar were probably at their peak. Mably's opening move, in fact, is to remind Wielhorski of the exigencies of the military situation facing the Confederation in 1770. The success of any effort to reform the Polish Republic depended upon nothing less than a complete Russian defeat in the present war and the total elimination of Russian influence in Polish domestic politics—a goal that Mably mistakenly believed was brought within reach by Turkish entry into the conflict.[6] At the same time, Mably continues, the fruits of military victory would be in vain if the Confederates had not already put into effect a comprehensive plan for restructuring the Republic, one that addressed the deepest roots of political disorder in Poland. Here Mably provides a brief sketch of Polish political history, which narrows to a focus on the two most famous features of the Polish constitution, whose final institutionalization dated from the later seventeenth century. The first is the notorious *liberum veto*, which bound deputies to the Sejm to mandates from local assemblies or dietines, and which imposed a rule of unanimity on the Sejm itself, such that it could be dissolved with a single negative vote—with paralyzing results, of course. The second is the recourse to "confederations," extraordinary assemblies operating outside the boundaries of established constitutional procedure—of which the Confederation of Bar itself was a prime example. There was nothing original in the choice of these objects of criticism: scandal over the *liberum veto* in particular was a staple of all commentary on Poland. But Mably hastens to add that these constitutional devices were not the primary causes of political weakness, but rather its symptoms. The deeper problem is simply the lack of any constitutional order proper, a kind of political vacuum at the center of the state.

The bulk of the first part of *Du gouvernement et des lois de la Pologne* is thus devoted to sketching a blueprint for a new constitutional order in Poland, designed to restore political power to its proper sphere and definition. Mably's basic recommendations are threefold. First, and foremost, there is the problem of legislative power, which at the time was shared among the two houses of the Diet and the king, producing the political paralysis of which the *liberum veto* was only the most salient symptom. The solution, Mably argues, is to situate full sovereign authority, once and for all, in a single legislative assembly, whose members would be drawn from and elected by the mass of the nobility as a whole—from the "equestrian class" alone, in other words.[7] A host of specifications follows: a rigorous periodicity and locale for the convocation of the Diet should be established, and any limits on the duration of its sitting removed; its representatives, meeting specific age and property qualifications, should be elected in equal numbers from the thirty-three provinces or "palatinates" of the Republic; voting in the Diet would take place by palatinate rather than by head, requiring the organization of each provincial delegation as a deliberative committee; and the *liberum veto* should be abolished, but not all at once—the first step would be to reduce its frequency by fighting fire with fire, and requiring unanimity *within* each palatinate before it could be invoked.[8] Finally, the placement of full legislative sovereignty in the general Diet means stripping the myriad local assemblies or dietines of the powers they currently possess: the dietines would continue to elect the representatives of each palatinate, but any species of binding mandate would disappear, together with the operation of the *liberum veto* at this level.[9] Where does this concentration of legislative authority in the hands of the general Diet leave executive power? Mably's second proposal is to dismantle the existing ministerial system, in which the main posts were held for life, replacing it with a new "Senate," reconstituted as an executive body: senators, meeting elevated age and property qualifications, would be elected for specific terms by the general Diet; the senate itself would be organized into four main administrative committees, made up of rotating "counselors" and presided over by more experienced "ministers." What role, finally, does this leave for a king? Mably's last proposal is not only to retain the monarchy, but also to render it definitively hereditary—a suggestion he knew was anathema to much of his Patriot audience, but which, he insists, is absolutely necessary if the monarchy were to serve as the visible symbol of a novel political stability and continuity in Poland. At the same time, the powers of the king should be entirely symbolic and ceremonial—rigorously excluded from the slightest involvement in even executive power.[10]

Such was Mably's advice to the Confederation of Bar, beyond the practical necessity of resistance to the Russians—in effect, a major remodeling of the constitution, at once concentrating political power at the center and dispersing it in an elaborate conciliar apparatus. For all its sweep, however, this reform program confined itself to constitutional matters, as they pertained to the *szlachta* alone. This left a number of ancillary issues, which Mably then pursued in a set of four concluding chapters, devoted to the administrative "departments" of the executive Senate. In regard to judicial matters, above all the monopolization of legal offices by the nobility, Mably counsels a prudent caution: if abandonment of this monopoly would be necessary in the long run, for the moment the reformers should confine themselves to reducing the juridical influence of the Church, and perhaps permitting bourgeois participation in the nomination of legal magistrates. Mably is bolder in regard to the *Conseil de Police* he projects: if the time was not yet ripe for the "full glory of the Roman censor," the Council of Police should nevertheless be charged with both systematic educational reform, designed to end the dismal reign of "superstition" over Polish minds and morals, and—it will come as no surprise—a meticulous commercial regulation along Swedish lines.[11] As for the third department, the Council of War, here Mably insists—with striking emphasis and energy—on the necessity of bringing the "military revolution" home to Poland, making the ancient martial vocation of the *szlachta* an up-to-date reality.[12] "Perhaps you will tell me," he admits to Wielhorski, "that it is quite surprising for a person of my background to dare to talk war with you at such length." But it is absolutely necessary:

> If the Poles truly wish to be free and to defend their freedom from both the efforts of domestic enemies and the injuries of foreigners, then they must become a military nation. I am deeply convinced that despite the wisest efforts to secure the empire of law and to prevent the advance of arbitrary power, a people will always fall into slavery at last, if each citizen does not believe himself destined to be a soldier as well.[13]

The question of finance and taxation, finally, brings Mably to the thorniest point of all: the necessity of extending participation in the Polish "nation" beyond the nobility proper. This, too, is not a reform for today, under the pressure of military emergency—but it cannot be put off indefinitely. In the long run, this of course means the abolition of serfdom and enfranchisement of the peasantry. But this had to be preceded by an even more pressing short-term goal, the restoration of rights of ownership and self-government to the inhabitants of Polish towns:

> Without that class of men known elsewhere under the name of bourgeois or third-estate, you will never know any industry, and you will lack even the most basic and necessary arts. In fact, it is only in this intermediary class that there develops the genius that too great or too miserable a fortune stifles in other citizens.[14]

Here too Mably finds it necessary, in light of his own reputation as a critic of "commercial society," to warn Wielhorski that he means what he says:

> You will not hesitate to tell me that you are extremely surprised at the doctrine I am preaching; for you are well accustomed to hear me attack commerce, and often in a very harsh manner. But I have the honor of replying that commerce is necessary among all peoples who are not savages and who wish to emerge from barbarism. In fact, I will even praise it when, without excess and without luxury, it serves simple needs and does not stir up our passions.[15]

This measured recommendation on behalf of bourgeois commerce and industry does indeed strike a new note in Mably's writing—a point to which we will return below. But it is consonant with the spirit of his advice to the Confederation as a whole. The dominant tone of *Du gouvernement et des lois de la Pologne* is one of pragmatic realism, focused narrowly on the immediate goal of securing Polish independence: for this end, Mably was perfectly willing to countenance measures—hereditary monarchy and economic "modernization"—that were otherwise unattractive to him.

Du gouvernement et des lois de la Pologne appears to have been the first Western response to Wielhorski's solicitation. Copies of the manuscript were distributed among the leadership of the Confederation of Bar in the fall of 1770; a number of written comments were then collected by Wielhorski and returned to Mably for a further response in the spring of 1771. In the meantime, Mably's text was among the documentation that Wielhorski bestowed upon Jean-Jacques Rousseau, once the latter had been persuaded to address the Polish crisis. On Jean Fabre's estimation, the composition of *Considérations sur le gouvernement de Pologne* was complete by April 1771. What was Rousseau's advice to the Confederation of Bar? The *Considérations* is a very different kind of text from that of Mably—indeed, the contrast between the two could hardly be greater. We have seen that Mably opens his writing with a reminder of the dire military situation facing the Confederation, which made the sweeping political centralization he advocated a matter of the highest urgency. Rousseau, by contrast, begins with a warning against any incautious tampering with a constitution that had evolved over so long a period. Instead, evoking the names of the three greatest "lawgivers" of antiquity, Moses, Lycurgus, and Numa Pompilius, Rousseau advocates what is in effect an *ideological* solution to the Polish dilemma:

> For the moment, I see only one way to give Poland the stability it now lacks: that is, to infuse, in a sense, the entire nation with the spirit of the confederates, and to establish the Republic in the hearts of the Poles, such that it will survive within them despite every effort of its oppressors. . . .

> If you see to it that a Pole can never become a Russian, then I guarantee that Russia will never subjugate Poland.[16]

The centerpiece of Rousseau's reform proposal is thus not a constitutional blueprint, of the kind offered by Mably, but rather a sketch for a national system of *education*, which had one central goal above all: "By the age of twenty, a Pole must not be any other kind of man: he must be a Pole."[17]

At the same time, the *Considérations sur le gouvernement de Pologne* does not lack for suggestions in the areas of politics and economics. But these, too, are as distant as they could be from the proposals of Mably. The key political problem in Poland, in the eyes of the latter, was a vacuum of sovereign authority in the state, the solution for which was to be found in a drastic centralization of power, under the aegis of a durable hereditary monarchy. Rousseau, by contrast, declaring that the "radical vice" of all modern governments was their excessive size, urges the Poles to engage in a preemptive partition of their own country and to yield territory before any one else can take it; failing that, he advises not centralization, but a reinvigoration of Polish *federalism*—breaking up the unitary state, parceling power out from the central Diet to local assemblies, and imposing strict mandates on delegates from these to the national Diet.[18] Economically, Mably urged the Poles, quite against the grain of his own thought, to adopt a program of modernization, promoting local industry and foreign commerce. Rousseau instead argues for a closing down of all economic contact with the external world, committing Poland to a kind of deindustrialization and agricultural autarchy. He then closes the *Considérations* with two further proposals, again at the antipodes from those of Mably. One is for an elaborate system of social ranking and promotion according to a schedule of public education and examination—described in astonishing detail, right down to the public costumes to be worn by the new Polish mandarinate.[19] Rousseau's final proposal directly reverses Mably's advice in regard to the Polish monarchy. Declaring that a hereditary monarchy would lead directly to a permanent tyranny in Poland, Rousseau instead sets forth a scheme for the periodic selection of nonhereditary Polish kings, by means of a complicated combination of election and sortition.[20] Both of these final proposals are presented as deliberately speculative and fanciful—and both consciously gestured back to Graeco-Roman models.

There is little doubt that Rousseau's *Considérations* is the one great masterpiece to have emerged from the debate over Poland. In effect, the peculiar circumstances of the Polish situation—where a national community risked extinction under the hammer of "partition"—seemed to have spurred Rousseau into a last, brilliant development of the key themes of his political thought. The result is what his editor Jean Fabre, happily echoing a later title by Barrès, has called the "first novel of national energy"—the earliest meditation on the ideological power of *nationalism* in the modern world. The price of Rousseau's extraordinary precocity, however, was a considerable abstraction from the actual realities of the Polish dilemma, not to mention the practical needs of the Confederation of Bar in 1770–71. Rousseau himself apologizes for his lack of research: Poland and its travails were far more the occasions for his *Considérations* than their true objects. This perhaps explains why Mably, who continued to focus his energies on the ongoing Polish struggle for independence, seems not to have taken the full measure of Rousseau's text when he responded to comments on his own proposals in the spring of 1771—if he saw the *Considérations* at this time at all. Instead, the shorter second part of *Du gouvernement et des lois de la Pologne*, dated 9 July 1771, is addressed chiefly to critics belonging to the Confederation of Bar, many of whom had fled to exile in Hungary. In a set of short chapters, Mably defends his critique of the Polish constitution, his suggestions in regard to the *liberum veto* and confederations, and above all his proposal for a hereditary monarchy, which was naturally offensive to "patriot" sensibilities. His chief interlocutor here seems to be Wielhorski himself, a diehard opponent of hereditary kingship, on both principled and pragmatic grounds; indeed, when Wielhorski published his own political testament in Polish in 1775, he boasted that the eminent French philosopher had finally conceded this argument to him.[21] At all events, the coda to *Du gouvernement et des lois de la Pologne* is a good deal more somber than the first part of the text. The military fortunes of the Confederation of Bar had looked fair enough a year earlier, but had suffered a series of serious blows in April and May 1771. Mably concludes his remarks with a grave plea to the Confederation to do more to cultivate its ties with the foreign powers on whom its fate, and that of Polish independence, now depended.

His anxieties were well-founded, of course, given the ease with which the Russian army wound up its military operations against the Confederation of Bar, paving the way for the First Partition in August 1772. General political and social anarchy persisted for some time after this. It took two more years to bring the war with Turkey to a successful conclusion, and it was only in 1775 that Russian political tutelage was firmly reestablished in Poland. In the meantime, Mably by no means lost interest in the country and its fate. He maintained his ties with Wielhorski, and it was in response to the latter's invitation that he left France for the one and only time in his life, to make a long visit to Poland in 1776–77. What did he find there? He left a vivid record of his impressions in two informal dialogues addressed to a Parisian friend. In the first, *Le banquet des politiques*, Mably describes his keen pleasure in discovering the extent of his own reputation in Germany, above all as the author of *Le droit public de l'Europe*. Pleasure turned to dismay, however, with his arrival at Krakow, where for the first time he came face to face with Polish social backwardness and economic misery: "On crossing from Silesia into Poland, I thought I had entered Tartary—what roads, what villages, what poverty! An unhappy republic, I told myself a hundred times over, is as miserable as an unhappy monarchy." Above all, he was surprised by the Poles themselves: "Here I began to see the Poles up close and to understand how different they are from the way they were described to me in Paris. The more deceived I was, the more ashamed I became at my credulity."[22] He goes on to describe an uncomfortable dinner party, at which he is hectored, in turn, by an opinionated Saxon general, a reactionary petty noble, and his host, a foolish and vacillating ex-minister of the Polish republic. The three disagree violently among themselves, but they share a common myopia and self-absorption that defeat Mably's every effort at argumentation. "But where have they fled," the abbé asks an acquaintance, once he has made his escape, "those republicans, those noble souls, those confederates who risked everything in order to defend the independence of their republic?" "Apparently," replies his sarcastic friend, "the Russians have killed them all."[23]

Mably's apparent condescension toward the Poles in *Le banquet des politiques* need not be taken too seriously. The overall tone of the dialogue is one of irony and playfulness, together with more than a hint of self-mockery.[24] But Mably clearly had decided that he had overestimated the talents and abilities of the Confederation of Bar in his earlier constitutional proposals. But what of his host, the leading intellectual light of the Confederation in the eyes of the West? *De la situation politique de la Pologne en 1776* records a conversation between Wielhorski himself and Mably. Its occasion is the announcement of the establishment of the new "Permanent Council" in Warsaw, which assumed the main executive functions of the Republic—under Russian direction—after 1775. For Wielhorski, this signals not only the end of the turmoil that flowed in the wake of the recent rebellion, but also a new opportunity for reform and perhaps for the restoration of Polish independence. Mably demurs: the price for the end of anarchy in Poland was submission to Russian political control, which ultimately pointed in the direction of further dismemberment and annexation. It is not just that Poland lacks the military force necessary to defend its liberty; it also lacks the will and self-direction to do so, as all the missed opportunities, from the reign of Sobieski to that of Poniatowski, demonstrated. Poland, Mably concludes somberly, would be absorbed by its neighbors—perhaps before the century was out. What role did this then leave for good republicans such as Wielhorski—or himself? As Mably explains, he too had learned to despair of ever seeing liberty restored in his own native land. His own response, which he urges on Wielhorski, has been to follow the example of his beloved ancients, who, after their final defeats, withdrew from public life and adopted an attitude of stoic *ataraxia*:

> In such circumstances, the enlightened citizen has no more duties to fulfill; he avoids, even flees from public functions, and devotes himself wholly to his philosophy; he contents himself with merely being a man. Nothing seems wiser or more instructive in this respect than the example of Cicero, after his defeat at the hands of Pompey.[25]

Wielhorski even enjoys an opportunity that his illustrious predecessor lacked: the extent of seigneurial authority in Poland makes it possible to undertake the political education of the peasantry, in a way that Cicero never dreamed of for his slaves. On this note, Mably takes his leave from Wielhorski: "Far away from you, I will wait for your news with the eagerness of a friend who is keenly interested in your glory. Whatever fate providence has reserved for your country, you will have done everything that philosophy demands of a wise and good citizen."[26]

The evolution of Mably's views on Poland can thus be seen to have reproduced something of the same trajectory as his hopes for France, albeit in briefer compass: presented with what seemed to be a favorable opportunity for political reform, he responded optimistically and energetically, with a proposal for a constitutional revolution that combined practical detail with sweeping ambition; once he judged this moment had passed, however, he promptly abandoned the field of action and retreated into a philosophic embrace of the harsh judgment of fate. In the case of Poland, too, Mably's extreme pessimism seems to have received a striking disconfirmation soon after his death, at least in the short term. For he greatly underestimated the impact of the First Partition on Polish political culture. Far from discouraging and dispersing its leadership, the ordeal seems finally to have prompted an enlightenment of sorts. The decade after 1775 saw both an influx of political writings from Western Europe, including Polish translations of Mably's own *De la législation* and Rousseau's *Discours sur l'inégalité*, and the development of progressive local traditions of noble and radical republicanism.[27] At the same time, there was a considerable recovery of urban life in this period, pointing to the development of precisely the commercial bourgeoisie Mably had thought necessary for political modernization in Poland. Profound differences of opinion continued to divide the landowning classes; but by the end of the 1780s, a consensus on behalf of a major recasting of the constitution seems to have emerged. Prussian encouragement and Russian distraction gave the "Four Years' Sejm" of 1788–91 its opportunity. A reform party, created from an alliance of progressive "patriots" and court officials, drafted a new constitution in secret in the winter of 1790–91, and then seized control of the state in a peaceful coup d'état in the spring. What is most striking about the constitution enacted in May 1791, from our point of view, is how close its main provisions—abolition of confederations and the *liberum veto*, declaration of popular sovereignty and a slight extension of the franchise, establishment of a hereditary monarchy, the separation of legislative and executive powers, and the creation of a modernized professional army—were to the proposals of Mably of some twenty years earlier.[28] However short-lived, the success of the Polish Constitution of 1791, the first written constitution of modern Europe, was also a testament to the depth and realism of Mably's practical insight.

Its fate, however, also revealed the accuracy of Mably's somber prediction to Wielhorski in 1776. The Russians used Lithuanian and Ukrainian resistance to the new order as a pretext for launching an invasion; the Constitution of 1791 was canceled within a year of its promulgation, and the Second Partition of 1792 divided three-fifths of the remaining territory of Poland between Prussia and Russia. This humiliation produced a final, fatal spasm in the dying state. The rebellion led by Kosciuszko in 1794 threatened to unite reactionary patriotism, petty-bourgeois radicalism, and peasant resistance in a single explosion, and it brought down the Russian hammer one last time. Warsaw fell to Suvorov's armies by the end of the year, and the Third Partition of 1795 erased Poland from the map of Europe. Could a reform of the constitution similar to that proposed in *Du gouvernement et des lois de la Pologne* have succeeded in 1768–71—and if it had, could this have helped to save the Polish state from its later extinction? Perhaps, but Mably was surely correct in judging that all chance for such salvation was permanently gone after the First Partition. For he had a keen sense of what rendered Poland so uniquely vulnerable to the predations of its neighbors—the failure of the Polish *szlachta* to submit to a durable and stable monarchy, capable of guaranteeing its security. Although Mably gravitated unhesitatingly to the "republican" camp in the debate over Poland, his insistence on the necessity of establishing a hereditary monarchy shows how prepared he was to let practical necessity take precedence over principle. When the old Polish Republic finally succumbed in 1795, it was according to the basic rules of absolutist warfare, whose analysis and critique Mably had written decades before in *Principes des négociations*.

The American Experiment

There is no doubt that the Polish tragedy clouded Mably's final years, deepening the mood of pessimism to which he was already inclined in the wake of the Maupeou "coup." Yet the outlook for political reform in the European world in these years was by no means uniformly bleak. For the last decade of Mably's life also saw the unfolding of a very different set of events on the other side of the globe. However great his dismay over the default of French politics, or his disappointment over reversals in Sweden and Poland, he could hardly have failed to be stirred by the drama of the American Revolution and its aftermath. In fact, as he was pleased to be able to report two decades later, Mably was one of the first French commentators to predict this course of events, insisting as early as the last edition of *Le droit public* in 1763 that a successful war for American independence from Great Britain was inevitable.[29] He naturally supported the American rebellion from the start and greeted the initial signs of its military success with enthusiastic approval.

At the same time, Mably's first extended comment on American affairs was not particularly celebratory—nor was it likely to be, given the complicated impact the colonists' success was bound to have on French politics. *Notre gloire ou nos rêves* is another of Mably's informal dialogues, published posthumously, but evidently written in 1779. In it, the abbé is accosted by a young friend named "Ariste" (obviously a descendent of *Entretien de Phocion*'s "Aristias," and perhaps a later incarnation of Chastellux), who is in a transport of enthusiasm: surely, he demands, Mably must be delighted by the current triumphs of foreign and domestic policy for France—the growing signs of British defeat in North America and Necker's successful experiment with provincial assemblies in Berry? Characteristically, Mably expresses reservations on both counts. Necker's provincial estates are mere window-dressing, which could be multiplied across France without the slightest effect on the declining fate of the monarchy as a whole. As for America, Mably's experience in Poland has taught him to beware of raising his hopes prematurely. It is not at all clear, he suggests, that the Americans have had the time to develop a "national character appropriate to a free people." Their revolt was inspired as much by the desire for economic advantage as political freedom, and has come unprofitably cheap, due more to English error than to their own zeal for liberty. "Ariste" responds to Mably with a vigorous defense of the *Insurgents*: he points to the high principles of the Declaration of Independence, with its clear statement of the eternal rights of popular sovereignty; he lauds the Americans for their genuine egalitarianism, deeply hostile to all forms of hereditary nobility; and praises the practical achievements of the new state constitutions, that of Pennsylvania above all, which should serve as a model for all the world.

In response, Mably affirms his own devotion to the principle of popular sovereignty. But he roundly rejects the idea that the Americans are somehow more egalitarian than their European ancestors:

> It is true that nobility is not recognized by the rebels; but although their families possess no special prerogatives, do you really believe that their differences in fortune do not give rise to special consideration? A gentleman always scorns a commoner—but still more does a rich man scorn a poor one. It is this regard for wealth that has banished liberty from Europe, and who will prevent it from establishing itself in America?[30]

As for Pennsylvania, Mably makes a detailed critique of its constitution, on the grounds that, despite its ultra-democratic appearance, its unicameral assembly and principle of legislative supremacy in fact make it uniquely vulnerable to *aristocratic* domination:

> It requires no great skill to avoid the tyranny of the poor by establishing that of the rich. It seems to me that in republics in which wealth is so disproportionately divided as in those of the colonists, and in which manners and customs have already established a considerable subordination, it is not against the ambition of the multitude that one must take precautions . . . the legislator must instead devote himself to restraining the rich, to try force them to submit to the rule of law.[31]

In Pennsylvania, Mably sees over and over "a particular predilection for aristocracy," which sorts ill with the republic's reputation for democracy. The result is a general turmoil and anarchy, which is in turn exacerbated, Mably argues, by the dangerous weakness of the central government of the American confederacy. Dismayed by the abbé's criticism of the Americans, "Ariste" finally tries a different tack: surely the success of the rebellion and humiliation of Great Britain is good for France, in and of itself? On the contrary, argues Mably. In the short term, Britain will soon recover from its losses, and soon seek to exact revenge on France, such that "we will come to regard the American revolution as merely another of our disgraces." In the long run, the Americans will themselves be unable to resist the lures of commercial wealth and imperial power, and may someday become "as strange and distant to us as China is today."[32]

Mably's gloomy predictions in *Notre gloire ou nos rêves*—which did not see print until some time after his death—were naturally a minority opinion. The views attributed to "Ariste" in the dialogue, on the other hand, are very close to what became the dominant French outlook on America, once the war for independence was under way. Prior to 1776, French comment on the New World had largely been confined to speculation and conjecture, in either a utopian (Voltaire's portrait of virtuous Quakers, Rousseauist celebrations of American primitivism, the anticolonialism of Raynal) or a dystopian (De Pauw's famous theory of "degeneration" in the New World, also repeated in the early editions of Raynal's *Histoire des deux Indes*) vein. Lexington and Concord altered this scene permanently. The chief agent of change here was Benjamin Franklin, who had already inspired a good deal of physiocratic interest in the economic life of the English colonies during his first visit to France in 1767. His diplomatic activity in France after 1777 permitted Franklin to organize a hugely successful publicity campaign on behalf of the fledgling American republic, which for the first time introduced American political thought to France.[33] A number of key works by American thinkers, including Franklin himself, Dickinson, and Paine, appeared in French in these years. But most important of all were translations of the major documents of American political *practice*—the Declaration of Independence, the Articles of Confederation, and the various new state constitutions. By early 1777, Franklin had overseen the publication of the Declaration, the Articles, and seven state constitutions and bills of rights, under the title *Affaires de l'Angleterre et l'Amérique*; six years later, he and Mably's patron La Rochefoucauld brought out a definitive collection, *Constitutions des treize Etats-Unis de l'Amérique.*

The constitutional materials first publicized by Franklin, accompanied by a flood of commentary in newspapers and journals, formed the basis for the great debate between French, American, and British political thinkers that extended down to the French Revolution and beyond.[34] As a final gesture, Franklin can also be said to have launched the debate itself, since it seems to have begun with his gift of a copy of Richard Price's *Observations on Civil Liberty* to Turgot, theorist of physiocracy and former controller-general, whose experimentation with a liberalized grain trade ended in debacle in 1775. Turgot wrote an enthusiastic letter of appreciation to Price in March 1778, congratulating him for what he saw as the only significant advance in British political thought in a century—in effect, for having introduced a tonic dose of French rationalism into England. At same time, Turgot also felt moved to provide Price with his assessment of the new American constitutions. On the whole, his view of the American scene was close to that which Mably ascribed to "Ariste" in *Notre gloire ou nos rêves*: the successful overthrow of British tyranny announced a new epoch in world history, for which the American conceptions of individual liberty and popular sovereignty would provide the guiding principles. Nevertheless, Turgot's comments had a critical edge missing in those of Mably's "Ariste." The constitutions themselves fell short of their promise, in his view. He criticized some for an insufficient separation between Church and State, others for permitting an excessive degree of economic intervention, in violation of "the sacred principle of freedom of trade." But above all, he saw in nearly all of them "the useless imitation of English customs"—by which he meant the complicated machinery of upper and lower houses, separated by arbitrary property qualifications, whose only purpose was the protection of a privileged class. This was the baleful shadow of the English version of the "mixed government": "Instead of bringing all the authorities into one, that of the nation, they have established different bodies, a house of representatives, a council, a governor, because England has a house of commons, a house of lords, and a king."[35] The one state constitution that pointed in another, more egalitarian direction was that of Pennsylvania, whose one-chamber assembly, which wielded absolute authority over a docile executive branch, approximated the ideal for Turgot.

Turgot's letter turned out to be the opening salvo in the debate over the American constitutions. It circulated widely after its author's death in 1781, and made its way into print in several languages soon after. By 1787, its arguments had been restated by a number of French thinkers, which in turn provoked a three-volume response by John Adams, in what was perhaps the most important work of American political thought prior to *The Federalist*, his *Defence of the constitu-*

tions of Government of the United States of America, against the attack of M. Turgot. Long before this, however, Adams had been instrumental in bringing Mably into the center of the controversy. The two men first met in December 1782, during the peace talks in Paris, and saw one another frequently in the months that followed. By this point, although he was well into his seventies, Mably had evidently decided to produce a major work on the American Revolution, a philosophical history in his grand style. On his own account, Adams argued against so ambitious an undertaking, which he believed to be premature, even for a much younger man; instead, he advised the abbé to attempt a briefer work, a commentary on the state constitutions.[36] Mably responded with his usual energy, and had completed his *Observations sur le gouvernement et les lois des Etats-Unis d'Amérique,* in the form of four letters addressed to Adams, by the end of summer 1783. Adams himself saw to the book's publication in Holland in autumn 1784; editions in English, Dutch, and Italian followed shortly thereafter. The last publication of Mably's lifetime, the *Observations* also provoked by far the most violent controversy. Well before its publication, rumors began to circulate to the effect that Mably had received an official invitation from the United States, via Adams and Franklin, to draft a new constitution for the American republic—a circumstance that Grimm, in his *Correspondence,* called "a great scandal for philosophy and for the *philosophes.*"[37] The *Observations* was greeted on its appearance by a number of violent denunciations in the philosophic press in France, while reports that Mably was being burned in effigy arrived from America. Adams, who otherwise remained loyal to the memory of Mably, felt it necessary, in *A Defence of the Constitutions,* to deny the legend of an official solicitation: the "request to the Abbé to write upon American affairs" had been nothing more than a "mere civility" on his part.[38]

What was in the *Observations sur le gouvernement et les lois des Etats-Unis* to provoke such a response? In and of itself, Mably's book seems innocuous enough, a characteristic combination of sincere respect and sober criticism. The opening letter, dated July 1783, serves as a kind of introduction. Mably begins by praising both the theory and practice of American politics:

> While nearly every nation of Europe flouts the constitutive principles of society, treating their citizens like beasts of burden to be ruled only for the advantage of their owners, one is astonished and inspired to find that your thirteen colonies have understood the dignity of mankind and have turned to the wisest philosophy for the basic principles according to which they wish to rule themselves.[39]

Having secured their freedom in a the justest of wars, the Americans wisely declined to follow the Dutch in a retreat toward a traditionalist authoritarianism. Instead, they created something infinitely more admirable—a Swiss-style federalism, whose original model was the "amphictyonic council" of ancient Greece. Among other practices, Mably singles out for particular praise the clement treatment accorded to freed slaves in the United States, at least in the North; and above all, the jury system, "the wisest institution ever created to establish a sort of equality between the strong and the weak, or rather a true equality."[40] Having expressed his hopes for the United States, however, Mably also feels constrained to express some reservations, chiefly political. For all that the Americans obviously owe to British political traditions, there is nevertheless a fundamental difference between their new forms of government and the English constitution. The latter is forever marked by its feudal origins, and has remained *monarchical* its basic principles. The American constitutions, by contrast, have been founded on "the true and wise principles of Locke on the natural liberty of mankind and the nature of government."[41] They are, in other words, fundamentally *democratic* in form, and democracy, Mably insists, "must serve as the basis for any government that hopes to bring out the best in its citizens." Nevertheless, he tells Adams, "you will agree that this democracy needs to be fashioned and tempered with the greatest possible care," if one is to avoid the violent contention between social orders that was the bane of the great republics of antiquity.[42] Here Mably repeats the fears expressed in *Notre gloire ou nos rêves*, that the Americans have perhaps made the transition from domination to democracy too precipitously, without having formed the "national character" necessary to sustain a free government.

The proving ground for these anxieties was to be found in the actual political life of the new republics. The heart of *Observations sur le gouvernement et les lois des Etats-Unis* is thus the second letter, in which Mably turns to a discussion of the constitutions of Pennsylvania, Massachusetts, and Georgia. It was the first of these that was the real crux in the debate over the American constitutions. From its framing in the summer of 1776, the Pennsylvania constitution was widely seen as the great test-case for the American experiment with radical democracy.[43] Its popularly elected unicameral legislature and weakened executive, its "Council of Censors" to keep watch over the constitution, its notorious Section 15, which required all bills to be submitted to popular scrutiny before becoming law—these and a host of other democratic devices seemed to be the very antithesis of the "mixed government" of English tradition, which is precisely what most excited the admiration of progressive philosophic thought in France, from Turgot to Condorcet. As for Mably, we have seen the reservations expressed in *Notre gloire ou nos rêves*. In *Observations sur le gouvernement et les lois des Etats-Unis*, he restates and amplifies these criticisms. In principle, a unicameral, popular democracy is indeed the best form of government. But its stable and durable operation demands certain conditions—the small size, relative equality of social conditions, and high degree of public spiritedness characteristic of the early Greek city-states—that are obviously missing in Pennsylvania. In such a highly stratified and competitive society, the necessary consequences of an untrammeled democracy—in addition to Section 15, Mably alludes to the extraordinarily low property and residency qualifications for office, the low age for voting rights, and the popular election of the executive council—would paradoxically be social turmoil and ultimately aristocratic domination. The specific fear he conjures up for Pennsylvania is the erection of a Florentine-style tyranny, Philadelphia falling under the control of its own Medici bankers.[44]

Mably's criticisms of the constitution of 1776 were neither extreme nor novel. In large part, they faithfully reproduce the position staked out by the "Republicans," led by James Wilson and Robert Morris, who faced off against the loyal "Constitutionalists" in the great factional struggles over the reform of the Pennsylvania constitution in the 1780s—these struggles were in fact particularly intense in the years 1783–84.[45] What is Mably's own remedy for the excessive democracy of Pennsylvania? He is relieved to turn his eyes northward to Massachusetts—intimately associated, of course, with the name of his friend and addressee, Adams—whose constitution, with its bicameral legislature, checked by a suspensive legislative veto, is an excellent approximation of the mixed government of antiquity, and far superior to the English model on which it is based. Mably explains the practical advantages of Massachusetts over Pennsylvania in terms which, if they are rather more elitist than is typical for him, were certainly bound to appeal to his friend Adams:

> I do not doubt that those who think only of the dignity and the common rights that all men possess by nature, will prefer the government of Pennsylvania to that of Massachusetts. But I am also convinced that they will change their minds, once they abandon their metaphysical speculations in order truly to study the human mind, which is so limited in most men. . . . In requiring a very different level of wealth to enter the chamber of the senate, than that of the representatives, you have, I believe, estab-

> lished a very wise balance, which will prevent the wealthiest citizens from monopolizing all authority. That, I believe, is the arrangement mostly likely to permit you to temper aristocracy by a kind of mixture with democracy.[46]

In fact, however, Massachusetts is not Mably's favorite among the American constitutions. Revealingly, he concludes his second letter with a warm description of the constitution of Georgia, which, with Vermont, modeled on Pennsylvania, was the only other state to feature a unicameral legislature. There were in fact some differences from Pennsylvania: Georgia had somewhat more stringent property and residency requirements, and an Executive Council that functioned as a kind of shadow upper chamber. But what principally makes it possible for Georgia to dispense with the precaution of a mixed government, in Mably's view, are the relatively compact size of the state and the simplicity of its largely agricultural economy, which together created an egalitarian ethos missing in the North. "It seems to me," he concludes admiringly,

> that this republic has found the middle ground between Pennsylvania and Massachusetts. It is not enough there simply to pay taxes in order to be elevated to the dignity of representative; yet the fortune that is required is too modest to be compatible with anything other than a democracy. On the other hand, the legislators have distanced themselves from aristocracy, by declining to establish a two-chamber legislature, as in Massachusetts. It is clear that equality is precious to the Georgians, since they refuse to recognize as a citizen any person who has not sincerely renounced those titles imagined by petty vanity, which seem to designate a sort of nobility in England.[47]

Mably's preference for what he saw as the noncommercial and egalitarian republic of Georgia will have come as no surprise to readers familiar with his thought. The final two letters of *Observations sur le gouvernement et les lois des Etats-Unis* are addressed explicitly to "ideological" and economic issues. Pennsylvania, Massachusetts, and Georgia are each to be congratulated, Mably writes at the start of the third letter, for the attention—or at least the promise of attention—they have given to public education. But the states need to devote an equal amount of care to the religious life of their citizens, perhaps developing, if possible, some version of an antique-style public cult. Any reader who doubts the power of education and religion to determine the fate of a republic, Mably suggests, should consult the famous book by the British moralist John Brown, *Estimate of the Manners and Principles of the Times*—"I know of no more profound work on politics" Mably insists—a book that accurately predicted the current decadence of British political character.[48] The Americans have succeeded in creating a Swiss-style political confederation: they need to remember that the Swiss have preserved their freedom over the centuries only by maintaining a strict control over private passion and public morality. The Americans are especially vulnerable to corruption, Mably argues in the fourth and last letter, given the extent to which they have become dependent on manufacture and commerce in their economic lives. The umbilical cord joining commerce and corruption has been established not only in Brown's *Estimate*, but, above all, in the masterpiece of Cantillon, "a man of the most penetrating and far-seeing genius."[49] For commercial republics such as those of the United States, it can hardly be surprising that the aristocratic constitution of Massachusetts may well be preferable to the democratic one of Pennsylvania, as a bulwark against tyranny. Fortunately, Mably explains, the Americans have one obvious remedy at hand for the dangers by which they are menaced. He concludes his *Observations* with a recommendation for a considerable increase in the authority of the Continental Congress to regulate and direct the moral and economic lives of Americans; the model for such an authority is to be found in the Roman Tribunate, as theorized by Cicero in his *Republic*.[50]

In the controversy ignited by the publication of *Observations sur le gouvernement et les lois des Etats-Unis*, it was often suggested that the book was a relatively feeble performance, in which the now elderly philosopher at last showed the signs of his age. In fact, there is little evidence of intellectual slippage in the letter of the text. On the contrary, Mably seems to have lost none of his diagnostic or imaginative powers in his *Observations*. His criticisms of the state constitutions in question echoed or presaged those of any number of American critics during the transitional period of the early 1780s; his positive recommendations were perfectly logical and even creative extensions of the great themes of his own political thought, applied to the novel terrain of American constitutional practice. If the *Observations* nevertheless provoked so vitriolic a response, the explanation is to be sought in a particular conjuncture of ideological pressures and cross-currents. Mably's book was published at the moment when the torch of American diplomatic and intellectual leadership in Europe was being passed from Franklin to Jefferson, who was named American plenipotentiary minister to France in 1784. Jefferson's chief task was to overcome the risk of diplomatic isolation of the United States, now that the war for independence had been won. But there was also a challenge to meet on the ideological plane—to respond to a new wave of criticisms of the American political achievement, of which Mably's book was only one example. Jefferson may have lacked Franklin's personal flair for the dramatic, but he exceeded the latter in his ability to marshal or inspire European intellectual talent in support of the United States. The later 1780s thus saw a great counteroffensive on the part of French thinkers allied or associated with Jefferson, designed to answer British and French critics of the American republics.[51] Nearly all of these writers, whose ranks came to include Chastellux, La Fayette, Morellet, Mirabeau, and Condorcet, were intellectual descendants in one way or another of Turgot, whose own original letter to Price had now made its way into print as well—that is, harsh critics of any conception of "mixed government" and doctrinaire defenders of free trade and commercial modernity.

The fact is that Mably had the misfortune, in what amounted to the last public political intervention of his career, of providing Turgot's successors with a perfect polemical target—all the more tempting, given his own critique of physiocracy and hostile relations with the intellectual mandarins of the later Enlightenment. Indeed, *Observations sur le gouvernement et les lois des Etats-Unis* became the chief whipping-post of the most famous of all these works, the *Recherches historiques et politiques sur les Etats-Unis* of Filippo Mazzei, the Tuscan publicist whose emigration to Virginia had made him first neighbor and then intellectual lieutenant of Jefferson.[52] Mazzei's book, written in 1786 and published the following year, was a hastily assembled potpourri of information and invective, which included a historical introduction to the American Revolution and a long attack on Raynal as well. But its centerpiece is what Mazzei intended to be a total demolition of *Observations sur le gouvernement et les lois des Etats-Unis*. In practice, this turned out to be a scattershot, overblown effort, in which Mably is portrayed, improbably enough, as a kind of crypto-aristocrat. But Mazzei's diatribe at least has the merit of pointing to a crucial parting of the ways in French political thought of the 1780s—the growing fissure between the emergent bourgeois radicalism of the Turgot school and the classical republicanism of Mably, which could now seem to be retrograde by comparison. In fact, this divergence was always at the heart of the international debate over the American constitutions, whose echoes reverberated in Atlantic political thought for decades to come. Shortly after the appearance of Mazzei's book, Adams published his gargantuan counterattack on Turgot and his successors, his *Defence of the Constitutions of Government of the United States* (1787–88). Adams was in turn rebutted by the New Jersey planter John Stevens, the French translation of whose rejoinder was destined to play a crucial role in the intellectual struggles of the French "pre-Revolution." The Philadelphia Convention and the ratification of the new federal constitution in the United States marked a new epoch in the debate, but it did not end it—the *Federalist Papers* were merely one more of its products. Adams himself produced a lengthy restatement of his position in his *Discourses on Davila*; nearly three decades later, he was still passionately debating his views with Jefferson, in the famous twilight correspondence that the two former presidents exchanged in their retirement.

As for Mably, his own early contribution to the debate over the American constitutions can best be judged by comparing his position with that of his American friend and sponsor. It has long been a commonplace for historians of American political thought to see Adams as the greatest representative of the classical republican tradition in the New World. Indeed, for Gordon Wood, in the initial presentation of this view, the tenacity with which Adams clung to his traditional republican convictions was precisely what condemned him to "irrelevance" in the new era inaugurated by the 1787 Constitution—a fact of which Adams became bitterly aware in later years.[53] No doubt something of the same could be said of Mably, within the intellectual arena of late Old Regime France. There was obviously a considerable degree of overlap between the basic political outlook of Mably and that of Adams, a consonance that was especially pronounced in the major early works of the latter, the "Dissertation on the Canon and Feudal Law" and *Thoughts on Government.* The intellectual affinity between the two men was no doubt what permitted them to form a close friendship during Adams's residency in Paris, in Mably's last years. Nevertheless, there remained important differences of tone and emphasis in the republicanism of the two thinkers. On the one hand, Adams never shared the hostility toward commercial, financial, and even agricultural capitalism that was so central to Mably's political thought: amid constant warnings of the dangers posed by commercial relations in terms of "corruption," Adams always remained a vocal defender of economic modernity. On the other hand, Mably escaped the obsessive concern with aristocracy that formed the keynote of Adams's writing from the *Defence* onward: though hardly less convinced than Adams of the inevitability of the division of societies by unequal classes, Mably's work lacked the special pleading on behalf of aristocracy—what one might term its *pathos*—that became so marked in Adams's later public pronouncements and private correspondence. This is what lay behind the doctrinaire insistence on "mixed government" in Adams, for which he turned to the authority not of Mably, but of De Lolme—and behind him, of Montesquieu. Mably, on the other hand, as we have seen, could defend "mixed government" as a bulwark of social stability and liberty in a highly stratified society such as Massachusetts, yet at the same time express a preference for a purer form of democracy, where social conditions of greater equality made it possible, as he imagined they did in Georgia. What these differences point to, of course, is the far greater role that a specific kind of radical utopianism played in the classical republicanism of Mably, in comparison with Adams. Paradoxically enough, Mably's outlook always had something in common with the visionary egalitarianism of Adams's old friend and antagonist Jefferson—a thinker who was perhaps condemned to his own kind of "irrelevance" in the new world of nineteenth-century American politics.

The Consolation of Philosophy

We have seen that Mably consistently shunned public controversy throughout his career, avoiding both confrontation with political authority and polemical exchange with intellectual adversaries. Yet his characteristic caution seems to have deserted him at the end of his life: he spent his last three years embroiled in a series of well-publicized disputes. The first began late in 1782 with the publication of *De la manière d'écrire l'histoire*, a work whose tart comments about Hume, Robertson, Gibbon, and above all Voltaire provoked harsh responses in the philosophic press throughout the following year.[54] This was succeeded almost immediately by the uproar over Mably's intervention in the debate over the American constitutions—rumors about the imaginary invitation from American authorities circulated from January 1783 onward. Well before the actual publication of *Observations sur le gouvernement et des lois des Etats-Unis*, however, Mably stumbled into a third grave controversy. In January 1784, he published a long dialogue in three parts entitled *Principes de morale*. In this case, reaction came from another quarter entirely. The Theological Faculty of the Sorbonne, a stronghold of intellectual conservatism in France, erupted in protest, above all because Mably's book had been published with official royal permission.[55] By the end of January, Sancy, the censor who had approved the work, had been suspended from his duties. Mably entered into frantic negotiations with the Archbishop of Paris, in an effort to make peace with the religious authorities. He partly succeeded—Sancy was reinstated in June. But Mably could not prevent the Sorbonne from proceeding with its censure of the book. In July, *Principes de morale* was officially condemned by the Theological Faculty for "containing propositions respectively false, scandalous, erroneous, contrary to the word of God, injurious to the Christian religion, at variance with natural religion, dangerous for morals and damaging to society."[56]

The censure of *Principes de morale* might suggest that Mably had concluded his intellectual career with an abrupt about-face, by declaring his allegiance to the same Enlightenment he had sharply criticized for so many years. In fact, the Sorbonne almost certainly mistook its target in this instance. Beyond Mably's extremely mild deism, and a specific passage in which the author displayed a curiously lenient attitude toward prostitution, there was little in *Principes de morale* to offend even the most reactionary readers. The Sorbonne's censure tells us a good deal more about its embattled posture in French intellectual life in this epoch than any putative last-minute change of mind by Mably. For our purposes, the interest of *Principes de morale* lies in another direction entirely. In point of fact, the dialogue was not a new text at all. It had been drafted some years before, as early as 1773–74, and had circulated in manuscript in the meantime. Nor, as it turns out, was it isolated or unusual among Mably's later writings. For the publication of his *oeuvres complètes* by his literary executors in the 1790s revealed the existence of a very large number of dialogues devoted to similar subjects, most of them written in the last decade of his life. Mably's careful husbanding of their manuscripts, and his publication of the most substantial of them in his last year, make it clear that these dialogues can be regarded as his literary testament—his last word on the themes that had animated his intellectual career. Specifically, the late dialogues form a chain of interconnected reflections on the relations between "politics" and "morality." In other words, they mark a return to the terrain of *Entretiens de Phocion*, in much the same way that Mably's last works on Poland and the United States can be seen as an extension of the constitutional and practical political concerns of *Des droits et des devoirs du citoyen*. In this case as well, however, there were to be significant departures from his earlier position, in line with the darker outlook of his later years.

The first and most striking novelty of Mably's later dialogues, from *Principes de morale* onwards, is the far more explicit appeal to the philosophy of Condillac in them. We noted earlier the somewhat surprising omission of any reference to his brother's writing in *Entretiens de Phocion.* Mably and Condillac in fact remained in close contact throughout their adult lives; they collaborated intellectually on the latter's *Cours d'études* for the Prince of Parma; and their relations seem if anything to have become even more intimate in their last years—Mably ended up serving as Condillac's literary executor after his death in 1780, preparing the first complete edition of his works for publication. Of course the philosophy of Condillac—which covered an immense range, from metaphysics and ontology, logic and mathematics, to psychology, history, and economics—is notoriously ambiguous in its overall profile. In the epoch of the high Enlightenment, Condillac's transcription of Locke for a French audience could serve as the basis for the rationalist utopianism of thinkers such as Helvétius and Holbach; a generation later, his sensationalism provided the launching pad for a still more ambitious program of social remodeling in the work of Destutt de Tracy and the other *idéologues.* The modernist optimism of these figures was light years away from Mably, who found something else entirely in the writings of Condillac. Whether or not it was a more accurate reflection of the actual outlook of his brother, it is clear enough what Mably's appeal to the *Essai sur l'origine des connaissances humaines* and the *Traité des sensations* brought to his later writings. Condillac's philosophy provided Mably with a philosophical anthropology, whose main themes were the limits of human knowledge and the frailty of human reason. The explanation for both, according to this conception, was to be sought in the dual nature of mankind—half-animal, half-spiritual—which meant that reason and knowledge, at both the individual and collective levels, were subject to a difficult developmental process, with no guarantees of cumulative progress for either. Again and again in these late dialogues, Mably reproduced this same bleak picture of the human condition, nearly always invoking the name of Condillac as he did so.

As for the specific uses to which this new, darker anthropology was put, these are on most vivid display in *Principes de morale* itself, the earliest and in many ways the most substantial of the later dialogues. Set, like most of the works that followed, in the Luxembourg Gardens, it describes three successive conversations between Mably and a set of friends bearing Greek pseudonyms—in this case, the already familiar "Ariste," together with "Eugène" and "Théante." Its occasion was the recent news of the papal dissolution of the Jesuit Order, which, together with references to escalating tensions between the

British and their North American colonists, would place the dialogue in 1773–74. The first conversation serves as an introduction and does not, in fact, stray far from the outlook of *Entretiens de Phocion*. In it, Mably himself outlines a very conventional theory of the passions, according to which there are two extremes to be avoided in morality, for creatures like ourselves, composed of body and soul: "Epicureanism," or the belief that the passions are wholly reliable guides to happiness, and "Stoicism," the notion that it is possible to submit the passions entirely to the guidance of reason.

In the second conversation, however, where the chief speaker is not Mably but "Eugène," the argument begins to move in a novel direction. First, the balance struck between Epicureanism and Stoicism in the first talk is upset: "Eugène" begins with a long attack on rationalism alone, represented in this case by the figure of Malebranche, whose theory of the virtues vastly underestimates the sheer weakness of the human mind in the face of the passions, as well as the degree of human interdependence necessary for happiness.[57] From here, "Eugène" moves to an actual catalogue of the virtues, one that differs significantly from the version found in *Entretiens de Phocion*. Where the earlier dialogue had demoted "temperance" to the second tier of virtues, "Eugène" restores it to the first rank, thus reinstating the classical quartet of justice, prudence, courage, and temperance. More important, where in *Entretiens de Phocion* Mably had abstained from specifically ranking the virtues, "Eugène" proceeds to just that: citing the authority of Cicero, and again emphasizing the extent of human weakness in regard to the virtues, he places "prudence" ahead of "justice," and moves "courage" to the last position. Finally, in still another departure from the earlier dialogue, "Eugène" denies any political application for the theory of the virtues he has sketched: out of reach for the vast majority of mankind, the truly virtuous life is possible only for a small circle of genuine philosophers, prepared to devote themselves solely to study, the pursuit of truth, and the love of equality.

This drift away from the outlook of *Entretiens de Phocion* is completed in the final conversation of *Principes de morale*. Its speaker is "Théante," whose first move is without precedence in Mably's earlier writings, but became a staple of the later dialogues: he sketches a genetic account of the development of the passions in the individual, from infancy to adulthood, based on a direct appeal to Condillac's philosophical psychology. It was the specific problems posed by the awakening of sexual desire in adolescence that produced the passage most offensive to the theologians of the Sorbonne:

"Théante" suggests that philosophically inclined young men might have recourse to the services of a prostitute, not only "without weakness, without error, and without prejudice," but also "without stain"—a phrase that his literary executors replaced with "without attachment" in the *oeuvres complètes*, at the request of the chastened author.[58] This "Epicurean" relaxation of moral austerity is of course very slight. But it is consonant with the posture of "Théante's" presentation as a whole, whose main theme, again, is the extreme weakness of human reason, which generally comes, if at all, as a late arrival, and nearly always remains in a fatal dependence on the passions. "Théante" concludes by repeating the earlier claim that the moral theory being expounded should not be expected to yield a political program. On the contrary, he asserts, the great majority of people are dominated wholly by their passions, which are in turn determined largely by the form of government under which they happen to live; only a happy few can lead virtuous lives, and only by turning their backs on politics. It is this theme, of course, that suggests the distance traveled between *Entretiens de Phocion* and *Principes de morale*. As we have seen, the earlier dialogue was pessimistic enough in its outlook. But it still proceeded from the assumption that morality and politics formed a single coherent field, and was still animated by what might be termed the "neo-Stoic" ideal of a rational political society as a whole. By the time of *Principes de morale* the assumption and the ideal alike seem to have been abandoned by Mably, or at least thrown radically into question.

A glance at any of the dialogues written in the succeeding years confirms this. For the most part briefer works than *Principes de morale*, their standard démarche is to explore the implications of that work's philosophical anthropology at the collective rather than the individual level. If the results tend to be still more gloomy, this is part owing to a further argument that it is only hinted at in *Principes de morale*, but that is highlighted in most of its successors—the notion, also ascribed to Condillac, but that obviously owed no less to Rousseau, of a fatal tension between political virtue and progress in the arts and sciences. *Du développement, des progrès, et des bornes de la raison*, for example—also set in the Luxembourg Gardens, in 1778—describes a conversation with a friend named "Valère," who attempts to stage a confrontation between two opposed theorists of natural law, Hobbes and Cumberland, to the benefit of the latter. Mably's response, introduced with the requisite appeal to the authority of Condillac ("whose principles I have merely applied to moral and political matters"[59]), is to "historicize" this opposition with a genetic account of the slow progress of reason in societies as a whole. Not only does reason advance slowly, he argues, it also often divides and turns against itself: the record of both ancient and modern history shows not only that political-moral and scientific-artistic rationality develop at different rates, but are frequently at odds with one another. Citing the famous denunciation of "avarice" in Longinus, Mably reminds "Valère" that advances in the arts and sciences have typically proved fatal for morality and politics alike.[60]

As often happens in these later works, these roles are then reversed in a follow-up dialogue, entitled *L'oracle d'Apollon ou de la connoissance de soi-même.* Here it is "Valère," musing on Juvenal, who expresses a lethal skepticism, not merely about reason in general, but about the possibility of genuine human self-knowledge, given the unfathomably tangled web of the passions. Mably dissents, arguing that the educational theories of his friend Stanhope show that a genuine self-knowledge and self-direction are possible, even in a corrupt society—though again this privilege is reserved only for a tiny elite who have withdrawn from political life. In any case, Mably returned to the Rousseauesque notion of a fatal discrepancy between politics and the arts and sciences at still greater length in *Du beau,* apparently drafted around 1780.[61] Here a character named "Cléophon" again attempts to mediate between the rival claims of Epicureanism and Rationalism by means of an appeal to Condillac. The price, however, is a striking collapse in the direction of moral and aesthetic relativism, as the "beautiful"—or perhaps the "good"—is divided into a multiplicity of competing types and spheres. "Cléophon" concludes by repeating the melancholy observation that moral and political excellence seem to depend on a certain degree of economic and cultural simplicity, while the arts and sciences typically flourish in the midst of political and moral decay.

The basic practical recommendation of the dialogues written in the wake of *Principes de morale* is in fact always the same—abandonment of the field of politics for the consolations of philosophy, in imitation of Cicero and so many other illustrious figures from antiquity. In other words, "Epicureanism" for the passionate Many, "Stoicism" for the sober Few. This is not to say that Mably ever succeeded in turning his back entirely on politics. On the contrary, these late dialogues themselves are full of ironic references to the abbé's resolve never to speak of politics again—a resolve that is always shown to be in vain, since he and his interlocutors always return to the subject, and to the rough and tumble of contemporary events, with obsessive regularity.

Nevertheless, in only one of these works did Mably explicitly attempt to coordinate their themes with the central concerns of his earlier historical and constitutional writings. This work, which thus forms the true complement to *Principes de morale,* was *Du cours et de la marche des passions dans la société,* which is also set somewhat apart from the others by its setting—the record of a long conversation with an unidentified pupil, which took place in Poland during Mably's visit in 1776–77. The text begins in fact with an appealing description of Mably acting as a "doctor of natural law" on his travels, patiently attempting to teach Locke's *Two Treatises of Government* to puzzled Polish squires in weekly tutorials.[62] But the main work of the dialogue is to apply the view of the passions set forth in *Principes de morale,* where its object was chiefly individual psychology, to human history as a whole. In the first section, Mably makes the now-standard presentation of Condillac's dualist ontology, and adds that there are generally three psychological types as a result: the very small number of true sages, in whom reason predominates; the slightly larger number of intelligent and energetic individuals, who are consistently dominated by a single passion; and then the normal run of mankind, subject neither to reason nor to a single passion, but to a confused and often incoherent skein of passions, woven by event and circumstance. Mably then moves to a genetic account of the origins of societies, by reference to a concept we have seen often enough in his historical writings: at their origins, he argues, societies typically acquire a "national character," which, once formed, then acts as a powerful and durable causal factor throughout their subsequent history, acting like an "instinct" for the people involved.

"National character," however, turns out to be only one of a number of determinants examined in *Du cours et de la marche des passions dans la société.* At the start of the second part of the dialogue, Mably shifts to the specifically political plane, to consider the impact of forms of government on the passions—and vice-versa. For what follows is a presentation of the classical cycle of governments, in which the passions are first determined by the form of government, only to serve as the motors of historical change in the transition to the next form—in this case, democratic passion leading to the establishment of aristocracy, then aristocratic passion prompting the creation of monarchy, and so on. But this is only a very general model, Mably immediately adds. "National character" itself can alter, reverse, or suspend the cycle, as happened in the case of the Roman Republic; in some rare cases, even human will and intention can have an impact—for which the supreme model remains the "mixed government" of Lycurgus, which stayed the hand of time in Sparta for half a millennium. At the other end of the spectrum from human self-direction, there are the natural determinants of geography and climate; these must be given their due, although, Mably hastens to add, climate is not the *deus ex machina* it is assumed to be by so many theorists in Paris—it can often be resisted or overruled by "moral causes."

Du cours et de la marche des passions dans la société thus canvasses a wide range of social determinations, working on and through the passions—the historical impact of national character, the structural effects of forms of government, the intervention of political will and imagination, the scene-setting of geography and climate. But all of these causes are trumped in the end, Mably argues at the start of the last section of the dialogue, by one ultimate determinant—the "secret poison" that brings the life of every government and society to its appointed end. For the creations of mankind are no less mortal than the individuals who compose them; the most fine-tuned balance of passions and interests in a society will ultimately fall victim to this law of decay—as can be seen, again, in the Spartan and Roman mirrors. As for modern Europe, Mably suggests that it has been exceptionally fortunate in postponing its own decadence, chiefly through a happy fermentation of contrasting passions. Nevertheless, most of the states of Europe are far weaker than they seem, many teetering on the brink of their final ruin. "What can we do, my dear pupil," Mably asks at the end of the conversation, "when societies refuse all help? It is necessary to submit respectfully to the decrees of providence, without whose permission nothing happens in this world. Since we ourselves are mortal, why should we complain to find that our creations are subject to the same fate?"[63] Such was the extent of Mably's valedictory pessimism—for this prediction of the general ruin of Europe, in accordance with the iron laws of "providence," was of course an exact reversal of the optimistic outlook of his central works of the 1750s and 1760s, when the prospects for the recovery of liberty in France and elsewhere had looked so fair.

It seems unlikely that either *Du cours et de la marche des passions dans la société* or *Principes de moral* brought much consolation to their author. Their chief themes—the defeat of reason by the passions, the "secret poison" that menaced modern Europe with a fatal corruption—instead suggest a painful awareness on Mably's part of the limits of his own thought. Yet the imaginative depth and intellectual energy of these texts, and of the shorter dialogues that accompanied them, at least demonstrate that Mably's final pessimism had other springs than simply the toll of the years or his alleged bitterness over the triumph of the Enlightenment.

The real sources of the darkening of his outlook in his last years were twofold. In the first instance, as we have seen in this chapter, Mably's loss of intellectual optimism was prompted by the series of genuine political defeats, as he saw them, that he witnessed or experienced in the years after 1770: the ending of twenty years of parlementary agitation and "republican ferment" in France with the Maupeou Coup; the retirement of the "Age of Liberty" in Sweden with the restoration of royal authority by Gustavus III; the defeat and dismemberment of the Polish Commonwealth; even the democratic anarchy that seemed to flow in the wake of the American Revolution, and the risk of its capture by "commercial" despotism. It is to Mably's credit that despite his own disappointments over these events, he remained remarkably clear-headed about their meaning and causes. His final insistence that the French monarchy was no longer capable of reforming itself was of course correct; if Mably failed to understand that this made a French revolution inevitable rather than impossible, his own analysis of the dead weight of monarchical tradition in *Observations sur l'histoire de France* certainly helps to explain the tumultuous and convulsive character of the revolutionary process, once it was under way. As for Mably's late writings on Poland and the United States, what is striking in both is what might be termed the *sociological* insight he brought to the problems at hand. His later visits to Poland confirmed what he had already seemed to suspect in *Du gouvernement et des lois de la Pologne*, that what rendered the prospect of Polish reform so unlikely was the lack of any specific class *agent* to bring it about, given the reactionary outlook of the Polish nobility and the embryonic character of the Polish bourgeoisie. In regard to the United States, Mably was obviously wrong about the prospects for a major restructuring of the American polity at the federal level—but he was certainly not mistaken about the class character and outlook of the agents of change in this instance.

Beyond these local reverses and defeats, however, there was of course a deeper determinant of Mably's final pessimism. As we have seen, from start to finish his intellectual career revolved around the contrast between classical antiquity and European modernity, and the nature of the transition from one to the other. In *Parallèle des romains et des français*, the young royalist declared the superiority of modernity and ascribed its advance to the work of a benign providence. Mably's subsequent conversion to republicanism of course involved a reversal of this polarity and the abandonment of any such notion of providence. But it did not betoken any loss of political optimism. On the contrary, the basic assumption of Mably's major works of the 1750s and 1760s was that, while the heights of Spartan or Roman achievement might be beyond the grasp of modern Europeans, the classical republics could still provide a practical working model for a transition beyond absolute monarchy in Europe. The post-absolutist regimes of England and Sweden, together with the persistence of free city-states in Switzerland, Italy, and Germany, were there to show how much could be done; the political ferment in France at mid-century, the struggle for liberty in colonial America and even in feudal Poland suggested to Mably something like a further collective move in a republican direction. This optimism was never more than precarious, of course. Once these local hopes were dashed, and the immediate explanations for this or that reversal had been canvassed, Mably was left to confront the deeper mystery of the unattainable *superiority*, as he saw it, of ancient over modern civilization. What enabled the ancient Spartans or Romans to create political regimes so orderly, so free, and so durable that their memory still dazzled two millennia later? What prevented modern Europeans from even beginning to repeat those achievements? It goes without saying that Mably was incapable of providing any satisfactory answers to such questions, from within the confines of his own categories of thought. The economic laws of motion governing the rise and decline of classical civilization and the subsequent transition to feudalism in Europe—not to speak of the gathering transition to capitalism of Mably's own time—were naturally invisible to him, as they were to the overwhelming majority of his contemporaries. Acutely aware of the effects of these great structural shifts for the political lives of the states involved, yet unable to account for their causes, Mably unsurprisingly resorted to a familiar repertoire of Enlightenment explanatory devices, from the variable effects of climate to the molding force of "national character." In the end, however, he had recourse to the more desperate solutions of his last dialogues, whose chief themes—the frailty of human nature and the mortality of all political creations—were the sure signs of the limits of the classical republican vision, at the end of the Old Regime.

Fittingly, then, Mably ended his career by embracing a pessimism that accurately echoed that of his beloved ancients. Still, it is important not to exaggerate the darkness of his final outlook. Contrary to legend, Mably's pessimism never issued into bitterness or produced a loss of intellectual balance. This can perhaps best be seen in one of the shortest and most attractive of the later dialogues, which provides us with an appropriate end-point for our tour through his thought. In *De la superstition*, apparently written in 1777–78, Mably is confronted yet again by "Ariste," who remarks that the abbé has never addressed himself to this subject. It is, of course, the Enlightenment itself that is at stake here, since "superstition," or the problem of false belief, particularly in the religious realm, was one of the most central objects of its intellectual and political energies. Among other things, *De la superstition* proves yet again that Mably was never tempted to adopt an anti-Enlightenment stance *tout court*; here, as elsewhere, he appears merely as a sympathetic critic of its excesses. He first remarks that for all the evils caused by false beliefs and fanaticism, it is important to remember that "superstition" nevertheless seems to have consistently served indispensable social functions in the past—the glue of all known "primitive societies," it was also inseparable from the martial and cultural achievements of classical antiquity. As for the present-day campaign to extirpate all "superstition," Mably gently suggests that the philosophical work of Locke and Condillac themselves should lead to a certain epistemological modesty: how can we be sure that the thought of Newton will not be superseded in a century, as was that of Descartes? At the least, there is something "superstitious" and fanatical about the Enlightened campaign against superstition itself. We are social creatures, Mably concludes, destined to be governed for some time to come by the passions: the upshot is that we must learn to live with superstition, to tame rather than to abolish it, while waiting patiently for the gradual development of a more rational society.[64] Nothing could be more characteristic of Mably's temper than this cool and judicious appraisal of the enthusiasms of his contemporaries—expressing an outlook that combined, one might say, adapting the famous maxim of a later radical thinker, a classical pessimism of the intellect, and a modern optimism of the will.

CHAPTER 8

Conclusion: Classical Republicanism in Eighteenth-Century France

Mably died in Paris on 23 April 1785. The description of his last hours made by his friend and eulogist Pierre-Charles Levèsque suggests that he met his final illness and death with Socratic fortitude and good humor.[1] In fact, aside from the relatively small number of letters he left behind, the chief sources of information about Mably's life remain the two *éloges historiques* by Levèsque and the abbé Brizard, which shared a prize sponsored by the Royal Academy of Inscriptions and Belles-Lettres in 1787. There are slight differences between the two portraits of his character and temperament. Brizard's *éloge* is the more formal and pious, obviously animated by a concern to establish Mably's credentials as "a Spartan who wrote in Athens." He highlights Mably's willingness to sacrifice power and prestige in order to maintain his intellectual and moral independence, describing in detail his efforts to avoid election to the Académie Française.[2] Brizard also lays special stress on the real expressions of Mably's egalitarian social convictions—his scorn for the wealthy and well-born, his sympathy and generosity for social classes below his own, as well as the "virtuous poverty" of his own mode of life. Levèsque's profile is at once warmer and more critical of its subject. He concedes that Mably suffered from a certain inflexibility of character and rashness of judgment, which made him a stranger to compromise and conciliation; and he does not shrink from describing Mably's intemperate breach with Tencin, which was so decisive for the shape of his adult life, as "a mistake."[3] Mably himself seems to have been aware of the flaw: the anecdotal evidence adduced by Levèsque suggests that his friends often witnessed scenes that began with angry explosion and ended with rueful self-reproach.[4] At the same time, Levèsque also stresses the warmth and intensity of Mably's devotion to his circle of intimates, many of whom in turn remained faithful to his memory long after his death. Indeed, behind a public face of irascibility and misanthropy, there is every sign of a deep streak of kindness and solicitude toward others in Mably's character—Brizard and Levèsque were both impressed, for example, by the economies he imposed on himself in his last years in order to establish a legacy for his sole domestic servant.

At all events, the anecdotal evidence about Mably, as slight as it is, accords well enough with the more narrowly intellectual profile sketched in these pages. What are the main lines of our portrait of him as a thinker? They can be summarized as follows. Mably began his career as a political royalist whose thought initially found expression in a form of philosophical history. *Parallèle des romains et des français*, it might be said, joined the intellectual method of Montesquieu to the political values of Voltaire, in a characteristic early-Enlightenment mélange. Mably's commitment to philosophical history as a mode of social thought never wavered thereafter. But his original political convictions were soon abandoned, together with what had been a promising career in the service of the Bourbon monarchy. An apologist for French absolutism in 1740, Mably had become by mid-century a committed republican—a *classical* republican, for whom the egalitarian city-states of ancient Sparta and Rome served henceforth as the central models for political thought and action. At the same time, his mature thought plainly owed a more proximate debt to the English commonwealth tradition, which he always regarded as the most vital modern incarnation of Graeco-Roman republicanism, and to which he paid homage in *Des droits et des devoirs du citoyen*. As the latter work reveals, however, the real horizon of Mably's thought was always France itself. His own radicalization coincided with the "republican ferment"—in Franco Venturi's phrase—that overtook France in the 1750s. Mably's major works of the decade or so after 1758 were all written in a spirit of measured optimism, buoyed by his belief that a *"révolution ménagée"*—on the model of the Dutch Revolt, the English revolutions of the seventeenth-century, or the installation of Estates rule in contemporary Sweden—was at last possible in France. This optimism did not last, of course. The Maupeou Coup of 1771, which brought to an end the parlementary agitation of the 1750s and 1760s, and the repeated failure of Enlightened reform from above, both in France and elsewhere, combined to make the prospects for a general recovery of "liberty" in Europe seem increasingly remote to Mably. He ended his intellectual career in a somber mood. The common theme of his last writings might be termed the *failure of agency*—the tragic inability of mankind, individually and collectively, to master its fate by escaping from the constraints of custom and circumstance. But this final pessimism reflected more than mere political disappointment. It was also the inevitable expression of his classical republican outlook—that of a genuine "Machiavellian moment" prolonged, as it were, into the disconcerting context of late-eighteenth-century France.

This, of course, has been the central purpose of this study: to make a case for reading Mably as an authentic republican thinker, a French heir to Machiavelli and to Harrington. Indeed, it seems clear enough in retrospect that the features of his thought that have most attracted the attention of modern commentators—his radical egalitarianism, his insight into the tactics and strategies of political reform and revolution, his hostility to the Enlightenment and to "commercial society"—all spring from this same source. Why then has Mably's status as a republican thinker not been recognized earlier or more often? The answer seems to be that he has been the victim of accidents of geography and timing within the currents of modern historiography. As we have seen, Mably *was* in fact known as a classical republican at one time. In the eyes of early liberals such as Constant or Thierry, Mably was perhaps the most important of the promoters of "ancient liberty" who paved the way for the Jacobin Republic of Virtue and the Terror that accompanied it. But "classical republicanism" in this sense gradually disappeared from the agenda of French historiography, at the same time that Mably himself acquired the permanent label of *philosophe utopiste.* Neither the cult of the Greek city-states among Rousseau, Mably, and Helvétius, nor the Jacobin and Napoleonic imitation of Graeco-Roman institutions and symbolic forms—phenomena that once seemed so central to such diverse thinkers as Constant and Marx—have attracted the sort of attention that might have been expected from twentieth-century historians. As we noted in the introduction, however, there are in fact signs that this long period of neglect may finally have come to an end. Prompted by the recovery and reconstruction of the classical republican tradition *elsewhere* in early-modern Europe, from Renaissance Italy to Colonial America, a number of scholars have begun the work of extending these perspectives to the case of eighteenth-century

France. This brings us then to the question of the larger import of this intellectual biography of Mably. Assuming that the profile of his life and thought sketched in these pages is an accurate one, what does it have to contribute to a broader understanding of early-modern republicanism?

For obvious reasons, any response to this question must be speculative and provisional. Nevertheless, the evidence surveyed in this study of Mably's thought does point to certain general conclusions, beyond the purposes of intellectual biography proper. In the first place, a consistent attempt has been made throughout to define Mably's place within a larger narrative account of classical republicanism in the era of the decline and overthrow of French absolutism—it is clear that Mably was neither the first nor the only civic humanist thinker of his epoch. How might this wider history be characterized? In effect, Mably's own career suggests that a narrative account of classical republicanism in eighteenth-century France can best be approached in terms of three broad phases of development—the first running from the last decades of the reign of Louis XIV to mid-century, the second from the epoch of the High Enlightenment to the eve of the Revolution, and the third focusing on the decade of the Revolution itself.

The remote origins of French republicanism can thus be traced to certain signs, at the end of the seventeenth century, of novel polemical uses for references to classical antiquity—both to launch criticisms of Bourbon absolutism and to express anxiety over various programs of economic "modernization." Above all, there was the famous "Quarrel of the Ancients and the Moderns" itself, the acrimonious squabble among intellectual and literary elites that clouded the last quarter-century of the reign of Louis XIV, as well as the debates over "luxury" and "commerce" that flowed in the wake over the debacle of the Law System and the first arrival of Mandevillian ideas in France in the 1720s and 1730s. Far more important than either of these disputes, however, was a development somewhat further offstage—the appearance of what was unmistakably the language of classical republicanism in the service of aristocratic resistance to absolutism. As we have seen, the pivotal figure here seems to have been Boulainvilliers, whose historical writings of the first two decades of the century never ceased to be read down to the Revolution itself. Two features stand out in these works: first, Boulainvilliers's explicit depiction of the "feudal government" of the Dark Ages as a kind of Greek *polis*—a martial, egalitarian "mixed government" erected over a dependent labor force—which then gradually fell victim to monarchical "despotism"; and second, the fact that this aristocratic republicanism was mediated through an appeal to English political thought, as its proximate inspiration and source. Here, in other words, was one conduit for the importation of radical Commonwealth political ideas into France.

In any case, all three of these strands—the Quarrel of the Ancients and Moderns, the debate over luxury, and the emergence of aristocratic republicanism—formed the intellectual background for the greatest single work of political philosophy of the century. The publication of *De l'Esprit des lois* in 1748 can serve to mark the close of this first period of development: Monstesquieu's theory was, of course, founded on an explicit and deeply felt contrast between classical antiquity and European modernity, of the kind that lay behind the famous Quarrel. Within this framework, Montesquieu appeared as a moderate advocate of economic modernity, in which the interests of commerce were expected to soothe the passions of monarchical honor, the egalitarian virtue of the ancient republics belonging in any case to an irretrievable past. Finally, this position was then complicated by coded criticisms of Bourbon "despotism" and Montesquieu's cryptic depiction of the libertarian English constitution, which together suggest something of a paler version of Boulainvilliers's aristocratic republicanism. There is no more vexed issue than the question of Montesqieu's precise *parti pris* in politics. In fact, the delphic ambiguity of his political outlook was a reflection of the relative calm of the first half of the eighteenth century in France, when it was still possible to avoid hard political choices. As Judith Shklar has suggested, Montesquieu was central to the history of civic humanism in France, not because he *was* a "republican" in any direct sense, but because he established the terms in which republicanism was to be discussed for the rest of the century.[5]

At all events, the emergence of republicanism proper as a viable political program in French thought came only after Montesquieu's death, in the last three decades before the Revolution—the second major phase in this larger account. The conditions of possibility for this emergence seem to have been twofold: on the one hand, the sudden delegitimizing of the Bourbon monarchy, in the wake of continued military defeat and a series of bitter collisions between court and judicial elites over issues of fiscal imposition and reformation-style religious controversy; and, on the other, the major reception of radical English political thought in France, with the translations of both the canon of major Commonwealth thinkers and republicanized versions of Locke. This "republican ferment" provided the context and impetus for the appearance of at least two major versions of a French civic humanism, both reaching their maturity in the 1760s. The most striking and original of these theories was that of Jean-Jacques Rousseau. Paradoxically enough, it is only in the past few years that the effort to rewrite Rousseau's thought in terms of classical republicanism has gotten under way, despite Pocock's own description of him as "the Machiavelli of the eighteenth century." No doubt the complexity of Rousseau's thought, and his privilege as the most innovative thinker of the age, was owing to his position at the crossroads of *both* the major political languages of his time, natural law or contract theory, and classical republicanism. The hallmark of his thought, from a more conventional republican standpoint, was thus its determinate *abstraction*, whether expressed in the stadial theory of historical evolution in the *Discourse on Inequality*, or in the program for political legitimacy set forth in *The Social Contract*, founded on the novel concept of the "general will."

Meanwhile, the other commanding figure of French civic humanism was, of course, Mably, whose thought was perhaps less original than that of Rousseau, but for precisely that reason was probably more important in "naturalizing" classical republicanism in the French context. In the first place, Mably's debt to English thought, both to Commonwealth thinkers and to Locke, was far more explicit. At the same time—setting aside for the moment the flirtation with utopian communism that secured his later reputation—Mably produced what was arguably the major contribution to the central ideological dispute of the epoch, the debate over the history of the French monarchy. His legacy to his countrymen included a thoroughly republican interpretation of the national past, and a set of extraordinarily insightful meditations on the practical problems of effecting a revolutionary passage from absolutism to his cherished "mixed government," which were both to have an enormous impact during the years of the "pre-Revolution."

Whatever differences remain between the outlooks of Rousseau and Mably—and other names could be mentioned here as well—their thought taken together signaled the arrival of a new kind of republicanism on the French scene. Shorn of much of the aristocratic and nostalgic cast given it by Boulainvilliers and Montesquieu, classical republicanism could now assume a far more central place in the "public sphere" of the Old Regime. Nor was the impact of this republicanism confined to political thought alone, in the narrow sense of the term. There exists no more accurate or memorable description of what can properly be termed its "structure of feeling" than the chapter on eighteenth-century *opera seria* in Charles Rosen's *The Classical Style.* Rosen's object is the musical "naturalism" of Gluck, but the neoclassical outlook he describes, with its characteristic tension between "instinct" and "doctrine," is unmistakably that of Ledoux and David, Rousseau and Mably as well.[6] At the same time, a further feature of this new republicanism might be mentioned. From this point onward dated a distinctive trait of French civic humanism, which seems to have no clear precedents in earlier versions of the same political language. This was the ongoing debate between proponents of Sparta and Athens—a debate that continued through the Revolution itself, leaving its mark on the thought of Constant and others in the Restoration.[7]

What was the fate of French republicanism after Rousseau and Mably? The last decade before the Revolution is one of the murkiest in the history of eighteenth-century political thought, as established signposts and positions began to buckle under the pressure of the impending collapse of the Old Regime. What remains to be established by further research are the ways in which the relatively sophisticated intellectual programs of Rousseau, Mably, and others were diffused outward from the aristocratic salons that furnished their first audiences, and filtered downward along the social scale. For there is no doubt that these programs played important roles during the "pre-Revolution" and the outbreak of the Revolution proper. Specifically, the historical writings of Mably seem to have been absolutely central to the pamphlet wars of 1788–89; while the principles of *Du contrat social* are easy enough to read in and between the lines of the Declaration of Rights of 1789 and other revolutionary documents.[8] Nevertheless, classical republicanism in the precise sense of the term remained only one ideological option among many in the first years of the Revolution, and certainly not the most important. It is worth noting, for example, that the central token of Mably's political thought, "mixed government," seems to have made its one and only appearance during the Revolution with the "Monarchien" or Anglophile constitutional offensive of the summer of 1789, before being ushered off the stage permanently in September of that year. At the same time, another notable feature of this period was the earliest signs of the emergence of what can properly be called a *modern*—that is to say, specifically *anti*classical—republicanism in France, in the thought of Sieyès or Condorcet.

In the meantime, however, this period of ideological drift and dislocation in the first years of the Revolution also saw the incubation of a novel form of classical republicanism, still more popular and democratic than that of Rousseau and Mably. No doubt an important transitional figure here was that of Camille Desmoulins, whose advocacy of an "Athenian" model of republicanism dated from the summer of 1789 onwards. Desmoulins's debt to Mably and Rousseau, as well as to the Anglo-American radicalism of the Wilkes era, is evident; at the same time, he seems to have been among the earliest to introduce the positive vocabulary of *sans-culottism*.[9] In any case, the preconditions for an explosive phase of what might be called a republican "unity-of-theory-and-practice" had by now assembled themselves: the default of revolutionary leadership, the cancellation of monarchical legitimacy at Varennes, the onset of war with Austria and Prussia, and the upswing in urban insurgency. The establishment of the First Republic in September 1792 can thus be said to mark the start of a third great phase in the history of classical republicanism in France, after the moments of Boulainvilliers-Montesquieu and Mably-Rousseau—in effect, the moment of Jacobinsim proper. Now this is not, of course, to suggest that the political thought and practice of the First Republic can be subsumed under that rubric entirely, as if the Jacobin cult of antiquity could somehow provide us with an exhaustive explanation of the movement and its fate in these years. Nevertheless, it seems clear enough that the idealization of Graeco-Roman antiquity in the thought of Saint-Just, Robespierre, Billaud-Varenne, and others, should not only be seen as constitutive of the Jacobin outlook, but also that this outlook should be viewed as a highly distinctive variant of the tradition of early-modern republicanism as a whole. If this is true, then it also means that a narrative history of civic humanism in France would find it necessary at this point to turn its attention from the theory of politics to its practice; that is, from the writings and speeches of Saint-Just and Robespierre, and their various constitutional and educational schemes for the Republic of Virtue, to the actual record of governance during the Dictatorship of the Year II. In other words, the narrative would have to address such phenomena as the uneasy coalition between intellectual and political elites and their petty-bourgeois shock troops, the triumphant prosecution of the war and the rather less successful direction of the economy, the mounting of the great public festivals of the epoch, and the fatal recourse to the Terror.

Did the history of classical republicanism in France end with the deaths of Robespierre and Saint-Just? From one angle, the answer is obviously yes: there is a clear sense in which Thermidor would serve as the fitting conclusion to a narrative that began a century earlier with the "Quarrel of the Ancients and the Moderns"—modernity having at last won a decisive and irreversible victory over the fantasy of a return to antiquity. Yet even setting aside for the moment the rather different "civic humanism" of Gracchus Babeuf and his co-conspirators, there remains the problem of the persistent imitation of antique political nomenclature and institutional forms, right through the Directory and on into the Consulate and Empire themselves. No doubt a good argument can be made that an account of classical republicanism in France should be extended to include what might be termed the "classical imperialism" of the First Empire. At all events, whether one chooses to end such an account with Thermidor or with the Restoration, the proper coda to it would be some consideration of the wider impact of this story on contemporary thought. As we know, the fate of the First Republic, and the self-immolation of Jacobinism above all, was a decisive event in the intellectual history of the modern world, whose effects can be traced in at least two contrasting intellectual traditions, whose founding currents flowed in the wake of the Revolution. On the one hand, modern political liberalism now found its classic expression in the writings of Constant, whose tireless efforts to unlock the secret of the French Revolution returned insistently to the Jacobin attempt, as he saw it, to re-create France as a modern Sparta. Identifying Rousseau and Mably as the chief culprits behind this experiment, Constant argued that the lesson of the Jacobin catastrophe was that the "ancient liberty" of classical antiquity was lost forever to the modern world—which, however, did not prevent him from tinkering with plans to revive some paler, more tractable form of "ancient liberty" suitable to modern conditions. On the other side of the Rhine, Hegel drew not dissimilar conclusions in the founding texts of the German idealist tradition. *The Phenomenology of Spirit* featured a famous analysis of the Jacobin effort to revive the pristine unity of the ancient *polis* by sheer force of will, which necessarily ended in self-destructive failure. However, Hegel also went on in *The Philosophy of Right* to sketch a model for a society in which ancient collective liberty and modern subjective freedom would somehow be joined in a rational synthesis. Efforts to theorize one form or another of just such a synthesis have of course been a constant feature of modern political culture, right down to the present.

Such, then, is the shape of the narrative account of the fortunes of French classical republicanism suggested in this study of Mably's thought. What first emerged in France as an ideology of aristocratic resistance to absolutism was subsequently transformed into a contemporary outlook and program on a much wider social basis—aristobourgeois, one might say—by thinkers such as Rousseau and Mably. The space opened up by the Revolution then permitted a further radicalization of this republicanism, to the point where it could inspire and legitimate a brief and violent episode of revolutionary dictatorship, led by a bourgeois-popular coalition—an event that in turn left an indelible mark on modern intellectual life. If this sketch for a new history of French republicanism can be accepted, however, it leads us to a further question—what is its significance for the history of early modern republicanism as a whole? Specifically, it might be asked, what would J. G. A. Pocock's "Atlantic republican tradition" look like, were its canon widened to include the French thinkers mentioned above? Here a vast terrain opens up, which there is no question of exploring in any detail. The question can hardly be avoided, however, especially since this study has repeatedly advanced the claim that Mably's thought did indeed represent a Gallic variant of a wider republican tradition. If we confine ourselves to the specific concerns of Pocock, as the most authoritative and influential student of early modern republicanism, we can at least make some provisional suggestions.

The original thrust of the revisionism that produced *The Machiavellian Moment* was against what Pocock saw as the naive linearity of an entrenched view of the history of modern European political thought. Whigs and Marxists alike were held to have mistakenly confined this history to charting the gradual emergence and final triumph of Lockean liberalism over feudal hierarchy and monarchical despotism. To recover the lost history of early modern republicanism, Pocock argued, was to encounter what he described as "an enduring conflict between *two* post-feudal ideals, one agrarian and one commercial, once ancient and one modern."[10] The conflict between nostalgic republicanism and modernist liberalism, he frequently insisted, has never really been resolved in the modern world, least of all in the United States. Pocock's reconstruction of the "Atlantic republican tradition" and his consequent recasting of the history of modern political thought have tended in turn to provoke two kinds of criticism. On the one hand, some have rejected the entire notion of "classical republicanism" as a distinct or coherent category, much less a unitary tradition of thought stretching from Renaissance Italy to early nineteenth-century America. Specifically, there are few members of Pocock's republican canon whose thought cannot, from another angle, be described as "liberal"—and vice-versa, for no small number of founding fathers of liberalism. On this account, the idea of an "enduring conflict" between liberal and republican ideals seems more of an anachronistic retrojection of late twentieth-century concerns than anything else.[11] On the other hand, Pocock has also often been criticized for failing to provide adequate contextual explanations for the phenomena he describes, leaving his sweeping republican "tradition" without convincing grounding in the realities of economic, political, and even ideological history. Indeed, he has been charged with having gradually abandoned the responsibility of connecting the history of political thought with the history of politics proper, in his own version of an inward "linguistic" or "discursive" turn.[12]

These criticisms are not without force. But their case would appear rather different, had *The Machiavellian Moment* extended its embrace to include eighteenth-century France—had the names, say, of Mably, Rousseau, and Robespierre been added to those of Machiavelli, Harrington, and Madison. On the one hand, there would seem to be a good deal less difficulty in distinguishing the "republican" and "liberal" traditions, once one arrives on French soil. In part, this is because the hallmark of eighteenth-century French republicanism, in any comparative perspective, was its sheer *radicalism*, in so many respects: its shift of attention from Roman models to the more "primitive" Greek city-states, its heightened hostility to commerce and capital, its far greater commitment to egalitarian and communitarian ideals. It may be possible to dispute the republican credentials of a Harrington or a Madison—but this seems far less plausible in regard to a Mably or a Robespierre, neither of whom are likely in turn to be mistaken for "liberals" of any kind. On the other hand, once the connections between the world of Anglo-American civic humanism explored by Pocock and a wider continental republican tradition are restored, a rather different picture of the relation of this republicanism to real political history emerges. Few will dispute that the language of civic humanism originated in the communes of medieval Italy, where it served to legitimate political resistance to the despotic authority of Emperors and Popes. The decisive question, as J. H. Hexter once put it in a famous review of *The Machiavellian Moment*, is "how the devil" did a political ideology forged in so unique a context, for such particular purposes, manage to find an audience far to the north of the Mediterranean, in the world of post-Renaissance, monarchical Europe?[13] The answer seems to be that an ideology that was useful for defending the liberty of Italian city-states proved no less serviceable for legitimating revolution in emergent European nation-states. For the career of classical republicanism seems to have tracked fairly faithfully what was once seen as the initial chain of great bourgeois revolutions against absolutism—the Dutch Revolt, the English Civil War, the American War for Independence, and the French Revolution. Within this series, this brand of republicanism initially played what was essentially a secondary or cameo role, since in the Netherlands and England it had to contend with much more entrenched religious idioms and local ideologies of ancient constitutionalism. But in the more secular and commercialized world of the eighteenth century, the tradition was prepared to arrive at its explosive maturity. On the account of Pocock and his followers, classical republicanism acted as a decisive catalyst in the American Revolution, and, even after its defeat, survived as a permanent and recurrent counterpoint in American political culture. In France, if the account suggested above is accurate, a variant of this republicanism played a still more central role in the Revolution and its dénouement, making an unforgettable impression on modern thought, whether as inspiring memory or as cautionary tale.

Of course, the legacy of eighteenth-century French republicanism went beyond memory alone. It may well be the case, as Perry Anderson has suggested, that other varieties of early modern civic humanism were essentially "ideological misfits," whose nostalgia for an illusory past robbed them of real political effect and relegated them to the margins of history.[14] But this seems a slightly less accurate judgment in regard to the political thought of Rousseau or the revolutionary balance sheet of Jacobinism. Defeated in the short term, Jacobinism helped to effect a permanent delegitimizing of monarchism in France, and no doubt paved the way for the emergence of the decisive French contribution to *modern* republicanism, the political culture of the Third Republic. At the same time, Jacobinism also turned out to have been the *fons et origo* of a variety of modern revolutionary traditions, bourgeois and socialist alike: it provided a kind of template for the bourgeois radicalism of the nineteenth century, as well as for Leninism in the twentieth.

But there is a further consideration here, one that will return us, finally, to Mably himself. There is no more insistent gesture in Pocock's historical writing than the reminder that from the Greeks to the present there has been a nearly continuous record of hostility toward "commercial" or "market" society, which has really only been challenged in the modern age:

> In every phase of the Western tradition, there is a conception of virtue—Aristotelian, Thomist, neo-Machiavellian or Marxian—to which the spread of exchange relations is seen as presenting a threat. In this perspective, those thinkers of the seventeenth through the nineteenth centuries

> who argued on individualist, capitalist or liberal premises that the market economy might benefit and transform human existence appear to be the great creative heretics and dissenters.[15]

What is more, Pocock's work is littered with hints that there were in fact very real connections, of influence and inheritance, between the "neo-Machiavellianism" that has formed his own object of study and the early socialist tradition—connections, that, if uncovered, would "end by establishing a kind of continuity between the days of Swift and those of Marx, and showing that there was in fact no moment at which the ideology of commerce was immune from the criticisms which the neo-Harringtonians had launched."[16]

In actually specifying such "linkages" between late civic humanism and early socialism, Pocock has typically confined himself to gestures in the direction of Rousseau. He has not been alone in this: no less authoritative a figure than Lucio Colletti once argued that the early political thought of Marx was to all intents and purposes identical with that of Rousseau.[17] At the same time, however, it is clear that the question of the relationship between early modern classical republicanism and the modern socialist tradition is not to be reduced to that of the influence of one individual thinker upon another—for which the evidence in any case happens to be rather weak in regard to Rousseau and Marx.[18] Instead, these connections are obviously to be sought in the wider tradition of French republicanism, to which Rousseau was merely one contributor among many. For there is no great mystery about the history of socialist thought prior to Marx, whose roots are largely to be traced within a single national tradition, the "French socialism" spoken of by Lenin in his famous article of 1913 on "The Three Sources and the Three Component Parts of Marxism." Indeed, behind the great "utopian" figures of Fourier and Saint-Simon, everything leads back to a single enigmatic figure and a single punctual gesture—the abortive coup d'état against the Directory led by a Jacobin extremist named Babeuf, who had already changed his first name to "Gracchus," and who conceived of the restoration of the Constitution of 1793 as merely a prelude to the establishment of a genuinely communal property regime in the First Republic.

But the "Conspiracy of the Equals" that founded the socialist tradition proper was not born out of thin air. Babeuf's claims at his trial that he had merely been inspired by a gallery of the most eminent thinkers—Rousseau, Diderot, and Mably above all—have sometimes been seen as no more than a tactical attempt to lend a spurious prestige to his cause. In fact, Babeuf was clearly a lineal descendent of the classical republican tradition described above, and by no means the least of its thinkers. The appeal to classical precedent in his writings was no less central to his outlook than it was to less extreme forms of Jacobinism.[19] As for Mably, we have taken some pains to try to distinguish his position from that of the genuinely utopian thinkers of his era with whom he is typically grouped—Meslier, Morelly, and Dom Deschamps—and who also contributed something to the intellectual background of Babeuvism. But it is important not to deny the utopian element in Mably's thought altogether. An intense preoccupation with the *communauté des biens* as an ideal of social organization dominated his writing in the decade after 1758, the most creative years of his intellectual career. Mably was no doubt driven to this preoccupation by the properly republican conviction—one shared with Rousseau—that the distribution of property was the decisive feature of any society, governing its evolution, its stability and durability, and, ultimately, the happiness or misery of its citizens. But Mably's concern with the ideal of communal property went beyond anything found in Rousseau. Though he claimed merely to be following in the footsteps of Plato and More in this respect, there are good reasons, as we have seen, to believe that Mably himself had felt the direct influence of his utopian contemporaries. This need not detract in the least from the *essentially* republican character of his thought. Instead, what this record of affinities and influences suggests is the essential accuracy of Pocock's instinct about the connections between the later republican tradition and the emergence of socialism in European thought. It has been some time since the question of the intellectual prehistory of socialism, and especially its relation to the specific crucible of the French Revolution, has been tackled in depth by any historian, but it seems perfectly clear what the appropriate terrain of any such inquiry must be.

In a number of respects, then, a genuinely comparative look at the fortunes of civic humanism in eighteenth-century and revolutionary France promises to alter our sense of the history of early modern republicanism as a whole—giving us an "Atlantic republican tradition" more easily distinguishable from liberalism, standing in a clearer and more decisive relation to the history of revolution, and with still closer and more intimate connections with early socialist thought. But it is time now to set these speculations aside, for other occasions. It is enough here to recall the main purpose of the study at hand—to argue that whatever final judgments are made about the shape and fate of classical republicanism in France, Mably himself will be seen to have played a central role in its history.

Reference Matter

Abbreviations

Although I occasionally refer to other editions of Mably's works, references are generally to the *Collection complète des oeuvres de l'Abbé de Mably*, published in fifteen volumes in 1794–95, the most widely available of the *oeuvres complètes*. The following abbreviations are used to refer to specific titles, which will be followed by the volume and page numbers in the *Collection complète*.

B	*Du Beau* (vol. 14)
BP	*Le banquet des politiques* (vol. 13)
CG	*Du commerce des grains* (vol. 13)
CMPS	*Du cours et de la marche des passions dans la société* (vol. 15)
CR	*Le compte rendu* (vol. 15)
DDC	*Des droits et des devoirs du citoyen* (vol. 11)
DPBR	*Du développement, des progrès et des bornes de la raison* (vol. 15)
DPPE	*Doutes proposées aux philosophes économistes sur l'ordre naturel et essentiel des sociétés politiques* (vol. 11)
DPE	*Le droit publique de l'Europe* (vols. 5–7)
EH	*De l'étude de l'histoire* (vol. 12)
EP	*De l'étude de la politique* (vol. 13)
EPh	*Entretiens de Phocion sur le rapport de la morale avec la politique* (vol. 10)
GLP	*Du gouvernement et des lois de la Pologne* (vol. 8)

GR	*Notre gloire ou nos rêves* (vol. 13)
LPL	*De la législation ou Principes des lois* (vol. 9)
MEH	*De la manière d'écrire l'histoire* (vol. 12)
MPT	*Des maladies politiques et de leur traitement* (vol. 13)
OA	*L'oracle d'Apollon ou de la connoissance de soi-même* (vol. 14)
OGEUA	*Observations sur le gouvernement des Etats-Unis d'Amérique* (vol. 8)
OHF	*Observations sur l'histoire de France* (vols. 1–3)
OHG	*Observations sur l'histoire de la Grèce* (vol. 4)
OR	*Observations sur les Romains* (vol. 4)
PM	*Principes de morale* (vol. 10)
PN	*Principes des Négociations* (vol. 5)
RN	*La retraite de M. Necker* (vol. 15)
S	*De la superstition* (vol. 13)
SPP	*De la situation politique de la Pologne en 1776* (vol. 13)
T	*Des talents* (vol. 14)

Notes

Chapter 1

1. Constant, p. 501. Unless otherwise indicated, all translations are my own.

2. Constant did not deny the immense allure of "ancient liberty"—his appreciation for it was in fact far warmer in this text, written on the eve of the assassination of the duc de Berry and the Ultra resurgence that accompanied it, than in any earlier formulation of the same theme. His willingness to find a role for a tempered version of "ancient liberty" in the modern world has of course made his recuperation by twentieth-century liberalism all the easier, as is evident throughout Stephen Holmes's study *Benjamin Constant and the Making of Modern Liberalism.*

3. The one major exception may be *Lettres à Mme la Marquise de P . . . sur l'opéra*, a book published anonymously in 1741 that is often attributed to Mably. Recent commentators have expressed a wide range of opinion about the attribution, from Maffey's skepticism (*Il pensiero politico*, p. 16) to Stiffoni's recognition of Mably's "mode of discussion" in the *Lettres* (*Utopia e ragione*, p. 24). At all events, a proper treatment of this work exceeds the competence of the present study. For some brief remarks on its place in eighteenth-century musical thought, see Girdlestone, pp. 73, 108, 145, 179, 185, 532–53, and Haeringer, pp. 15, 17, 109.

4. *EPh*, 10: p. 72.

5. Two works in fact may be numbered among the best-sellers of the epoch: *Le droit public de l'Europe*, which attained textbook status in several languges; and *Entretiens de Phocion*, which saw twelve editions in French alone, prior to the Revolution. For the balance sheet on Mably's publications, see Schleich, *Aufklärung und Revolution*, pp. 90–105.

6. The hostility was reciprocated, for the one place where Mably's works met with a consistently disparaging and dismissive reception was in the *Correspondance littéraire* edited by Grimm and his colleagues, the house organ, as it were, of the French Enlightenment. For some examples, see *Correspondance littéraire* 5 (May 1763): 293–94 (review of *Entretiens de*

Phocion); and ibid., 6 (April 1765 and December 1766): 253–54, 507 (on *Observations sur l'histoire de France*). A review of *Observations sur l'histoire de Grèce* characteristically concludes: "But the dreams of Montesquieu are at least ingenious, those of a great man, while those of M. de Mably belong to a mediocre man who sees no further than the end of his nose." *Correspondance littéraire* 7 (December 1766): 188.

7. For a detailed account of these personal collisions, see Galliani, "Mably et Voltaire."

8. A fact that the arch-anti-*philosophe* Fréron attributed directly to philosophic malice: "Here then is the great crime of M. the abbé de Mably and the principle cause of the kind of obscurity into which he fell in the last years of his life: he consistently refused to bend his knee before the idol of the day; his pure hands never burned incense at the altar of the Grand Lama of the empire of letters—that is to say, he dared to attack the Patriarch of Ferney on his throne. . . . From that point onward, the partisans of Voltaire, who throng through all the great houses of Paris, who direct the opinion of high society and distribute the certificates of genius according to their whim, took care to bury the good Abbé de Mably, to the point that one hardly knew he ever existed"; Fréron, pp. 305–10.

9. Rabaut de Saint Etienne, p. 85.

10. Mounier, p. 17.

11. For detailed documentation on the various aspects of Mably's revolutionary cult, again see Schleich, *Aufklärung und Revolution*, pp. 150–85.

12. This is amply documented in Harpaz, "Mably et la postérité."

13. Constant, p. 503.

14. Thierry, p. 64.

15. Lerminier, p. 95

16. Franck, p. 111.

17. Cited in Harpaz, "Mably et la postérité," p. 34.

18. See Marx, p. 436, and Engels, pp. 25 and 27.

19. See, for example, Lichtenberger, pp. 221–46, and Espinas, pp. 91–97. The former remains a valuable brief exposition of Mably's thought.

20. Gay, p. 18.

21. Guerrier's book opened with this statement: "Among the illustrious writers of the eighteenth century, there is only one who has been almost totally and unjustly neglected by our epoch: the abbé de Mably. . . . History offers us few examples of so striking a contrast in the destiny of a writer: an almost scornful indifference rapidly succeeded the reputation and exaggerated glory he enjoyed in his lifetime" (Guerrier, p. 1). Nearly fifty years later, Whitfield was still insisting that Mably should be "reinstated in the position from which he has been unjustly banished" (Whitfield, p. 33).

22. Galliani, "Quelques aspects de la fortune," p. 549.

23. Ibid.

24. Procacci, p. 219.

25. An exception is the article by Apih, in which Mably's thought is compared with that of Linguet.

26. See the three articles by Harpaz: "Mably et la postérité," "Mably et ses contemporains," and "Le social de Mably."

27. See Maffey, *Il pensiero politico*, pp. 103–33, in particular.

28. Ibid., pp. 9–10.

29. See Lecercle, "Mably et la théorie de la diplomatie," where *Principes des négociations* is described as "the first systematic attempt to found diplomatic practice as a rigorous science" (p. 899); Gauthier; Furet and Ozouf; and Baker, "Memory and Practice."

30. For a definitive demonstration of the point, see Baker, "A Script for a French Revolution."

31. *LPL*, 9: 43.

32. See the resumé of Eastern European literature on Mably in Galliani, "Quelques aspects." A representative sample can be seen in the article by Safronov, "Les idées politiques et sociales de Mably."

33. See Composto; Lecercle, "Utopie et réalisme politique"; and Galliani, "Quelques aspects."

34. See in particular the final chapter of *Utopia e ragione*, "Communismo egualitario come political dell'utopia e progretto riformatore," pp. 331–72.

35. Thamer, p. 185.

36. See Lehmann, pp. 196–98.

37. "The result of our *Rezeptionsgeschichte* of Mably is to suggest that we can turn the conspiracy thesis 'on its head': if one considers the 'metamorphoses' of this political philosopher—who changed from the leading figure of a conservative, anti-Enlightenment resistance, to an undisputed 'father of the Revolution' who experienced hostility only from conservative forces—then the Enlightenment did not 'make' the Revolution, but rather the Revolution made the Enlightenment. That is, the revolutionaries' own belief—as it has uncritically been received in the historiography of the Revolution—that they were implementing the goals of the Enlightenment has conditioned our image of the Enlightenment to such an extent that we project the revolutionaries' point of view back on the formation of the Enlightenment before the Revolution" (*Aufklärung und Revolution*, pp. 210–11)—a thesis that is perhaps less novel or heterodox today than Schleich imagines it to be.

38. The term is that of Elizabeth Rawson, in her invaluable study of *The Spartan Tradition in European Thought*.

39. See Schleich, "Der zweitbeste Staat."

40. Maffey, *Il pensiero politico*, pp. 161–62.

41. Where the subject has been kept alive, it is chiefly among classicists; see, for example, the articles by Vidal-Naquet and Loraux. Rawson, meanwhile, devotes three chapters to eighteenth-century France.

42. Pocock, *The Machiavellian Moment*, p. 504.

43. Even friendly critics expressed surprise at the notion of an "Atlantic republican tradition" that excluded the First Republic: see Gilbert, pp. 307–8, and Shklar, "Review of *The Political Works of James Harrington*," pp. 558–61.

44. Venturi, *Utopia and Reform*, pp. 47–69.

45. Cf. Gilbert's comment on *The Machiavellian Moment*: "But if one

thinks when in European history a Machiavellian moment occurred, neither the English Civil War of the seventeenth century nor the happenings in the British colonies of America come first to mind: one thinks of the French Revolution and of the reforms in Prussia. There we find hope for the beginning of an entirely new era, the appeal for a complete renewal of the social organization. There we have the demand for an active participation in politics by every member of society, and there we see the creation of a citizen army. We have the call for a conversion to true virtue—whether this call is uttered in France by the virtuous Robespierre, or in Prussia, promoted by the young military men of the Tugenbund" (p. 308).

46. Even with these two major thinkers, it is remarkable how slow scholars have been to make use of the recent literature on classical republicanism. It has taken until Viroli's *Jean-Jacques Rousseau and the 'Well-Ordered State'* (1989) for the question even to be broached in regard to Rousseau; meanwhile, there is no discussion at all of Montesquieu's relation to the republican tradition, even where it might be expected, as in Shklar's *Montesquieu*.

47. See Baker, "A Script for a French Revolution" and "Memory and Practice."

Chapter 2

1. Preface to *OR*, 4: 225–26.

2. Brizard, p. 101.

3. For a description of the Mably household in Lyon, see Aurenche. It was there that Mably first made the acquaintance of Rousseau.

4. Condillac, for his part, was ordained, but said mass no more than once, according to legend. For comments on the largely honorific title of "abbé," see Marion, p. 2. These abbés were often the objects of criticism and ridicule, the most famous example of which was the mordant attack of Voltaire in the *Dictionnaire philosophique*.

5. See Barthélemy, pp. 221–310. Barthélemy's "La vie privée de M. l'abbé de Mably" was published in a volume falsely attributed to Mably, *Le Destin de la France*.

6. Mably, *Parallèle*, 1: v.

7. For recent examinations of Montesquieu's own historical practice in his *Considérations*, see Shklar, *Montesquieu*, pp. 49–66, and Womersley, pp. 9–19.

8. Mably cites a passage from the sixth book of Polybius's *Histories*: *Parallèle*, 1: 45; the *Histories* of Tacitus are cited, 1: 174, and the *Annales*, 1: 237.

9. Mably also refers to Leibniz's *Essai sur l'Origine des Français*: *Parallèle*, 1: 232. By this time, he was acquainted with Pufendorf's *De jure naturae et gentium* as well: see *Parallèle*, 1: 236.

10. For useful general discussions of the uses of history in early-modern French political culture, see Lemaire, Keohane, and Grell.

11. This is already evident in the brilliant philippic, commonly attributed to the Protestant publicist Pierre Jurieu, written in the middle of Louis XIV's reign, *Les soupirs de la France esclave* (1689). This work anticipated many of the arguments of the gathering aristocratic opposition. Written from exile, however, its impact was postponed until well into the eighteenth century.

12. The fourteen *Lettres* were probably written between 1716 and 1718; they were published posthumously, in two versions: *Histoire de l'ancien gouvernement de la France, avec XIV lettres historiques sur les parlements ou états généraux de la France* (1727), and *Etat de la France, contenant XIV lettres sur les anciens parlements de France* (1728). For the complex history of Boulainvilliers's manuscripts, see the definitive study by Ellis, "Boulainvilliers Ideologue and Publicist," especially the bibliographical appendix, pp. 778–844.

13. The one indispensable study of the debate remains that of Carcassone, which, however, should be supplemented with Ellis, "Montesquieu's Modern Politics," and Baker's essays in *Inventing the French Revolution*.

14. Mably, *Parallèle*, 1: 106–7, 136; 2: 6–7.

15. See Ferrier-Caverivière, pp. 351–59.

16. "It is true that Athens was free; it was the center of a republic; its citizens were equal; they were not ashamed of one another; they walked, alone and on foot, into a clean, peaceful, and spacious town, in whose shops and markets they bought themselves their necessities; the emulation of a court did not force their exit from a common life. . . . There they assembled in order to deliberate on public affairs; here they conversed with foreigners; elsewhere, the philosophers taught their doctrines and lectured to their students. These places were then the scenes of both pleasure and business. There was something so simple and popular in these activities, which so little resemble our own . . ." (La Bruyère, p. 36).

17. See the summary of the "modernist" position in Ferrier-Caverivière, pp. 366–79.

18. See Kortum and Ross.

19. The notion of a "parallel" history also may owe something to Montesquieu, for the fourth chapter of the *Considérations* is devoted to a "parallel" between Carthage and Rome.

20. Mably thus repeatedly echoes the famous tributes that Machiavelli made to the "struggle of the orders" in Book I of the *Discorsi*. "To whatever degree of perfection the quarrels between the nobility and the people brought the particular policies of the Romans, this was not the greatest advantage they produced. They distributed sovereign power among the different parties, and the equality that this established among the citizens reinforced the marvelous order of this government." (Mably, *Parallèle*, 1: 44–45).

21. Ibid., 1: 59.

22. Ibid., 1: 86–91.

23. Ibid., 1: 92.

24. Ibid., 1: 90–91.

25. Ibid., 1: 106–7.

26. For the classical origins of the idea, see von Fritz; for its medieval career, see the recent study by Blythe.

27. Montesquieu, *Considérations*, in *Oeuvres complètes*, 1: 405.
28. Vertot, 1: 125–26.
29. Mably, *Parallèle*, 1: 113–30, 223–27.
30. Ibid., 1: 256–60, 310–11.
31. Ibid., 1: 340–46.
32. Ibid., 1: 170–71.
33. Ibid., 1: 265–66.
34. Ibid., 1: 266.
35. Ibid., 1: 333–34.
36. Ibid., 2: 351.
37. See Chapter VIII of Book I, "Refléxions sur la bonté absolue et la bonté relative des gouvernements."
38. Mably, *Parallèle*, 1: 52. The concept of a "contradiction" between a given institutional form and the *moeurs* of a people is of course a central token of Montesquieu's sociology, from which Mably undoubtedly derived it.
39. Ibid., 1: 323.
40. Ibid., 1: 314. "A government founded on the same principles as that of Sparta and Rome would not revive the *moeurs* of the ancients. These will never be seen again, unless by some revolution impossible to predict all the arts are lost, and by a series of events that it would be absurd and chimerical to expect, men somehow find themselves once more in the same circumstances as the Spartans." (Ibid., 1: 56.)
41. Ibid., 1: 318.
42. Mably in fact explicitly recommends Melon's *Essai politique sur le commerce* to his readers in a note: 1: 322.
43. Commenting on the conventional comparisons between the struggle of the orders in Rome and the civil strife recorded in English history, Mably insists that their mixed governments were still fundamentally dissimilar: "In England there are laws that prevent the prince, the nobility, and the commons from uniting. There is no circulation among the three orders of the state such as to give them one single interest." (Ibid., 1: 77–78.)
44. Montesquieu, *De l'Esprit des lois*, 1: 139.
45. To be fair, Mably does pay a conventional tribute to the historical role of the *Gens de Robe*: "The magistrates contributed a good deal to the perfection of the government: they were the guardians of the law and they made its authority felt; this was a new yoke for the nobility, which in no way rendered the king hateful." (*Parallèle*, 1: 178). But he is quite silent on any role played by the *noblesse de robe* or *parlements* subsequent to the medieval period.
46. Mably, *Parallèle*, 1: 271.
47. "Besides establishing the order of succession that is least likely to render these rights litigious, and the fact that it is marvelously apt to promote the enlargement of the state . . . the Salic Law also ties more intimately the subjects to the sovereign, and the sovereign to his subjects." (Ibid., 1: 355.)
48. The reviewer in the latter wrote: "This work can only bring honor to its author, in every way. It is solid in its reasoning, just and fair in the conclusions it draws, and the parallels it establishes are very judicious. Its style is pure, correct, and strong. Although its author's name is little known

in the republic of letters, one risks nothing in placing him among its ranks; all the more so, if this book were indeed his first effort." (*Bibliothèque raisonnée* 28, January–June 1742: p. 306.)

49. Voltaire, 35: 392.

50. She also had the honor of guiding *De l'Esprit des lois* through the press in 1748, and was rewarded with the first copy to reach Paris. For Madame de Tencin's life, see the biography by Masson.

51. If his biographers can be trusted, Mably was engaged in work of considerable importance. According to Brizard, it was Mably who negotiated secretly with the Prussian minister in 1743, and drafted the treaty conveyed to Frederick by Voltaire; later, he had the honor of carrying the day in the Council of War, when his advice to initiate a campaign in the Low Countries happened to coincide with the designs of Frederick; finally, it is claimed, he prepared the instructions for the French delegates to the negotiations at Breda in 1646. See Brizard, pp. 97–98, and Levèsque pp. 10–14. The only extant record of Mably's diplomatic activity, however, is the collection of five short *mémoires* he drafted, preserved in the Archives du Ministère des Affaires Etrangères at Paris; they are printed as an appendix to Stiffoni, "Da 'royaliste' a 'democrate,'" pp. 122–37.

52. See Maffey, *Il pensiero politico*, pp. 24–25, 214–15.

53. "One will not find here the sort of commentary with which Rousset has honored the editions of my work issued by the booksellers of Holland. This commentary, produced, no doubt, with too great haste, is unworthy of the reputation that its author has acquired in the republic of letters. . . . At times he affects not to understand me, in order to rehash arguments that are as useless as they are long; at other times, he accuses me of concealing my thoughts, and in attempting to bring me out, he has me saying things I am very far from having thought. If one is reading only for instruction and for the pursuit of the truth, the commentary by Rousset is perfectly useless to my work." (*DPE*, 4: 242–43.)

54. For example: Rousset had protested a reference in the 1746 *Droit public* to the "usurpation of William III"; in 1764 this was replaced with: "his conduct in regard to James II." For this and other alterations prompted by Rousset's criticisms, see the discussion in Lecercle, "Mably et la théorie de la diplomatie," pp. 904–8.

55. Brizard p. 98.

56. See Friedemann, "Neues zur Biographie Mablys," pp. 361–68.

57. On this occasion, Mably wrote a revealing letter (7 October 1766) to the Duc de la Rochefoucauld: "I am very sure of the pleasure that the news of my pension brings to you, or rather the pension of Madame the duchesse d'Enville. . . . In truth, Monsieur le duc, after having spent thirty years convincing yourself that it is easier to do without a fortune than to make one, you feel very rich indeed when your income is doubled all at once; you feel, in a sense, flooded with superfluity, as if you were suddenly transported to the mines of Peru." (Sarreil, p. 69.)

Chapter 3

1. Mably, *Observations sur les Grecs*, n. p. [p. 2]. The Virgilian epigraph of the book—"Rerum cognoscere causas" (Georgics, II.490)—is an appropriate motto for Montesquieuean historiography in general, as David Womersley remarks: Womersley, p. 11.

2. *OHG*, 4: ii–iv.

3. Herodotus, Thucydides, Xenophon, Polybius, Plutarch, Livy, Dionysius of Halicarnassus, and Tacitus are all cited with considerable frequency. This erudition had its limits, however, for the Greek works are quoted in Latin or French translation: there is no evidence that Mably read Greek.

4. Mably, *Observations sur les Grecs*, p. 10; *OHG*, 4: 9.

5. *OHG.*, 4: 14.

6. Ibid., 4: 16.

7. Mably's description of Lycurgus is notable for the emphasis he places on both the radicalism of the reforms and the coercive character of their imposition: "Lycurgus opposed his genius to that of the Spartans, and dared to take up the hard task of making them into a new people. He did not believe it impossible to involve everyone, by hope or by fear, in the revolution he planned. He found a handful of worthy friends willing to appear armed in the public square where he would declare his laws; and, without any right other than that conferred by a love of the good and the safety of the people, he forced the Lacadeamonians to become wise and happy" (ibid., 4: 16–17).

8. Ibid., 4: 18.

9. Ibid., 4: 19–20.

10. *OR*, 4: 280–83.

11. See the *Discorsi*, Book 1, Chapter 3. This also induced Mably to read the functions of the tribunate back into the ephorate of Sparta, as the quotation above from the *Observations* on Greece makes clear.

12. *OR*, 4: 289.

13. The standard historical work on the terminology of "powers," W. B. Gwyn's *The Meaning of the Separation of Powers*, attempts to treat the two as separable, but Gwyn's own evidence clearly belies this. It seems to be the case, as von Fritz assumes in *The Theory of the Mixed Constitution in Antiquity*, that every theory of "mixed government," from Aristotle and Polybius to Mably and John Adams, inolves some differentiation of governmental "powers" and various calls for their "separation" or "balance."

14. For the interpretation of the *Discorsi* as a "systematic dissent from the Venetian paradigm," see Pocock, *The Machiavellian Moment*, pp. 183–218.

15. Machiavelli, pp. 145–46.

16. *OHG*, 4: 20–21.

17. Ibid., 4: 22.

18. *OR*, 4: 269–70.

19. *OHG*, 4: 23.

20. *OR*, 4: 426.

21. Ibid., 4: 444.

22. Ibid., 4: 462.

23. A feature that recommended the work to several of the American

founders: see Reinhold, pp. 236–37.

24. *OHG*, 4: 10–11.

25. Ibid., 4: 211.

26. Ibid., 4: 245–46. "In reading their history," Mably continues, "we feel ourselves renewed; if we still possess in our hearts some germ of virtue, our souls take flight, and seem to soar beyond the narrow confines in which the corruption of our century has kept us."

27. Ibid., 4: 60.

28. "The spoils of Plataea gave the Greeks a love of riches; the Spartans themselves dared to take part of the booty and to profane their city with Persian gold, while the Athenians, not realizing that too great a prosperity always announces an immediate decadence, gave themselves over to an insane presumption" (ibid., 4: 55).

29. "I do not blame her [Sparta]," Mably writes, "for having finally succumbed, since this was inevitable; but I do blame her for having taken none of the precautions suggested by common prudence, in order to evade or at least put off the dangers with which she was menaced" (Ibid., 4: 116-17).

30. Ibid., 4: 123.

31. *OR*, 4: 535.

32. Ibid., 4: 302–3.

33. Ibid., 4: 375.

34. Ibid., 4: 421.

35. *OHG*, 4: 154–55.

36. Mably, *Observations sur les Grecs*, pp. 197–98.

37. *OHG*, 4: 165–66.

38. Ibid., 4: 168.

39. Ibid., 4: 213–14.

40. Ibid., 4: 226.

41. Ibid., 4: 248.

42. *DPE*, 5: 241.

43. For accounts of the strategic decline of France in the long-term, see Doyle, *The Old European Order*, pp. 265–91; and Wallerstein, Chapter 6.

44. For these effects, see the recent account by James C. Riley.

45. *PN*, 5: 11–12.

46. Ibid., 5: 38.

47. As noted above, *Principes des Négociations* has been called "the first systematic attempt to found diplomatic practice on a rigorous scientific basis" (Lecercle, "Mably et la théorie de la diplomatie", p. 899).

48. *PN*, 5: 19–20.

49. Ibid., 5: 19.

50. Ibid., 5: 37–38, 48–56, 60–72.

51. "The interest of a prince of the second order is not to attempt to expand at the expense of the dominant powers. In this way, he will make no enemies; for, whatever reasons they have to complain about him, they have so many more to forgive him and to seek out his friendship" (Ibid., 5: 85). "I might blush at the Machiavellian maxims I have just set forth," Mably comments, "if it were not possible to extract from them some consequences useful to men" (Ibid., 5: 83–84).

52. "The division of public power," Mably continues, considerably underestimating the martial abilities of the English, "has not been made in England in the proportions necessary to give the state a common interest and a constant conduct in regard to foreigners" (Ibid., 5: 34–35).

53. Ibid., 5: 27.
54. Ibid., 5: 70.
55. Ibid., 5: 68.
56. For a survey of attitudes towards war and commerce in Europe, from Bodin to Smith, see Silberner.
57. *PN*, 5: 196.
58. Mably mentions no particular edition; French translations of Hume's essays were published in both Paris and Amsterdam in 1752 and 1754. See Rochedieu, pp. 161–62.
59. It is notable, however, that in "Of Luxury" (Hume changed the title to "Of Refinements in the Arts" in later editions of the *Political Discourses*), the defense of luxury takes up nine pages, while the criticisms Hume promises are given only two. See Hume, pp. 268–80.
60. Ibid., p. 265.
61. *PN*, 5: 199–200.
62. "[T]he most systematic, the most lucid, and at the same time the most original of all the statements of economic principles before the *Wealth of Nations*" (Blaug, p. 20). Cantillon's work was published in French in 1755, but apparently circulated in French and English manuscripts several decades prior to this; a useful edition has been edited by Takumi Tsuda. For Cantillon's life and work, see the recent biography by Antoin E. Murphy.
63. *PN*, 5: 200.
64. For the history of the doctrine of the "specie-flow mechanism," from Mun to Hume, see Viner, pp. 74–87; and Blaug, pp. 11–13, 18–21.
65. See Hume, pp. 281–85. Mably seems not to be aware that Hume had presented an argument more or less identical to that of Cantillon.
66. Although he does not cite it here, Mably would later refer frequently to Cantillon's notorious declaration that "Once a state has arrived at the point of greatest wealth, supposing as always that the comparative wealth of states consists principally in the respective quantities of money that they possess, it will not fail to decline into poverty by the ordinary course of things" (Cantillon, p. 231).
67. Hume, p. 264.
68. *PN*, 5: 198.
69. *DPE*, 6: 519–20. Mably's citation only slightly modifies the original: see Cantillon, p. 241.
70. *DPEDPE*, 6: 534.
71. Ibid., 6: 510.
72. Ibid., 6: 515.
73. Hume, p. 260.
74. Ibid., p. 258.
75. Ibid., pp. 259–60. Hume adds, somewhat surreptitiously, "Not to mention the great equality of fortunes among the inhabitants of the ancient republics, where every field, belonging to a different proprietor, was able to maintain a family, and rendered the numbers of citizens very considerable, even without trade and manufactures."

76. *DPE*, 6: 534.
77. Ibid., 6: 528–29.
78. *OR*, 4: 253.

Chapter 4

1. *EP*, 13: 128. Cf. a similar statement at the beginning of *De l'étude de l'histoire* (12: 23): "For many years I studied history without method or guide, and it is only by stumbling over a good many obstacles that I learned to recognize them as such. I lost much time. . . ."
2. James C. Riley, p. xix.
3. For the history of the late-medieval and sixteenth-century Estates-General, see Major, and Lewis, pp. 3–24.
4. His only successful effort in this regard was to require that remonstrances *follow*, rather than precede, registration, after 1673: a temporary imposition rescinded in the settlement that inaugurated the Regency in 1715.
5. "The relationship between crown and *parlements* under Louis XV was not, in fact, a conflict between irreconcilables. It was not a struggle for sovereignty between legitimate government and insubordinate subjects determined by rebelling to secure a share of power. It was, rather, a highly effective way of involving the governed in government, a stable political system working by well-understood rules" (Doyle, "The Parlements," p. 162).
6. For a brief résumé of the history of Jansenism and Gallicanism in the seventeenth and early eighteenth centuries, see the first chapter of Van Kley, *The Jansenists and the Expulsion of the Jesuits from France*.
7. The standard account of relations between the monarchy and the magistrature is Egret's *Louis XV et l'opposition parlementaire*, 1715–75. For an effective narrative of the events of the decade, including the activities of the *mouvement philosophique* itself, see Diaz, pp. 13–82.
8. For a detailed analysis of this conjuncture, turning on the attempted assassination of Louis XV, see Van Kley, *The Damiens Affair and the Unravelling of the Ancien Régime*; for an incisive account of the religious *de*legitimation of the monarchy over the long term, see Merrick.
9. For the history of parlementary ideology in this period, see Bickart, Joynes, and Van Kley, *The Damiens Affair*, pp. 166–225.
10. See *EP*, 13: p. 145, where Mably refers to "a manuscript that I know on *Des droits et les devoirs du citoyen*."
11. *Correspondance littéraire*, 15: 413.
12. For information on both Stanhope and Mahon, see *Dictionary of National Biography*, 18: 888–92. For more extended reflections on the identity of "Stanhope," see Lecercle, "Introduction," pp. xx–xxiii.
13. *OA*, 14: 17.
14. For an extended discussion of the physical setting of the dialogue and its meaning, see Roelens.

15. *De republica*, III, xxii.
16. Mably, *Des droits et des devoirs du citoyen*, p. 10.
17. Ibid., p. 11.
18. Ibid., p. 12.
19. Rousseau, 3: 123.
20. Mably, *Des droits et des devoirs*, pp. 12–14.
21. Ibid., p. 15.
22. Ibid., pp. 16–17.
23. Ibid., pp. 22–23.
24. Ibid., p. 27.
25. Ibid., p. 40.
26. Ibid., pp. 44–45
27. Ibid., p. 59.
28. Ibid., pp. 68–69.
29. Ibid., p. 76.
30. Ibid., pp. 91–92.
31. For this interlude, see ibid., pp. 103–14.
32. Ibid., p. 114.
33. Venturi, *Utopia and Reform*, p. 73.
34. See Dedieu, pp. 73–74; and Rochedieu.
35. For the history of both the conservative and radical wings of the rights tradition in the seventeenth century, see Tuck, *Natural Rights Theories*.
36. For remarks on Barbeyrac, see Derathé, *Jean-Jacques Rousseau*, pp. 89–92.
37. Mably plainly relished the notion of his noble patron studying so radical a text, for the letter begins: "A *corps de garde* would be, I believe, astonished if he knew the sort of ideas with which you are occupied; it is the first time that someone has written there on Locke and on natural right, and this novelty is well worthy of you. Your conduct must be scandalous, for I imagine that within the Regiment of the King, as at Paris, people are content enough with their prejudices that they do not care to trouble themselves about the truth" (Letter of 2 June 1764; see Maffey, "Un'ottava lettera del Mably," p. 65).
38. *DP*, 13: 143–45.
39. "We English, for example," explains Stanhope, "have up to the present not had very sound ideas in regard to royal power, and under the name of prerogative we leave a far too extensive authority to the king, in order one day to be able to erect a perfect Republic on the ruins of the monarchy. We are not worthy of governing ourselves as did the Romans" (Mably, *Des droits et des devoirs du citoyen*, pp. 44–45).
40. See Mastellone and Jacob.
41. Baker, "A Script for a French Revolution," pp. 241–42, 248–49.
42. See the recent examination of Sidney's thought in Scott, pp. 14–42.
43. See the remarks of Sonenscher, *Work and Wages*, pp. 333–38.
44. See Maffey, *Il pensiero politico*, p. 31.
45. Mably's chief source being, of course, Plutarch's *Life of Phocion*.
46. Rulhière, p. 39. On Mably and Chastellux, see Varnum, pp. 22–23, and Schliech, *Aufklärung und Revolution*, pp. 35–36.
47. In a note (p. 35), Mably suggests that this speech is nearly identical in spirit to the famous "funeral oration" attributed to Pericles by Thucydides—Pericles of course being the author of the disaster of the Peloponnesian War.

48. *EPh*, 10: 48–49.

49. Hume, *Treatise*, p. 415. Hume's own departures from the natural law tradition have, of course, themselves been exaggerated often enough; the most balanced assessment of this issue can be found in Forbes, pp. 55–91.

50. Diderot, *Oeuvres*, pp. 9–10.

51. Helvétius, p. 268.

52. Rousseau's usage of the concept of a "volonté générale" is better known, of course, but Diderot's article on "Droit naturel" was no less daring, in its own way: ". . . if one accepts the idea of species in a perpetual flux, the nature of *natural right* would not change, since it would always be relative to the general will, and to the common desire of the entire species" (Diderot, *Encyclopédie*, 11: 371–72).

53. *EPh*, 10: 46–47.

54. Ibid., pp. 47–48.

55. Ibid., pp. 50–51.

56. Ibid., pp. 51–52.

57. It is not surprising that Rousseau gave his stamp of approval to *Entretiens de Phocion*, in a letter to Prince Louis-Eugène of 26 May 1764: "I accept with gratitude the work that you have had the kindness to send to me, and when I reread this work, I will always use the volume you have given me. These dialogues are not really those of Phocion, but of the abbé de Mably, brother of the abbé de Condillic famous for his excellent works of metaphysics, and well-known himself for various political writings, very fine as well of their kind. . . . Also, although I know the abbé de Mably to be an honest man full of very sound views, I was still surprised to see him elevate himself in his latest work to so pure and sublime a morality. It is for that reason, no doubt, that these dialogues, besides very well done, have only had a middling success in France, but have enjoyed a very greater one in Switzerland, where I see with pleasure that they have been reprinted" (Leigh, 20: 93). As we shall see, Rousseau later did Mably the further honor of accusing him—unjustly—of plagiarism in *Entretiens de Phocion*.

58. *EPh*, p. 63.

59. Ibid., pp. 74–75.

60. For this theme in Montesquieu, see Meyer, pp. 845–91. Rousseau's formulation in *Emile* is famous: "It is necessary to study society by men, and men by society; those who try to treat politics and morality separately will never understand either" (Rousseau, 4: p. 128). For Helvétius's claim in *De l'Esprit* that "the science of morality is nothing other than the science of legislation itself," see Helvétius, p. 163 (Discourse II, Chapter XVII).

61. *EPh.*, p. 100.

62. Ibid., p. 102.

63. Ibid., p. 120. In a note (p. 121), Mably defends Phocion's exclusion of the propertyless from citizenship: "What Phocion adds here, that it is necessary to regard artisans as slaves, will perhaps strike some readers as an outrageous and cruel sentiment; but it is important to try to enter into his thought in this regard, which is easy enough to do, and then one soon will see its truth. Phocion was no doubt too knowledgeable about the rights of humanity, to suggest that artisans should be deprived of their liberty and

reduced to slavery; what he meant was merely that men who could possess none of the sentiments of citizens, like slaves, should have no part in public administration, and he was right."

64. Ibid., p. 126.

65. Ibid., pp. 139–40.

66. It is important, however, not to exaggerate Machiavelli's distance from the classical conception of the place of the "virtues" in political life. Referring to the exclusion of "justice" from Machiavelli's list, Quentin Skinner writes: "This represents an epoch-making break with the classical republican analysis of the cardinal virtues; its suddenness and completeness can hardly be overemphasized. But it is scarcely less important to emphasize that this represents Machiavelli's sole quarrel with his classical authorities. The rest of his analysis of *virtù* is impeccably Ciceronian in character" (Skinner, "The idea of negative liberty," pp. 215–16).

67. See Tuck, "The 'Modern' Theory of Natural Law," pp. 115–19.

68. *EPh*, 10: 148–58.

69. Ibid., pp. 175–76.

70. Ibid., pp. 185–93. Mably rejects Cantillon's own contention that an "able minister" is always able to "restart" the economic cycle, restoring the military power of a "poor" nation: "If Cantillon, instead of considering merely the effects of wealth and commerce, had studied, and no one was more capable of it than he, the entire body of society, then he probably would have agreed with Phocion. Far from counselling a republic whose finances had been ruined by too great a prosperity, to *attempt to restore a real balance of commerce annually*, he would have advised it to take advantage of its decadence in order to prohibit luxury and avarice, give itself some character, make poverty attractive, or at least learn to do without superfluous wealth. Wouldn't this policy be superior to that of his minister, who dreams only of resuming the circle of wealth and poverty described by Cantillon?" (Ibid., p. 192).

71. Ibid., p. 193.

72. Hirschman, pp. 20–31.

73. *EPh*, 10: 214–15.

74. Ibid., pp. 231–32.

75. Ibid., p. 221.

76. Ibid., p. 28.

77. Ibid., pp. 232–33.

78. See Diderot, *Encyclopédie*, 11: 409–14, where Boucher d'Argis defines natural law as "certain rules of justice and equity that natural reason alone has established between men, or, to put it better, that God has engraved in our hearts. . . . Natural law is inscribed in our hearts in characters so beautiful, expressions so forceful and strokes so luminous, that it is impossible to fail to recognize it"—terms nearly identical to those used by Mably in his two dialogues.

79. It appears, for example, that Diderot's own essay was conceived as a specific response to that of Boucher d'Argis; while it in turn provoked the denunciation of guardians of the "traditional" conception of natural law, among them the antiphilosophe André Chaumeix in his *Préjugés légitimes contre l'Encyclopédie* (1758–59) and the editors of the highly conservative

journal *La Religion vengée*. For these exchanges, in the context of a brief survey of natural law theory in the French Enlightenment, see Grimsley, pp. 93–108.

Chapter 5

1. Mably, *Des droits et des devoirs du citoyen*, pp. 107–8.
2. Ibid., p. 111.
3. Locke, p. 395 (IX.124).
4. See, for example, the famous denunciation of agrarian laws in *De Officiis*, II, xxi. 73. For a survey of Cicero's views on property, see Wood, *Cicero's Social and Political Thought*, pp. 105–19.
5. *LPL*, 9: pp. 52–53. For a similar passage, see *EH*, 12: 31–32.
6. *LPL*, p. 61.
7. *DPPE*, 11: p. 11. For similar passages, see ibid., pp. 38–39, and *LPL*, 9: 24–25.
8. *LPL*, 9: 90.
9. His claim, it should be noted, is not merely that struggles over property are the source of most domestic strife, but of most wars between nations as well; see *DPPE*, p. 14.
10. Or at least they will attempt to make it their instrument: "Once wealth has created a certain distinction, the wealthy necessarily attempt to usurp public authority." *LPL*, 9: 48–49.
11. The best extended statement is the second chapter of *LPL*, 9: 43–67.
12. Moreover, Mably could also explain the eventual demise of the Spartan polity by reference to its unjust treatment of its captive labor force and its introduction of property rights after Leuctra; see *EH*, 12: p. 35, and *DPPE*, 11: 7–8. He does not, however, attempt to account for the enormous time lags involved in such explanations.
13. The most comprehensive recent survey of these writers seems to be Rihs's, *Les philosophes utopistes*; but see also Baczko's *Lumières de l'utopie*, and the Manuels' *Utopian Thought in the Western World*, pp. 413–577.
14. See, for example, *MEH*, 13: 379–80.
15. Mably's works, in fact, may not be entirely devoid of references to the writers in question. In *Des droits et des devoirs du citoyen*, he writes: "It is true, continued [Stanhope], that your political writers, who do little more than comment on *l'Esprit des Lois*, which they regard as the code of nature, remain very far from having good principles . . ." (p. 128). As Lecercle remarks, Mably's meaning here is not entirely clear; but the use of the phrase "code de la nature" seems unlikely to have been accidental, especially given the fact that the subtitle of Morelly's book is "la véritable Esprit de ses loix." Elsewhere, when he refers to "my system of the community of goods," this may well be a gesture in the direction of Dom Deschamps' *Vrai système*.
16. See, in particular, Meslier, 2: 16–18, 29–30, 48–67.
17. The title of the second chapter of *LPL*, 9: 43.
18. *DPPE*, 11: 13.

19. Mably, *Des droits et des devoirs du citoyen*, p. 108.

20. Le Mercier de la Rivière, p. 2.

21. *DPPE*, 11: 30–31.

22. Ibid., 11: 37.

23. Ibid., 11: 32–33.

24. See Mably, *Des droits et des devoirs du citoyen*, pp. 107–14; *EH*, 12: 30–45; *DPPE*, 11: 11–12, 18–20, 22–32; *LPL*, 9: 92–114.

25. Mably, *Des droits et des devoirs du citoyen*, p. 113.

26. *LPL*, 9: 97–98.

27. Ibid., 9: 111–12.

28. That Mably's social program is conceived as an accommodation to the "second best" has been widely noticed; see, in particular, Schleich, "Der Zweitbeste Staat."

29. *DPPE*, 11: 222.

30. *LPL*, 9: 109.

31. Mably, *Des droits et des devoirs du citoyen*, p. 102.

32. *DPPE*, 11: 223–24.

33. For summaries, see Mably, *Des droits et des devoirs du citoyen*, pp. 178–213; and *EH*, 12: 46–62.

34. ". . . but if it is impossible to attain perfection, must one give up trying to approach it? Why not establish a specific patrimony for each order? We find in Sweden the beginning of such a practice; there are lands there that can be owned only by nobles, others only by bourgeois. . . . If the fortune of each citizen can change within his class, shrinking or growing, the fortune of the order itself would at least remain the same." (*LPL*, 9: 146–47).

35. *DPPE*, 11: 251. The second chapter of *Entretiens de Phocion* argues that "the principle object of politics is the regulation of *moeurs*" (10: 61).

36. *LPL*, 9: 357–474.

37. *EH*, 12: 130.

38. Mably, *Des droits et des devoirs du citoyen*, p. 43.

39. France, Russia, Switzerland, Poland, the Italian maritime republics, Germany, Holland, England, and Sweden—the last was always Mably's model of the best performance by any European government, largely owing to its inclusion of the peasantry in the local Estates system. See *EH*, 12: 130–273.

40. Mably, *Des droits et des devoirs du citoyen*, p. 40.

41. *EH*, 12: 316.

42. This is, in effect, the judgment of Rihs, who confers the label of "hesitant communitarian" on Mably, together with Rousseau and Brissot de Warville, distinguishing all three from Meslier, Morelly, and Dom Deschamps; see Rihs, pp. 71–85.

43. See Skinner, "Sir Thomas More's *Utopia*," pp. 146–47.

44. *MEH*, 13: 380.

45. *DPPE*, 11: 1–2. As we have seen, Mably was not without interest in economic thought, even if largely for opportunistic purposes. He provides a brief history of physiocratic doctrine in *Du commerce des grains*, in which

he reveals his own associations with Gournay, whose calls for economic liberalization preceded and influenced the thought of Quesnay; see *CG*, 13: pp. 290–98.

46. Le Mercier, p. 30.
47. Ibid., p. 22.
48. Ibid., pp. 91–137, 156–74.
49. Ibid., pp. 50–51.
50. *DPPE*, 11: 171.
51. Le Mercier, pp. 122–27.
52. Montesquieu, *De l'Esprit des lois*, 1: 189.
53. Ibid., 1: 302.
54. *DPPE*, 11: 233–34.
55. Ibid., 11: 205–6.
56. Montesquieu, *De l'Esprit des lois*, 1: 293.
57. "Political liberty, for a citizen," Montesquieu writes, "is that peace of mind that comes from the opinion he has about his safety; and, in order for such liberty to exist, the government must be such that a citizen has nothing to fear from another citizen" (ibid., p. 294). See Shklar, *Ordinary Vices*, pp. 197, 217ff, 235ff.
58. *DPPE*, 11: 70–71.
59. Le Mercier, p. 20.
60. *DPPE*, 11: 29.
61. Hobbes, p. 266.
62. Constant, p. 502.
63. Ibid., p. 183.
64. In its later incarnations, the idea of differing "ancient" and "modern" concepts of freedom has of course tended to be overlaid and displaced by the even less useful notion of a Manichean struggle between a putative "negative" and "positive" liberty. The most influential and crudest version of this is Berlin's essay "Two Concepts of Liberty," where we are assured that: "The desire to be governed by myself, or at any rate to participate in the process by which my life is to be controlled, may be as deep a wish as that of a free area of action, and perhaps historically older. But it is not a desire for the same thing. So different is it, indeed, as to have led in the end to the great clash of ideologies that dominates our world" (p. 131). For a famous demonstration of the incoherence of the whole notion of "negative" liberty, see Taylor.
65. *Le Mercier*, 11: 25.
66. Mably, *Des droits et devoirs du citoyen*, pp. 22–23.
67. For a recent exploration of the concept of republican liberty in Machiavelli's texts, together with criticisms of current liberal assumptions on this subject, see Skinner, "The idea of negative liberty."
68. *DPPE*, 11: 179–80.
69. See Kaplan, 1: 150–214, 2: 590–613.
70. *CG*, 13: 245.
71. Ibid., 13: 251–52.
72. Ibid., 13: p. 255. Mably continually teases his opponent with praise of Colbert, the *bête noire* of the physiocrats. Perhaps following James Steuart, he also proposes the establishment of "*greniers d'abondance*" by the state, stockpiling grain for times of dearth—see 13: 268ff.
73. Ibid., 13: 271–72.
74. Ibid., 13: 278.
75. Ibid., 13: 287–88.
76. Ibid., 13: 276.

77. See Rousseau, 1: 282–83, 287, 407.

78. "One thing that has upset me a great deal is having just read the *Lettres de la Montagne.* All my ideas about Rousseau have been overthrown. I believed him to be an honest man, that his morality was sincere, in his heart, and not at the tip of his pen. Despite myself, I shall have to change my thinking, and this sorrows me" (Letter 3867, Mably to Madame Saladin, 11 January 1765; Leigh, 23: 87–88).

79. "If my misfortunes have not made you forget our old ties and the friendship with which you honored me," wrote Rousseau, "I beg you to maintain this last, with a man who has not deserved to lose it, and who will always be fond of you" (Letter 3983, 5 February 1765; Leigh, 23: 291–92).

80. Rousseau, 1: 621.

81. Letter 4014, Mably to Rousseau, 11 February 1765; Leigh, 23: 335.

82. Mably's last word on the subject may be found in a late dialogue: "Rousseau, whom we all knew, is a grand example, and perhaps unique, of everything that the imagination can produce, both for good and for ill. . . . Where you and I would have only the slightest suspicions, he believed he had conclusive proof. Instead of a virtuous friend, who, perhaps, was sometimes a bit slow, cold or distracted, he saw merely a dishonest man, even a villain. . . . I linger too long over so sad a subject: but I do not want to lose any occasion to do justice to a man whom I knew and loved, who had the misfortune to have lost his mind, but who was not malicious, unjust, or a calumniator" (*T*, 14: 178–84).

83. Rousseau, 3: 931.

84. Though where it has been recognized, it has typically resulted in the designation of Mably as a "disciple" or even "plagiarist" of Rousseau. The best comparative look at these two thinkers can be found in Lehmann, esp. pp. 196–98, where Lehmann describes the unique combination of radicalism, reformism, and conservatism that characterizes their thought.

85. Mably uses the phrase "general will" only in very late works, and only in passing; see, for examples, *GLP*, 8: 27, and *GR*, 13: 430.

86. It becomes merely one of "different forms of government" discussed in Book III of *Du contrat social,* where it is accorded no special privilege or attention.

87. Rousseau, 3: 371–72.

88. This passage from *Doutes proposées aux philosophes économistes* is typical of Mably's indifference to the question: "But finally, why should it seem so bizarre to our author that men, who have common interests and who are placed in society only order to see to them mutually, should assemble themselves in order to discuss them, if their number is small, or if they are spread over a vast territory, that they choose representatives to speak and to decide on their behalf?" (11: 182–83); see also *LPL*, 9: 294. For Rousseau's attack on representation, see *Du contrat social,* Book III, Chap. XV, "On deputies or representatives."

Chapter 6

1. In the Preface to *Observations sur les Romains* (1751), Mably wrote: "Rather than attempt to correct my incorrigible parallel in order to publish a new edition, I decided it was better to write two completely new works. Today I publish the one on the Romans—I will indeed be fortunate, if, in trying to correct a first error, I do not make a second!" (*OR*, 4: 245).

2. Although Keith Baker's recent collection of papers on *Inventing the French Revolution* goes a long way toward filling this gap for the second half of the century. The other major works in the field, Lemaire and Carcassone, are indispensable, but now quite dated.

3. The phrase is that of Pocock, *The Ancient Constitution*, p. 53.

4. Burke, pp. 116–17.

5. At the price, however, of the incomprehension of most of his readers: "Contemporary opinion seems to have concluded either that a *History* which was not obviously Whig could only be Tory or Jacobite, or else that it was inconsistent. Hume's programme was self-defeating. His bi-focal vision of the conflict of king and commons was too subtle for his critics." (Forbes, p. 291).

6. For Burke's relation to ancient constitutionalism, see Pocock, "Burke and the Ancient Constitution."

7. For an insightful discussion of Dubos's historiography in its political context, see Kaiser.

8. On Moreau, see especially Baker, "Controlling French History."

9. Cited in Carcassone, p. 517.

10. Pocock, "Burke and the Ancient Constitution," p. 229. Significantly enough, Pocock uses the phrase here to describe the historical outlook of the Levellers, with its focus on the notion of the "Norman Yoke."

11. One of the achievements of Ellis's work on Boulainvillers has been to establish just this.

12. Boulainvilliers, 2: 186

13. Richet, p. 11.

14. This is Carcassone's own judgment of Montesquieu's achievement; see Carcassone, pp. 88–94, 673–74.

15. On Le Paige's work in the context of the crisis of the *refus des sacrements*, see Van Kley, *The Damiens Affair*, pp. 184–91.

16. Le Paige, 1: 51.

17. Ibid., 1: 4–5.

18. Ibid., 1: 33.

19. Mably, *Des droits et des devoirs du citoyen*, p. 136.

20. Ibid., p. 76.

21. *EH*, 12: 337 88.

22. *OHF*, 1: 124–25.

23. Mably, *Des droits et des devoirs du citoyen*, p. 116.

24. Baker, "A Script for a French Revolution." The following discussion of *Des droits et des devoirs du citoyen* is much indebted to this essay.

25. "Despite the philosophy of which our century is so proud, but which we apply only to frivolous matters," Stanhope comments, "we go on thinking, without realizing it, according to the admirable principles of our ancestors. We regard the king as the unique and universal end of society; we consider him as the master, not the leader of the nation; it is the king we serve, and not the fatherland; it is to the good of the crown, and of the treasury, that we look first, and then, if we can, that of the subjects. The private reason of the king is the universal and general reason of his realm. . . . Accustomed as we are to regarding despotism as the wisest of governments, and liberty as an unnecessary encumbrance, and to forgiving everything in a prince who is only moderately stupid or wicked, we have had a hundred occasions for making ourselves free, but it has never occurred to us to take advantage of them" (Mably, *Des droits et des devoirs du citoyen*, pp. 123–24).

26. Ibid., pp. 133–34.

27. See ibid., pp. 128–29.

28. Ibid., p. 127.

29. Ibid., pp. 137–38.

30. See Marion, pp. 216–17; Doyle, *Origins of the French Revolution*, p. 66.

31. Mably, *Des droits et des devoirs du citoyen*, p. 155.

32. Ibid., p. 175.

33. Ibid., pp. 188–91.

34. Ibid., pp. 161–62.

35. Ibid., p. 176. In an earlier passage (p. 149), he claims that his goal, at the start at least, was no more than to create a "feudal republic, liable from the start to flatter, stir up, and enliven people's minds, but which would finally enlighten them enough so that they will desire something better."

36. Ibid., p. 212.

37. Ibid., p. 162.

38. Ibid., pp. 164–65.

39. Ibid., p. 168.

40. Ibid., p. 170.

41. Ibid., p. 181.

42. Earlier, Stanhope suggests that this agitation was directly inspired by the example of English political thought: "You learn English, you translate our works, and you learn to appreciate them; some of your writers even devote themselves to politics, which demonstrates that this kind of study is not an idle matter for your nation" (Ibid., p. 128).

43. Ibid., pp. 183–84.

44. Ibid., p. 173.

45. Ibid., p. 212.

46. Ibid., pp. 214–15.

47. Mably was of course not completely alone in his predictions: cf. the famous lament of Lamoignon in 1756: "I have long felt that our state is threatened by revolution. I did not however believe that I would live to see it; but now it seems so imminent that, old as I am, I begin to think that I shall have the misfortune of seeing it come to pass" (Cited in Flammermont, 2: xxvi).

48. Mably described the book in a letter to Madame Dupin: "Since one can speak one's mind with a little liberty these days"—referring, no doubt, to the clement atmosphere for publication created by Malesherbes—"one must take advantage of it. I have revised this work, and without betraying

the truth, I have substituted polite expressions for some hard words, which occurred to me while studying the history of a country whose inhabitants have almost never done what they ought to have done" (Letter of 21 September 1764; in Villeneuve-Guibert, p. 443). Despite Mably's emendations, the *Observations* still required the protection of Choiseul in order to appear in France; see Brizard, pp. 106–7.

49. *OHF*, 1: 121.

50. Mably also makes extensive use of the barbarian law codes, the earlier *Historiae Francorum scriptores* of Duchesne, Dumont's *Corps universel diplomatique,* and Du Cange's *Glossarium,* among other sources. For a detailed inventory of the antiquarian scholarship that sustained the great debates of the eighteenth century, see Cox, pp. 110–50.

51. For the history of the concept in this period, see Koselleck, pp. 706–25; Goulemot, pp. 81–122; and Baker, "Inventing the French Revolution," pp. 204–9.

52. See p. 31 above. The term is found frequently in Montesquieu's writings as well: Book XXXI of *De l'Esprit de lois,* for example, is entitled "Theory of feudal law among the Franks, in the relation it has with the revolutions of their monarchy."

53. *OHF*, 1: 133.

54. Ibid., 1: 145.

55. Ibid., 1: 155–56.

56. Ibid., 1: 249.

57. Ibid., 1: 252–53.

58. Ibid., 1: 250.

59. Ibid., 1: 289.

60. Ibid., 1: 192.

61. Ibid., 2: 29.

62. Ibid., 1: 332–33. On Dubos, see also 1: 140–41, 327–41, 344–49.

63. The fundamental affinity of the outlook of Boulainvilliers and Mably—one of whose sources surely was the predominance of republican language in their writings—is discussed in greater detail in Furet and Ozouf.

64. *OHF*, 1: 325, 358–60, 389–99.

65. Montesquieu, *De l'Esprit des lois*, 2: 317.

66. *OHF*, 1: 406.

67. Ibid., 1: 407.

68. Nowhere else in *De l'Esprit des lois* is Montesquieu's own *parti pris* quite so evident: "It has been claimed that it was during the disorders of the second dynasty that the vassals usurped control over jurisdiction in their domains. . . . But these jurisdictions do not owe their origin to usurpation; they derive from the original establishment, and not from its corruption" (XXX.xxii). For Mably's response, see *OHF*, 1: 366–82, 406–11.

69. Ibid., 1: 398.

70. Echeverria, *The Maupeou Revolution*, p. 221.

71. As Furet and Ozouf point out, the extent of agreement between Boulainvilliers and Mably is still very striking: "What separates the two is important in regard to political opinion: Boulainvillers is a narrow aristocrat, while Mably restores the third estate to the nation. But this difference is negligible in two other respects: both participate in the liberal defense of society against power, for which the nobility was the natural spokesman.

Above all, each writes the same history intellectually, woven out of the same institutions, played by the same actors: the 'nation' permits them to think of the social and the national at the same time, in contradistinction to the nineteenth century, which could not see beyond the nation." (Furet and Ozouf, p. 448.)

72. *OHF*, 2: 32–33.

73. Mably comments on the myopia of the nobility in this instance: "This is not the place to meditate the dignity of men, or to consider under what circumstances slavery may be useful or harmful to society. I leave these great questions aside: but I cannot help noting that the lords greatly reduced their own respect, power, and wealth, by selling their liberty to their serfs" (Ibid., 2: 128).

74. Ibid., 2: 91–92.

75. Ibid., 2: 168.

76. Ibid., 2: 39.

77. Ibid., 2: 51.

78. Ibid., 2: 250–51.

79. Ibid., 2: 254–55.

80. Ibid., 2: 277. "As a profound historian who has addressed himself to this issue notes," Mably continues, referring to Hume, "moderate men from the two parties, which is to say, the body of the nation, thought the same way about essentials; they worked towards the same end, and disagreed only about the means necessary to secure both royal prerogative and the liberty of citizens at the same time. . . . The government preserved its ancient form, and parliament aimed at nothing more than bringing the dignity of the prince and that of the nation into a happy balance with one another" (ibid., 2: 280–81).

81. See *EH*, 12: 237, for an example.

82. Acomb, pp. 35–38. Acomb did, however, note some ambiguity here: "Mably himself was not entirely consistent. When he wished to show that England was more free than France because she had a constitution and France (so he said) did not, he took an almost Anglophile attitude toward party. But his prevailing sentiments were hostile to it" (ibid., pp. 37–38).

83. Mably's claims here are not fantastic, it is worth noting. They are frequently echoed by sober twentieth-century historians such as Mollat: "Without the temporizing hesitance of the regent Charles and the excesses of Etienne Marcel, which compromised his cause, the Great Ordinance of 1357 might have done for France what Magna Charter and the Provisions of Oxford did for England" (Mollat, p. 67).

84. *OHF*, 2: 243.

85. Ibid., 2: 249–50.

86. Ibid., 2: 282–83.

87. On the Maupeou "coup," see Egret, Chap. V; and Doyle, "The Parlements of France."

88. *OHF*, 3: 298–99.

89. Baker, "Memory and Practice," p. 49.

90. *OHF*, 3: 154.

91. Ibid., pp. 161–62.

92. Ibid., 3: 357.

93. Ibid., 3: 346.

94. Ibid., 3: 425.

95. For Voltaire's attitudes towards the *parlements* and his own re-

sponses to the Maupeou "coup," see Echeverria, pp. 147–68.

96. *OHF*, 3: 300–301.

97. Ibid., 3: 257.

98. Ibid., 3: 310.

99. Ibid., 3: 313.

100. Ibid., 3: 320.

101. For the controversy over Necker, past and present, see above all Bosher, Egret, *Necker*, and Harris.

102. See *CR*, 15: 83–111.

103. *RN*, 15: 133.

Chapter 7

1. See in particular the long discussion of Sweden in *De l'étude de l'histoire, EH*, 12: 241–73. These views were not mere fancies on Mably's part—they had a firm ground in historical reality, as can be seen in Michael Roberts's vivid portrait of eighteenth-century Sweden.

2. For the history of early modern Poland, see Anderson, pp. 279–98, and Davies, pp. 279–353; for the eighteenth-century scene, see Leslie, pp. 1–50.

3. See the survey of the West European debate in Venturi, *The End of the Old Regime in Europe*, 1768–1776, Chapter VII; for the French scene, see especially Diaz, pp. 471–505.

4. For a profile of Wielhorski, see Walicki, pp. 11–15.

5. See Fabre, "Introduction," pp. ccxxxii–vii.

6. See *GLP*, 8: 4–5.

7. From which both the "senatorial" elite and the monarch would be rigorously excluded: "I would be pleased if you declared in the clearest way possible that the king, the senators, and the ministers have no right to resist the decisions of the general Diet, and that the hommage that the latter makes to them before dispersing is at bottom nothing more than a polite means of communicating to them the wishes of the nation" (*GLP*, 8: 16–17).

8. Ibid., 8: 14–31.

9. Ibid., 8: 32–46.

10. Ibid., 8: 52–76. Of course, a question remained: who could be induced to accept so degraded a position? Certainly not Poniatowski, nor the Elector of Saxony, favored by Patriot opinion, but who, in Mably's eyes, harbored "despotic" designs as well. Pointing to the diplomatic advantages of an appeal to Austrian pride and protection, Mably suggests that the next king of Poland should be the Duke of Saxe-Teschen, son of Maria-Theresa.

11. "Without sumptuary laws, whose goal is to render riches less necessary and the love of glory more active, you cannot hope to establish a durable liberty" (Ibid., 8: 193).

12. In addition, he was pleased to endorse Wielhorski's own pet project of raising a peasant infantry of 30,000 to 40,000 troops who should be rewarded with land and liberty after their service, in Roman fashion, Mably added (ibid., 8: 204–6).

13. Ibid., 8: 204, 199.

14. Ibid., 8: 232–33.

15. Ibid., 8: 232–34.
16. Rousseau, *Oeuvres complètes*, 3: 959–60.
17. Ibid., 3: 966.
18. Ibid., Chapters V, VII–X.
19. Ibid., Chapter XIII.
20. Ibid., Chapter XIV.
21. See Walicki, pp. 14–15.
22. *BP*, 13: 68–69.
23. Ibid., p. 120.
24. This irony seems lost entirely on Fabre, who lashes Mably continually for his lack of confidence in the Poles, in his commentary on Rousseau's *Considérations*.
25. *SPP*, 13: 59.
26. Ibid., 13: 65.
27. See Leslie, pp. 21–25, and Walicki, pp. 16–27.
28. For the Constitution of 1791, see Palmer, pp. 422–29.
29. See *DP*, 7: 375–89.
30. *GR*, 13: 428.
31. Ibid., 13: 435.
32. Ibid., 13: 473–74.
33. For the standard account of French commentary on America, before and after the arrival of Franklin, see Echeverria, *Mirage in the West*, Chapters I, II.
34. The classic recounting of the course of the debate over the American state constitutions can be found in Palmer, I: 263–82; but see also Venturi's discussion in *The End of the Old Regime*, 1776–89 I: Chapter 1.
35. Cited in Palmer, p. 268.
36. For Adams's account of the genesis of Mably's *Observations*, see the "Postscript" to the first volume of *A Defence of the Constitutions of Government of the United States* (I: pp. 383–92), which reproduces a long letter to Mably on the sources Adams thought necessary for writing a history of the American Revolution. See also the remarks of Venturi, *The End of the Old Regime*, 1776–1789, I: 104–5.
37. Grimm, 13: 264.
38. Adams, I: 384.
39. *OGEAU*, 8: 340.
40. Ibid., 8: 349–50.
41. Ibid., 8: 354.
42. Ibid., 8: 351–53.
43. See the discussion in G. Wood, pp. 226–37.
44. *OGEAU*, 8: 361–80.
45. See the account in G. Wood, 438–53.
46. *OGEAU*, 8: 385, 388–89.
47. Ibid., 8: 393.
48. Brown, Anglican preacher and utilitarian commentator on Shaftesbury, published his *Estimate of the Manners and Principles of the Times* in 1757; a French translation, under the title, *Les Moeurs angloises, ou Appréciation des moeurs et des principes qui caractérisent actuellement la nation britannique*, was published the following year in The Hague. See Rochedieu, p. 35.
49. *OGEAU*, 8: 441–45.
50. Mably's recommendation includes a plan for a solemn festival to be held every ten or twelve years, to celebrate the independence of the nation; see Ibid., 8: 478–79.
51. For this episode, see Echeverria, *Mirage in the West*, Chapter IV.

52. On Mazzei's career and role in the debate over the constitutions, see Palmer, pp. 277–79, and Venturi, *The End of the Old Regime,* 1776-89, I: 81–94, 108–29.

53. G. Wood, pp. 567–92. For a recent update, see Appleby.

54. See, for example, the review of *De la manière d'écrire l'histoire* in Grimm, 12: 225–29, 234.

55. The only other of Mably's books to be approved in this way were *De la manière d'écrire l'histoire* and, all those years before, *Parallèle des romains et des français.*

56. For the progress of the controversy in 1784, and the condemnation of the Sorbonne, see the description in the *Mémoires secrets,* in Bachaumont, 25: 70 (29 January 1784), 75 (31 January), 197–98 (27 March); 26: 57–58 (18 June), 82 (6 July), 137–38 (7 August).

57. See *PM,* 10: 319–27.

58. See *PM,* 10: 419–20. If the Faculty of the Sorbonne was shocked by the moral laxity of the elderly philosopher, his mortal enemy, Grimm, permitted himself some sarcasm: "We hear that the poor abbé often found himself in a bad way for having followed his own advice. But it is worthy of his philosophy not to hold a grudge" (Grimm, 14: 488).

59. *DPBR,* 15: 26.

60. Ibid., 15: 74–81.

61. The counterpart to *Du beau* is the dialogue entitled *Des talents,* which included Mably's last word on the by-then deceased Rousseau.

62. *CMPS,* 15: 137–44.

63. Ibid., 15: 467.

64. See *S,* 13: 301–2, 313–14, 345–52.

Chapter 8

1. See Levèsque, pp. 31–32.

2. Brizard relates how, having been persuaded by the Maréchal de Richelieu to accept his sponsorship for entry into the Académie Française, Mably immediately went to Condillac to beg the latter to extract him from the obligation. "If I accept," he told his surprised brother, "I would be obliged to praise the Cardinal de Richelieu, in violation of my own principles; and if I do not praise him, in the presence of his grand-nephew, I would be guilty of ingratitude." Condillac succeeded in having Mably's name withdrawn. See Brizard, p. 118.

3. See Levèsque, pp. 14–16.

4. "A few years before his death, at the home of a woman celebrated for her talents and for qualities that assured her the lifelong devotion of her friends (Mme de Bocage), a touching anecdote was told. Everyone was moved except for Mably. When he was reproached by one of his friends (M. Dusaulx), the abbé responded: 'That is not in nature.' 'And how do you know that?' his friend demanded. 'From fifty years of experience and meditation.' 'You might enjoy twice that, my dear abbé, without having sounded the depths of the

human heart.' At these words, the abbé stood up and rapped his cane on the floor; everyone waited for a terrible explosion of anger. Instead, Mably took the arm of his friend and said: 'You are right, I am merely a fool.' " Ibid., p. 21.

5. See Shklar, "Montesquieu and the New Republicanism."

6. See Rosen, pp. 164–84.

7. For this debate, see the indispensable study by Guerci, *Libertà degli antichi e Libertà dei moderni.*

8. For Mably's "reception" in various phases of the Revolution, again see the exhaustive accounting in Schleich, *Aufklärung und Revolution*; for remarks on the Declaration of Rights of 1789, see my own "National Sovereignty and the General Will."

9. On Desmoulins, see the discussion in Parker, especially Chapter VI.

10. "Mobility of Property and the Rise of Eighteenth-Century Sociology," in Pocock, *Virtue, Commerce, and History*, p. 109.

11. For this and other criticisms of Pocock, see the useful discussion in Chapter 6 of Shapiro.

12. For an example, see Perry Anderson's comments in "A Culture in Contraflow," in Anderson, *English Questions*, pp. 290–93.

13. See "The Political Universe of J. G. A. Pocock," in Hexter, p. 288.

14. Anderson, *English Questions*, p. 293.

15. "Mobility of Property," in Pocock, *Virtue, Commerce, and History*, p. 104.

16. Pocock, "Cambridge Paradigms and Scotch Philosophers," p. 245.

17. See his "Introduction" to the Penguin edition of Marx's *Early Writings*, in Colletti, especially p. 46.

18. See Wokler's remarks in "Rousseau and Marx" in this regard.

19. For an appealing recent discussion, see Keaveney's essay on "The Three Gracchi: Tiberius, Caius and Babeuf."

Bibliography

Acomb, Frances. *Anglophobia in France, 1763–1789. An Essay in the History of Constitutionalism and Nationalism*. Durham: Duke University Press, 1950.

Adams, John. *A Defence of the Constitutions of Government of the United States of America*. 3 vols. London: C. Dilly, 1787–88.

Anderson, Perry. *Lineages of the Absolutist State*. London: Verso, 1974.

———. *English Questions*. London: Verso, 1992.

Apih, Elio. "Due conservatori francesi critici della storiografia illuminata." *Nuova rivista storica* 37 (1953), pp. 373–78.

Appleby, Joyce. "John Adams and the New Republican Synthesis." In *Liberalism and Republicanism in the Historical Imagination*, pp. 188–209. Cambridge, Mass.: Harvard University Press, 1992.

Aurenche, Louis. *Jean-Jacques Rousseau chez M. de Mably*. Paris: Société française d'éditions littéraries et techniques, 1934.

Bachaumont, Louis Petit de. *Mémoires secrets pour servir à l'histoire de la République des lettres en France, depuis 1762 jusqu'à nos jours; ou Journal d'un observateur* . . . 36 vols. London: J. Adamson, 1780–89.

Baker, Keith M. "Memory and Practice: Politics and the Representation of the Past in Eighteenth-Century France." In *Inventing the French Revolution: Essays on French Political Culture in the Eighteenth Century*, pp. 31–58. Cambridge: Cambridge University Press, 1990.

———. "A Script for a French Revolution: the Political Consciousness of the Abbé Mably." In *Inventing the French Revolution*, pp. 86–106.

———. "Controlling French History: the Ideological Arsenal of Jacob-Nicolas Moreau." In *Inventing the French Revolution*, pp. 59–85.

———. "Inventing the French Revolution." In *Inventing the French Revolution*, pp. 203–23.

Barthélemi, L. *Vie privée de M. l'abbé de Mably*. In *Le Destin de la France, par M. l'Abbé de Mably*. Paris: n. p., 1790.

Beik, William. *Absolutism and Society in Seventeenth-Century France: State Power and Provincial Aristocracy in Languedoc*. Cambridge: Cambridge University Press, 1985.

Berlin, Isaiah. "Two Concepts of Liberty." In *Four Essays on Liberty*, pp. 118–72. Oxford: Oxford University Press, 1969.

Bickart, Roger. *Les parlements et la notion de souveraineté nationale au XVIIIe siècle*. Paris: Félix Alcan, 1932.

Blaug, Mark. *Economic Theory in Retrospect*. Cambridge: Cambridge University Press, 1985.

Blythe, James M. *Ideal Government and the Mixed Constitution in the Middle Ages*. Princeton: Princeton University Press, 1992.

Bosher, J. F. *French Finances 1770–1795: From Business to Bureaucracy*. Cambridge: Cambridge University Press, 1970.

Boulainvilliers, Henri de. *Histoire de l'ancien gouvernement de la France*. 2 vols. Amsterdam, the Hague: n. p., 1727.

Brizard, Gabriel. *Eloge historique de l'abbé de Mably*. Paris: Demonville, 1787.

Burke, Edmund. *Reflections on the Revolution in France*. Edited by Conor Cruise O'Brien. Harmondsworth: Penguin, 1968.

Cambino, R. "Il garantissimo del Mably come prima costituzione teorica dello stato parlementare." *Sapienza* 14 (1961), pp. 503–8.

Cantillon, Richard. *Essay de la nature du commerce en générale*. Ed. Takumi Tsuda. Tokyo: Kinokuniya, 1979.

Carcassone, Elie. *Montesquieu et le problème de la constitution française au XVIIIe siècle*. Paris: Presses Universitaires de France, 1927.

Champeval, J.-B. "Lettres inédites de Maistre, Baluze et de Mably." *Bulletin de la Société des Lettres, Sciences et Arts de la Corrèze* (1906), pp. 445–67.

Chaussinand-Nogaret, Guy. *The French Nobility in the Eighteenth Century. From Feudalism to the Enlightenment*. Trans. William Doyle. Cambridge: Cambridge University Press, 1985.

Colletti, Lucio. "Introduction." In Karl Marx, *Early Writings*, pp. 7–56. Harmondsworth: Penguin, 1975.

Colloque Mably: La politique comme science morale. Actes du Colloque 6–8 juin 1991, Musée de la Révolution francaise, Château de Vizille. Vol. 1. Bari: Palomar, 1995.

Composto, R. "Le teorie sociale dell'abate Mably." *Belfagor* 10 (1955), pp. 468–76.

Constant, Benjamin. "De la liberté des anciens comparée à celle des modernes." In Marcel Gauchet, ed., *De la liberté chez les modernes: écrits politiques*, pp. 493–515. Paris: Librairie Générale Française, 1980.

Coste, Brigitte. *Mably: pour une utopie de bon sens*. Paris: Klincksieck, 1975.

Cox, Iris. *Montesquieu and the History of French Laws. Studies on Voltaire and the Eighteenth Century* 218 (1983).

Davies, Norman. *Heart of Europe. A Short History of Poland*. Oxford: Clarendon Press, 1984.

Dedieu, Joseph. *Montesquieu et la tradition anglaise en France*. Paris: J. Gabalda, 1909.

Derathé, Robert. *Jean-Jacques Rousseau et la science politique de son temps*. Rev. ed. Paris: J. Vrin, 1970.

———. "La Place et l'importance de la notion d'inégalité dans la doctrine politique de Jean-Jacques Rousseau." In R. A. Leigh, ed., *Rousseau after Two Hundred Years: Proceedings of the Cambridge Bicentennial Colloquium*, pp. 54–65. Cambridge: Cambridge University Press, 1982.

Diaz, Furio. *Filosofia e politica nel settecento francese*. Turin: Einaudi, 1963.

Diderot, Denis. *Oeuvres philosophiques*. Ed. Paul Vernière. Paris: Garnier-Flammarion, 1964.

Doyle, William. *The Old European Order, 1600–1800*. Oxford: Oxford University Press, 1978.

———. *The Origins of the French Revolution*. Oxford: Oxford University Press, 1980.

———. "The Parlements." In Keith Michael Baker, ed., *The French Revolution and the Creation of Modern Political Culture*. Vol. 1: *The Political Culture of the Old Regime*, pp. 157–67. Oxford: Pergamon Press, 1987.

Echeverria, Durand. *Mirage in the West. A History of the French Image of American Society to 1815*. Princeton: Princeton University Press, 1957.

———. *The Maupeou Revolution: A Study in the History of Libertarianism. France, 1770–1774*. Baton Rouge and London: Louisiana State University Press, 1985.

Egret, Jean. *Louis XV et l'opposition parlementaire, 1715–1775*. Paris: Armand Colin, 1970.

———. *Necker: Ministre de Louis XVI, 1776–1790*. Paris: Champion, 1975.

Ellis, Harold A. "Boulainvilliers Ideologue and Publicist: Ideologies of Aristocratic Reaction and the Uses of History in Early Eighteenth-Century France." Ph.D. diss., Washington University, 1981.

———. *Boulainvilliers and the French Monarchy: Aristocratic Politics in Early Eighteenth-Century France*. Ithaca: Cornell University Press, 1988.

———. "Montesquieu's Modern Politics: *The Spirit of the Laws* and the Problem of Modern Monarchy in Old Regime France." *History of Political Thought* 10 (Winter 1989), pp. 665–700.

Engels, Friedrich. *Anti-Dühring*. Moscow: International Publishers, 1947.

Espinas, Alfred. *La Philosophie sociale du XVIIIe siècle et la révolution*. Paris: Félix Alcan, 1898.

Fabre, Jean. "Introduction à *Considerations sur le gouvernement de Pologne*." In Jean-Jacques Rousseau, *Oeuvres complètes III: Du contrat social, Ecrits politiques*, pp. ccxvi–ccxlv. Ed. Bernard Gagnebin and Marcel Raymond. Paris: Gallimard, 1964.

Ferrier-Caverivière, Nicole. *L'image de Louis XIV dans la littérature française de 1660–1715*. Paris: Presses Universitaires de France, 1981.

Fink, Z. S. *The Classical Republicans: An Essay in the Recovery of a Pattern of Thought in Seventeenth-Century England*. Evanston: Northwestern University Press, 1945.

Flammermont, Jules, ed. *Remontrances du Parlement de Paris au XIIIe siècle*. 3 vols. Paris: Imprimerie nationale, 1888–89.

Fontana, Biancamaria, ed. *The Invention of the Modern Republic*. Cambridge: Cambridge University Press, 1994.

Forbes, Duncan. *Hume's Philosophical Politics*. Cambridge: Cambridge University Press, 1975.

Franck, Adolphe. "Mémoire sur le communisme jugé par l'histoire. Notice sur la vie et le système politique et social de Mably." *Séances et travaux de l'Académie des Sciences Morales et Politiques* 4 (1848), pp. 283–300.

Fréron, Elie Cathérine. *Année littéraire*, vol. 32 Paris: Le Jay, 1785.

Friedemann, Peter. "Introduction" to *Mably: sur la théorie du pouvoir politique*, pp. 7–54. Paris: Editions sociales, 1975.

———. "Die Konzeption der Repräsentation bei Mably." *Archiv für Rechts- und Sozialphilosophie* 56 (1970), pp. 415–41.

———. "Neues zur Biographie Mablys: Seine 'materiellen' Verhältnisse." *Francia* 1 (1972), pp. 361–68.

Fritz, Kurt von. *The Theory of the Mixed Constitution in Antiquity*. New York: Columbia University Press, 1954.

Furet, François, and Ozouf, Mona. "Deux légitimations historiques de la société française au XVIIIe siècle." *Annales E. S. C.* 34 (1979), pp. 438–50.

Furet, François, and Ozouf, Mona, eds. *Le siècle de l'avènement républicain*. Paris: Gallimard, 1992.

Galliani, Renato. "L'abbé Mably, le luxe, le commerce, les manufactures et les ouvriers." *Revue d'histoire économique et sociale* 53 (1975), 144–55.

———. "Mably et la censure." *Annales historiques de la Révolution française* 46 (1974), pp. 401–11.

———. "Mably et la communauté des biens." *Revue de l'Occident musulman et de la Méditerranée* 163 (1976), pp. 437–60.

———. "Mably et Voltaire." *Dix-huitième siècle* 3 (1971), pp. 181–94.

———. "Quelques aspects de la fortune de Mably au XXme siècle." *Studies on Voltaire and the Eighteenth Century* 88 (1972), pp. 549–65.

———. "Quelques lettres inédites de Mably." *Studies on Voltaire and the Eighteenth Century* 98 (1972), pp. 183–205.

Gauthier, Florence. "De Mably à Robespierre: un programme économique égalitaire, 1775–1793." *Annales historiques de la Revolution française* 259 (1985), pp. 265–89.

Gay, Peter. *The Enlightenment: an Interpretation*. Vol. 1: *The Rise of Modern Paganism*. New York: Alfred A. Knopf, 1966.

Gilbert, Felix. Review of *The Machiavellian Moment*. *Times Literary Supplement*, 19 March 1976: 307–8.

Girdlestone, Cuthbert. *Jean-Philippe Rameau. His Life and Work*. New York: Dover, 1969.

Grell, Chantal. *L'histoire entre érudition et philosophie: étude sur la connaissance historique à l'âge des lumières*. Paris: Presses universitaires de France, 1993.

Grimm, Friedrich Melchior von. *Correspondence littéraire, philosophique et critique par Grimm, Diderot, Raynal, Meister, etc.* 16 vols. Paris, Garnier, 1877–82.

Grimsely, Ronald. "Some Aspects of the Theory of Natural Right." In *From Montesquieu to Laclos: Studies on the French Enlightenment*, pp. 93–108.

Geneva: Droz, 1974.

Guerci, Luciano. *Libertà degli antichi e libertà dei moderni: Sparta, Atene e i "philosophes" nella Francia del '700*. Naples: Guida Editori, 1979.

———. "Pensiero politico e storiografia nel settecento francese: Mably et Condorcet." *Rivista storica italiana* 82 (1970), pp. 926–50.

Guerrier, M. W. *L'abbé de Mably, moraliste et politique. Etude sur la doctrine morale du jacobinisme puritain et sur le développement de l'esprit républicain au XVIIIe siècle*. Paris: Vieweg, 1886.

Gwyn, W. B. *The Meaning of the Separation of Powers*. New Orleans: Tulane University Press, 1965.

Haeringer, Etienne. *L'Esthétique de l'opéra en France au temps de Jean-Philippe Rameau. Studies on Voltaire and the Eighteenth Century* 279. Oxford: the Voltaire Foundation, 1990.

Harpaz, Ephraim. "Mably et la postérité." *Revue des sciences humaines* 74 (January–February, 1954), pp. 25–40.

———. "Mably et ses contemporains." *Revue des sciences humaines* 82 (July–September, 1955), pp. 351–66.

———. "Le social de Mably." *Revue d'histoire économique et sociale* 34 (1956), pp. 411–25.

Harris, Robert D. *Necker: Reform Statesman of the Ancien Régime*. Berkeley: University of California Press, 1979.

Helvétius, Claude-Adrien. *De l'esprit*. Ed. Jacques Montaux. Paris: Fayard, 1988.

Hexter, J. H. *On Historians*. Cambridge, Mass.: Harvard University Press, 1977.

Hirschman, Albert. *The Passions and the Interests: Political Arguments for Capitalism before its Triumph*. Princeton: Princeton University Press, 1977.

Hobbes, Thomas. *Leviathan*. Ed. C. B. Macpherson. Harmondsworth: Penguin, 1968.

Holmes, Stephen. *Benjamin Constant and the Making of Modern Liberalism*. New Haven: Yale University Press, 1984.

Hume, David. *A Treatise of Human Nature*. Ed. L. A. Selby-Bigge and P. H. Nidditch. Oxford: Clarendon Press, 1978.

Hume, David. *Essays, Moral, Political and Literary*. Ed. Eugene Miller. Indianapolis: Liberty Press, 1985.

Hunt, Lynn. *Politics, Class, and Culture in the French Revolution*. Berkeley: University of California Press, 1984.

Jacob, Margaret C. "In the Aftermath of Revolution: Rousset de Missy, Freemasonry, and Locke's *Two Treatises of Government*." In *L'età dei lumi: Studi storici sul Settecento europea in onore di Franco Venturi*. 2 vols. Naples: Govene, 1985. 2, pp. 487–521.

Joynes, D. Carroll. "Jansenists and Ideologues: Opposition Theory in the Parlement of Paris, 1750–1775." Ph.D. Diss., University of Chicago, 1981.

Kaiser, Thomas E. "The abbé Dubos and the historical defense of monarchy in early eighteenth-century France." *Studies on Voltaire and the Eighteenth Century* 267 (1989), pp. 77–102.

Kaplan, Steven L. *Bread, Politics and Political Economy in the Reign of Louis XV*. 2 vols. The Hague: Martinus Nijhoff, 1976.

Keaveney, A. "The Three Gracchi: Tiberius, Caius and Babeuf." In *La Storia della Storiografia Europea sulla Rivoluzione Francese*, pp. 417–32. Rome: Istituto Storico Italiano per l'Età Moderna e Contemporanea, 1990.

Kortum, Hans. "Frugalité et luxe à travers la querelle des anciens et des modernes." *Studies on Voltaire and the Eighteenth Century* 56 (1967), pp. 765–76.

Koselleck, Reinhart. "Revolution." In Otto Brunner, Werner Conze, and Reinhart Koselleck, eds., *Geschichtliche Grundbegriffe: Historisches Lexikon zur politisch-sozialen Sprache in Deutschland*, 5, pp. 706–25. Stuttgart: Ernst Klett, 1972.

La Bruyère, Jean de. *Les Caractères*. Ed. Robert Pignarre. Paris: Garnier-Flammarion, 1965.

Lecercle, Jean-Louis. "Introduction" to Gabriel Bonnot de Mably, *Des droits et des devoirs du citoyen*, pp. ix–l. Paris: Marcel Didier, 1972.

———. "Mably et la théorie de la diplomatie." *Studies on Voltaire and the Eighteenth Century* 88 (1972), pp. 889–913.

———. "Utopie et réalisme politique chez Mably." *Studies on Voltaire and the Eighteenth Century* 26 (1963), 1049–70.

Lehmann, Lutz. *Mably und Rousseau: Eine Studie über die Grenzen der Emanzipation im Ancien Régime*. Frankfurt and Bern: Lang, 1975.

Lemaire, André. *Les lois fondamentales de la monarchie française, d'après les théoriciens de l'ancien régime*. Paris: J. Gabalda, 1907.

Le Mercier de la Rivière, Pierre-Paul François Joachim Henri. *L'Ordre naturel et essentiel des sociétés politiques*. Paris: Geunther, 1910.

Le Paige, Louis-Adrien. *Lettres historiques sur les fonctions essentielles du parlement, sur le droit des pairs, et sur les loix fondamentales de royaume*. 2 vols. Amsterdam: n. p., 1753.

Lerminier, Jean-Louis. *De l'influence de la philosophie du XVIIIe sur la législation et la sociabilité de XIXe siècle*. Paris: Paulin, 1833.

Leslie, R. F. *Polish Politics and the Revolution of November 1830*. London: University of London Press, 1956.

Levèsque, Pierre-Charles. *Eloge historique de l'abbé de Mably*. Paris: Guillot, 1787.

Lewis, P. S. "The Failure of the French Medieval Estates." *Past and Present* 23 (1962), pp. 3–24.

Lichtenberger, André. *Le Socialisme au XVIIIe siècle: Etude sur les idées socialistes dans les écrivains français du XVIIIe siècle avant la révolution*. Paris: Félix Alcan, 1895.

Locke, John. *Two Treatises of Government*. Ed. Peter Laslett. Cambridge: Cambridge University Press, 1963.

Loraux, Nicole, and Vidal-Naquet, Pierre. "La formation de l'Athènes bourgeoise: Essai d'historiographie 1750–1850." In R. R. Bolgar, ed., *Classical Influences on Western Thought, 1650–1870*, pp. 169–222. Cambridge: Cambridge University Press, 1979.

Mably, Gabriel Bonnot de. *Collection complète des oeuvres de l'Abbé de Mably*. 15 vols. Paris: Desbrière, l'An III de la République [1794–1795].
———. *Le Droit public de l'Europe, fondé sur les traitez conclus jusqu'en l'année 1740*. 2 vols. The Hague: Jean Van-Duren, 1746.
———. *Des droits et des devoirs du citoyen*. Ed. Jean-Louis Lecercle. Paris: Marcel Didier, 1972.
———. *Doutes proposées aux philosophes économistes, sur l'Ordre naturel et essentiel des sociétés politiques*. The Hague: Durand, 1767.
———. *Entretiens de Phocion, sur le rapport de la morale avec la politique*. Amsterdam: n.p., 1763.
———. *De la manière d'écrire l'histoire*. Paris: Alexandre Jombert jeune, 1783.
———. *Observations sur le gouvernement et les loix des Etats-Unis d'Amérique*. Amsterdam: J. F. Rosard et Comp., 1784.
———. *Observations sur les Grecs*. Geneva: Compagnie des Libraires, 1749.
———. *Observations sur l'histoire de France*. 2 vols. Geneva: Compagnie des Libraires, 1765.
———. *Observations sur l'histoire de la Grèce, ou des causes de la prospérité et des malheurs des Grecs*. Geneva: Compagnie des Libraires, 1766.
———. *Observations sur les Romains*. Geneva: Compagnie des Libraires, 1751.
———. *Parallèle des Romains et des François, par rapport au Gouvernement*. 2 vols. Paris: Didot, 1740.
———. *Principes de Morale*. Paris: Alexandre Jombert jeune, 1784.
———. *Principes des Négociations, pour servir d'introduction au Droit public de l'Europe, fondé sur les traités*. The Hague: n.p., 1757.
Machiavelli, Niccolò. *Il Principe e Discorsi*. Ed. Sergio Bertelli. Milan: Feltrinelli, 1960.
Maffey, Aldo. *Il pensiero politico del Mably*. Turin: Giappichelli, 1968.
———. "Un'ottava lettera del Mably al duca di La Rochefoucauld." *Studi francese* 46 (1972), pp. 65–68.
———. "Recenti scritti sull'abate Mably." *Rivista internazionale di Filosofia del Diritto* 35 (1958), pp. 741–50.
Major, J. Russell. *Representative Institutions in Renaissance France, 1421–1559*. Madison: University of Wisconsin Press, 1960.
Malvache, Jean-Luc. "Correspondance inédite de Mably à Fellenberg, 1763–1778." *Francia* 19/2 (1992), pp. 47–93.
Manuel, Frank E. and Manuel, Fritzie P. *Utopian Thought in the Western World*. Cambridge, Mass.: Belknap Press, 1976.
Marion, Marcel. *Dictionnaire des institutions de la France au XVIIe et XVIIIe siècles*. New York: Burt Franklin, 1968.
Marongiu, A. "Mably e gli 'stati generali' francese." *Storia e politica* 6 (1967), pp. 563–604.
Marx, Karl. *Capital, Volume 2*. Trans. David Fernbach. Harmondsworth: Penguin, 1978.
Masson, Pierre-Maurice. *Madame de Tencin, 1682–1749: une vie de femme*

au XVIIIe siècle. Paris: Hachette, 1910.

Mastellone, Salvo. "Sur l'origine du langage constituionnel: une traduction anonyme de l'anglais (J. Locke et D. Mazel)." *Bulletin, Société de l'histoire du Protestantisme français* 125 (1979), pp. 757–78.

Mayer, Paul. "Politics and morals in the thought of Montesquieu." *Studies on Voltaire and the Eighteenth Century* 56 (1967), pp. 845–91.

Merrick, Jeffrey W. *The Desacralization of the French Monarchy in the Eighteenth Century*. Baton Rouge: Louisiana State University Press, 1990.

Meslier, Jean. *Oeuvres complètes*. Ed. Jean Deprun, Roland Desné and Albert Soboul. 2 vols. Paris: Editions anthropos, 1971.

Mollat, Michel. *Genèse médiévale de la France moderne: XIVe–XVe siècle*. Paris: Arthaud, 1977.

Montesquieu. *Oeuvres complètes*. Ed. André Masson. 3 vols. Paris: Nagel, 1950.

———. *De l'Esprit des lois*. Ed. Victor Goldschmidt. 2 vols. Paris: Garnier-Flammarion, 1979.

Morelly. *Code de la nature*. Ed. G. Chinard. Paris: Clavreuil, 1950.

Mounier, Jean-Joseph. *Les nouvelles observations sur les états généraux*. Paris: n. p., 1789.

Murphy, Antoin E. *Richard Cantillon, Entrepreneur and Economist*. Oxford: Oxford University Press, 1986.

Palmer, R. R. *The Age of the Democratic Revolution. A Political History of Europe and America, 1760–1800*. 2 vols. Princeton: Princeton University Press, 1959.

Pocock, J. G. A. *The Ancient Constitution and the Feudal Law. A Reissue with a Retrospect*. Cambridge: Cambridge University Press, 1987.

———. "Burke and the Ancient Constitution: A Problem in the History of Ideas." In *Politics, Language and Time: Essays in Political Thought and History*, pp. 202–32. New York: Atheneum, 1973.

———. *The Machiavellian Moment. Florentine Political Thought and the Atlantic Republican Tradition*. Princeton: Princeton University Press, 1975.

———. "Cambridge Paradigms and Scotch Philosophers: A Study of the Relations between the Civic Humanist and the Civil Juridprudential Interpretation of Eighteenth-Century Social Thought." In Istvan Hont and Michael Ignatieff, eds., *Wealth and Virtue: The Shaping of Political Economy in the Scottish Enlightenment*, pp. 235–52. Cambridge: Cambridge University Press, 1983.

———. *Virtue, Commerce, and History: Essays on Political Thought and History, Chiefly in the Eighteenth Century*. Cambridge: Cambridge University Press, 1985.

Procacci, Giuliano. "L'Abate Mably nell'Illuminisimo." *Rivista storica italiana* 63 (1951), pp. 216–44.

Rabaut de Saint-Etienne, Jean-Paul. *Précis historique de la révolution*. 5th ed. Paris: Treuttel et Würtz, 1809.

Rawson, Elizabeth. *The Spartan Tradition in European Thought*. Oxford:

Clarendon Press, 1969.

Reinhold, Meyer. "Eighteenth-Century American Political Thought." In R. R. Bolgar, ed., *Classical Influences on Western Thought, A. D. 1650–1870*. Cambridge: Cambridge University Press, 1979.

Richet, Denis. "Autour des origines idéologiques lointaines de la Révolution française: élites et despotisme." *Annales, E. S. C.* 24 (1969), pp. 1–23.

Riley, James C. *The Seven Years' War and the Old Regime in France: the Economic and Financial Toll*. Princeton: Princeton University Press, 1986.

Riley, Patrick. *The General Will Before Rousseau: the Transformation of the Divine in the Civic*. Princeton: Princeton University Press, 1986.

Roberts, Michael. *The Age of Liberty: Sweden, 1719–1772*. Cambridge: Cambridge University Press, 1986.

Rochedieu, C. A. *Bibiography of French Translations of English Works, 1700–1800*. Chicago: University of Chicago Press, 1948.

Roelens, Maurice. "Mably et Marly, ou les jardins de la politique." In *Modèles et moyens de la réflexion politique du 18ème siècle*. 2 vols. Lille: Publications de l'Université de Lille, 1979.

Rosen, Charles. *The Classical Style: Haydn, Mozart, Beethoven*. New York: Norton, 1972.

Ross, Ellen. "The Debate on Luxury in Eighteenth-Century France: A Study in the Language of Opposition to Change." Ph.D. dissertation, University of Chicago, 1975.

Rousseau, Jean-Jacques. *Correspondance complète de Jean-Jacques Rousseau*. Ed. R. A. Leigh. 26 vols. Oxford: the Voltaire Foundation, 1965–84.

———. *Oeuvres complètes*. Ed. Bernard Gagnebin and Marcel Raymond. 4 vols. Paris: Gallimard, 1959–64.

Rulhière, Claude Carloman de. *Discours prononcé à l'Académie française à la réception de M. Nicolay*. Paris: n. p., 1789.

Safronov, S. "Les idées politiques et sociales de Mably." *Recherches soviétiques* 4 (1956), pp. 47–87.

Sareil, Jean. "Sept lettres inédites de l'abbé de Mably au duc de la Rochefoucauld d'Enville." *Dix-huitième siècle* 3 (1971), pp. 61–72.

Schleich, Thomas. *Aufklärung und Revolution: Die Wirkungsgeschichte Gabriel Bonnot de Mablys in Frankreich (1740–1914)*. Stuttgart: Klett-Cotta, 1981.

———. "Die Resonanz Gabriel Bonnot de Mablys ausserhalb von Frankreich." *Francia* 8 (1980), pp. 213–44.

———. "Die Verbreitung und Rezeption der Aufklärung in der französischen Gesellschaft am Beispiel Mably." In Hans Ulrich Gumbrecht, Rolf Reichardt, and Thomas Schleich, eds., *Sozialgeschichte der Aufklärung in Frankreich*, pp. 147–70. Munich: Oldenburg Verlag, 1981.

———. "'Der zweitbeste Staat'. Zur Sicht der Antike bei Gabriel Bonnot de Mably." *Der Staat* 19 (1980), pp. 557–82.

Scott, Jonathan. *Algernon Sidney and the English Republic, 1623–1677*. Cambridge: Cambridge University Press, 1988.

Shklar, Judith N. *Montesquieu*. Oxford: Oxford University Press, 1989.

———. "Montesqueiu and the New Republicanism." In Gisela Bock, Quentin Skinner, and Maurizio Viroli, eds., *Machiavelli and Republicanism*, pp. 265–79. Cambridge: Cambridge University Press, 1990.

———. *Ordinary Vices*. Cambridge, Mass.: Harvard University Press, 1984.

———. Review of *The Political Works of James Harrington* by J. G. A. Pocock. *Political Theory* 6 (November 1978), pp. 558–61.

Shapiro, Ian. *Political Criticism*. Berkeley: University of California Press, 1990.

Silberner, Edmond. *La guerre dans la pensée économique, du XVIe au XVIIIe siècle*. Paris: Librairie du Recueil Sirey, 1939.

Skinner, Quentin. "The idea of negative liberty: philosophical and historical perspectives." In Richard Rorty, J. B. Schneewind, and Quentin Skinner, eds., *Philosophy in History: Essays on the Historiography of Philosophy*, pp. 193–221. Cambridge: Cambridge University Press, 1984.

———. "Sir Thomas More's *Utopia* and the Language of Renaissance Humanism." In Anthony Pagden, ed., *The Languages of Political Theory in Early Modern Europe*, pp. 123–57. Cambridge: Cambridge University Press, 1987.

Sonenscher, Michael. *Work and Wages: Natural law, Politics and the Eighteenth-century French Trades*. Cambridge: Cambridge University Press, 1989.

Stephen, Leslie, and Lane, Sidney. *The Dictionary of National Biography*. 22 vols. Oxford: Oxford University Press, 1921–22.

Stiffoni, Giovanni. "Da 'royaliste' a 'démocrate'. Gli anni da formazione del pensiero politico di Gabriel Bonnot de Mably." *Annali della Facoltà di Lingue et Letterature straniere di Ca'Foscari* 9 (1970), pp. 93–137.

———. *Utopia et ragione in G. Bonnot de Mably*. Lecce: Milella, 1975.

Taylor, Charles. "What's Wrong with Negative Liberty." In Alan Ryan, ed., *The Idea of Freedom: Essays in Honour of Isaiah Berlin*, pp. 175–93. Oxford: Oxford University Press, 1979.

Thamer, Hans-Ulrich. *Revolution und Reaktion in der französischen Sozialkritik des 18. Jahrhunderts: Linguet, Mably, Babeuf*. Frankfurt am Main: Humanitas-Studien, 1973.

Thierry, Augustin. *Récits des temps mérovingiens, précédés des Considérations sur l'histoire de France*. Vol. 1. Paris: Garnier, 1840.

Thom, Martin. *Republics, Nations and Tribes*. London: Verso, 1995.

Tuck, Richard. *Natural Rights Theories*. Cambridge: Cambridge University Press, 1979.

———. "The 'Modern' Theory of Natural Law." In Anthony Pagden, ed., *The Languages of Political Theory in Early-Modern Europe*, pp. 99–119. Cambridge: Cambridge University Press, 1987.

Van Kley, Dale K. *The Damiens Affair and the Unravelling of the Ancien Régime, 1750–1770*. Princeton: Princeton University Press, 1984.

———. *The Jansenists and the Expulsion of the Jesuits from France, 1757–1763*. New Haven: Yale University Press, 1975.

Varnum, Fanny. *Un philosophe cosmopolite du XVIIIe siècle: le Chevalier Chastellux*. Paris: Rodstein, 1936.

Venturi, Franco. *Utopia and Reform in the Enlightenment.* Cambridge: Cambridge University Press, 1971.

———. *The End of the Old Regime in Europe, 1768–1776. The First Crisis.* Trans. R. Burr Litchfield. Princeton: Princeton University Press, 1989.

———. *The End of the Old Regime in Europe, 1776–1789.* Trans. R. Burr Litchfield. 2 vols. Princeton: Princeton University Press, 1991.

Vertot, René Aubert de. *Histoire des révolutions de la république romaine.* 3 vols. Paris: L. Janet, 1819.

Vidal-Naquet, Pierre. "Une invention grecque: la démocratie." *Esprit* 197 (December 1993), pp. 5–23.

———. "Le mirage Grec et la Révolution française." *Esprit* 12 (December 1975), pp. 825–39.

Viner, Jacob. *Studies in the Theory of International Trade.* New York: Harper and Brothers, 1937.

Voltaire. *Oeuvres de Voltaire.* Paris: Garnier frères, 1877–87.

Walicki, Andrezej. *The Enlightenment and the Birth of Modern Nationhood. Polish Political Thought from Noble Republicanism to Tadeusz Kosciuszko.* Trans. Emma Harris. Notre Dame: University of Notre Dame Press, 1989.

Wallertein, Immanuel. *The Modern World System II: Mercantilism and the Consolidation of the European World-Economy, 1600–1763.* New York: Academic Press, 1980.

Whitfield, Ernest. *Gabriel Bonnot de Mably.* London: Routledge, 1930.

Wokler, Robert. "Rousseau and Marx." In David Miller and Larry Seidentop, eds., *The Nature of Political Theory,* pp. 219–46. Oxford: Clarendon Press, 1983.

Womersley, David. *The Transformation of* The Decline and Fall of the Roman Empire. Cambridge: Cambridge University Press, 1988.

Wood, Gordon S. *The Creation of the American Republic, 1776–1787.* New York: Norton, 1969.

Wood, Neal. *Cicero's Social and Political Thought.* Berkeley: University of California Press, 1988.

Wright, J. K. "Conversations with Phocion: the Political Thought of Mably." *History of Political Thought* 13 (1992), pp. 391–415.

———. "National Sovereignty and the General Will: The Political Program of the Declaration of Rights." In Dale Van Kley, ed., *The French Idea of Freedom: The Old Regime and the Declaration of Rights of 1789,* pp. 199–233. Stanford: Stanford University Press, 1994.

Index

Library of Congress Cataloging-in-Publication Data

Wright, Johnson Kent, 1957–
A classical Republican in eighteenth-century France: the political thought of Mably / Johnson Kent Wright.
p. cm.
Includes bibliographical references and index.
ISBN 0-8047-2789-9 (cloth: alk. paper)
1. Mably, abbé de, 1709–1785—Contributions in political science. I. Title
JC179.M25W75 1996
320'.092—DC21
97-6290 CIP

This book is printed on acid-free paper.